Woven in Wire

DIMENSIONAL WIRE WEAVING IN FINE ART JEWELRY

∘ SARAH THOMPSON ∘

 Interweave

fwcommunity.com

Interweave®

interweave.com

21 20 19 18   5 4 3 2

E-mail: enquiries@fwmedia.com
SRN: 18JM01
ISBN-13: 978-1-63250-622-1

**Editorial Director &
Content Editor** Kerry Bogert

Technical Editor Cindy Wimmer

**Art Director &
Cover Designer** Ashlee Wadeson

Interior Designer Pamela Norman

Illustrator Bonnie Brooks & Sue Friend

Photographer David Baum

contents

introduction

WHEN WRITING MY first book, I set out to teach and share with readers the technique at the heart of the jewelry I create, wire weaving with fine gauge wires. In *Fine Art Wire Weaving* I laid the groundwork for the solid foundation you and other jewelers need to successfully make pieces in my signature style. Now it's time to take things to the next level with new inspiration, using techniques for sculptural effects and dimensional designs, and increasing the complexity of your work. I'm setting out to challenge you, while providing guidance and support to grow your skills.

I'm often asked how I make my master designs and what techniques I use to pull them together. The answers are here in the pages of this book. I'm showing you everything from the tools and materials I prefer to the techniques I employ. You'll see each step of the process, but I will warn you, be prepared to invest time into the work we'll do together. Making the most of these techniques and achieving the level of beauty and intricacy of this style of jewelry requires patience. It isn't a skill mastered in an afternoon—practice is the key, and after all that practice you will be ready to transform your work into a masterpiece.

As we dig into the project chapters, we'll first explore Sculpting by applying sculptural techniques to wire weaving and using the moldable quality of wire to naturally enhance designs. With just a touch of dimension, I'll show you how to add life to your jewelry. From there we dive into Symmetry. By utilizing the symmetry techniques found in this book, I'll show you how to take your wirework to a professional level with truly sophisticated designs. In the final section, Transformation, we'll combine different design elements in creative ways that lead to breathtaking results.

Inspiration is found everywhere, and I hope by opening your eyes to how to layer more details, you will begin to find your own design path and have some real fun playing with wire.

Finishing Tools

When you've completed the weaving and construction of a piece of jewelry, there are a few final steps that give jewelry a true professional finish. Filing, adding patina, and polishing your work really make a world of difference in the quality of the end design.

Filing Tools

Filing is needed to take down any sharp edges that may touch the skin. A lot of my filing is done in small places, and I find **NEEDLE FILES** give me more control than larger files. There are two shapes I use the most: my flat file and an oval file. A **LARGE HAND FILE** is great to file exposed wire ends that don't have a clean flush cut. It removes a lot of material quickly and makes easy work of the job.

For finer work, I use **SANDPAPER** for rough prepolishing. The larger the reference numbers on the sandpaper, the finer the grit of the sand. You'll want to use graduated grits of 800, 1000, 1500, and 2000. You'll find this works very well to remove tool marks.

Patina

I don't feel like my jewelry is complete until I patina it. Patina brings out all the subtle details of the wire by creating light and dark contrast. I use **LIVER OF SULFUR** to achieve this effect. There are three forms of liver of sulfur available: solid, gel, and premade solutions. Out of the three, the gel form is the most stable and will last a long time. Liver of sulfur should always be stored in an airtight container in a dark, cool area.

STEEL WOOL

Polishing Tools

Once your jewelry is filed smooth and patina is applied, you'll need to remove some of that patina to reveal the details, depth, and dimension hiding under the oxidation.

STEEL WOOL is typically the first step to removing oxidation and starting the polishing process. Make sure to use Super Fine (0000 grit) steel wool to polish the patina off the high points of your design, leaving the crevasses dark. Coarser grits will scratch the surface of the wire. Super fine steel wool will leave a satin finish on your jewelry.

A **BRASS BRISTLE BRUSH** is an alternative to steel wool. Choose a soft brass jeweler's brush. It is more expensive, but will not scratch the surface of your jewelry. If starting with steel wool, you can follow it up with the brass bristle brush to remove any steel wool caught in the weave. I also find that this brush gives a nice polish as well.

PRO-POLISH POLISHING PADS are great for touch-up work after you have used the steel wool. They also can be used in place of steel wool, but it will take longer to polish and the texture of the wire weave will tear up your pad, shortening its life span. **POLISHING CLOTHS** can be used to buff jewelry, giving it a glossy finish, but it also takes more time.

My preferred method of polishing is to use a **TUMBLER WITH STEEL SHOT** or a **ROTARY TOOL** with a flex shaft. I love my tumbler; it creates a beautiful mirror finish on the jewelry, giving it almost a gunmetal look. A small 3-pound capacity tumbler is all that is needed with a pound of steel shot. If tumbling is not an option, then I turn to my rotary tool, either an all-purpose Dremel brand tool or a professional jeweler's flex shaft. With the polishing attachments available, you can achieve a mirror finish on your jewelry similar to the tumbler.

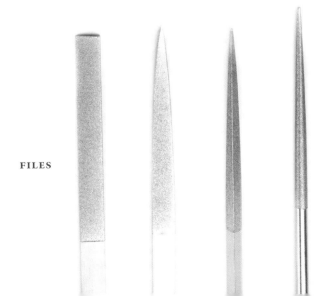

FILES

materials

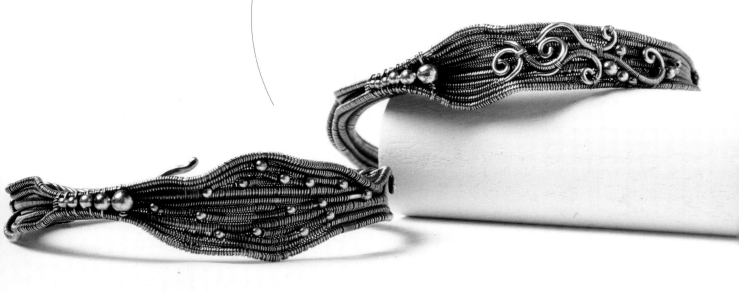

Choosing the Right Wire

Wire comes in a wide range of sizes, shapes, hardness ratings, and metals. I never really thought about the differences until I started teaching. I immediately saw that many students struggled, not because they weren't capable, but because they were using different wire than the rest of the class. You can create beautiful work with all types of wire, but working with the right wire will cut down on a lot of frustration and results in a more beautiful finished piece.

When it comes to wire, I like to keep it simple. Instead of having round, half round, and square on hand, I choose to only work with round wire. I find that round wire is very versatile, and I love the look I can get from manipulating it. Besides, if I want a flat surface then I simply hammer it into the wire.

Understanding Gauge & Hardness

Wire is measured by gauge—think thickness—and I break gauges into 3 categories: heavy, medium, and fine. I consider heavy gauge wires to be those that are 14–20 gauge. These are the wires I use as the base in my designs. They provide structure and can be shaped and layered together to create a more complex design. Medium gauges are wires ranging from 22–26 gauge in size. These gauges are great for embellishing finished designs with beads, creating head pins, and linking components together. Fine gauge wires measure 28 gauge or smaller and are what we'll use to weave and sew base wires in a design. Despite their thin nature, they add stability, strength, cohesiveness, and texture to the work.

Many types of wire are also measured by hardness—how stiff or how malleable the wire is. You'll see wires sold as full hard, half hard, and dead soft. Because of the extreme shaping that is needed in my style of wirework, I want the softest, most malleable wire available, which is dead soft. However, I have found that some wires labeled "dead soft" are not as soft as I would like, since there is a difference between manufacturers on the malleability of dead soft wire. You'll want to test wires from a few different suppliers before purchasing larger quantities.

Something else to consider when working with soft wire is how quickly it hardens and becomes brittle. This is particularly important with the smaller gauges. We want to be able to weave without having the wire break every time it gets a kink and be able to shape heavy gauge wires with ease. Other qualities I look for in wire: how nicely it anneals, how hammering affects it, how it oxidizes, and if a bead can be drawn on the end of the wire.

Types of Wire

The metal from which wire is made can have a dramatic impact on how easily you're able to perform certain techniques, which will directly affect the finished quality of your work.

FINE SILVER

Also known as pure silver, fine silver is my wire of choice. It is soft and malleable, allowing me to shape very intricate designs with ease. Plus, when needed, it anneals and reshapes wonderfully. Fine silver does not get as brittle as some wires; this means that 28-gauge wire won't break as frequently compared to other wires as you weave with it. The weave also compacts better and has less spring to it. So even if I am using sterling silver as my base wires, I always weave with fine silver.

STERLING SILVER

I rarely use sterling silver. Sterling wire work-hardens quickly, making it difficult to finish intricate, three-dimensional shaping. As you shape the wire, it tends to stay in that shape, which makes it more difficult to reshape if you make a mistake. Sterling silver doesn't torch as nicely, and when drawing a bead, the balls on the end of the wire tend to be slightly pitted. If you do choose to use sterling silver, you should know that after torching the wire you have to use pickle—an acid that removes fire scale—to clean it. Sterling silver will also oxidize more quickly over time, so it will require periodic cleaning as well. These attributes are all due to the small percentage of copper that sterling silver contains.

To combat these negative attributes, I use sterling silver for the base wires when I want a more structurally sound foundation, such as in a bracelet. Also, I make sure my design is simpler so I don't get frustrated trying to shape the sterling silver wire into an intricate design.

ARGENTIUM SILVER

Argentium Silver is a newer form of silver that is known for not oxidizing as quickly as traditional sterling silver. Unfortunately, its benefits stop there. For my style of wirework, I find it challenging because it quickly becomes brittle, to the point that it will break if heated or hammered. It doesn't draw a bead well when heated, but rather curls onto itself. While it is possible to anneal this wire, you must heat it just right and cool it properly or again it becomes brittle. The dead soft form of this wire quickly hardens and becomes unmanageable to shape into complex designs. All these qualities make Argentium Silver wire more difficult to work with, so I don't recommend it for these projects.

TIP MARKING

To mark my silver wire, I draw a bead on one end. This bead tells me at a glance whether the wire is fine silver or sterling silver, so I can store my silver wires together.

COPPER

It may sound surprising, but I prefer working with a good dead soft copper wire to sterling silver wire. However, not all dead soft copper is equal. I get my copper in 4 oz. to 1 lb. spools from Rio Grande, Monsterslayer, Rings & Things, or Metalliferous and have been pleased with the softness and quality of the metal. I have found most copper wire sold in smaller packages in craft stores tends to be harder and more difficult to work with. If you are struggling with your copper wire, try a different source. You can torch copper and create balls on the ends of the wire, but the balls are pitted. Copper can be annealed just like fine silver and sterling silver, and oxidizes very quickly.

> **NOTE** *You must pickle copper wire after torching to remove fire scale.*

CRAFT WIRES

In my experience, those who use generic craft wires struggle when learning wire-weaving techniques. Even though it is labeled "dead soft," it is still harder than most wire of the same gauge, so it is more difficult to shape. When wire weaving, 28-gauge craft wire has the most spring to it and tends to break more often than other wires. If you are using copper craft wire, you want bare copper. Those labeled "natural copper" have an anti-tarnish coating. The only time I recommend craft wire is if you're looking for vibrant colors that only craft wire can provide.

PLATED WIRES

I personally prefer not to use plated or filled wire as it limits my design abilities. It can't be hammered or heated without damaging the plating. Tool marks often expose the base wire beneath, and polishing can sometimes remove the plating as well. I do make an exception for gold-filled wire because of the price of working in gold.

Beads

I chose to work with crystals and pearls in this book, since they are materials that are easy to find and come in standard sizes and uniform shapes. Feel free to switch out the beads to fit your own personal tastes. Part of the fun of working with wire is that it can be easily altered and formed around almost any bead.

Some things to think about when selecting beads to include in your jewelry are the hole size, durability, and how they're affected by patina and polishing. The size of the hole in your bead needs to accommodate the gauge of wire you're using. Forcing a bead onto a wire that is thicker than the hole can cause breakage, and a bead on a wire that's too fine for the hole size can mean the bead moves and slips on the wire. If you plan to polish your finished jewelry in a tumbler, be sure your beads are durable enough to withstand the agitation in the drum. Some AB finishes on crystals, for example, will come off during tumbling. You may also find that some softer natural stones will break in the tumbler. Lastly, if adding patina to your piece, you'll want to test how liver of sulfur will affect your beads. If it damages the bead, then plan to add the bead after you have finished oxidizing and polishing your jewelry, or be careful of the bead as you polish with steel wool.

techniques

Before You Begin

Before you even attempt any technique or project in this book, it is important to start out on the right foot. The goal is to create elegant, refined jewelry with a sculptural touch. The best way to do this is to be mindful of your wire from the beginning. Take care to insure your base wires are straight or parallel to each other. Strive for neat, precise, and tight stitches when weaving. Inconsistency will lend to a more rustic style that, in some cases, can detract from the elegance and overall workmanship.

Every little detail matters and helps the jewelry become a work of art. So before diving into the projects, practice these techniques to develop good habits. It will lead to a higher level of craftsmanship in the end. This careful attention to detail, precision, and consistency is what will set your jewelry apart. Take the time to get it right, be okay with going slow, and know that with time you will get faster. The more you work, the more it will become second nature, and less time will be spent making sure that the wires are aligned and shaped correctly. It will always take a level of patience and a care for details, but the results are well worth it.

Handling Wire

Your hands are the best tools you have, and they tend to be underappreciated and not used to their full potential. There is a tendency to reach for a tool to do the work when your fingers can do a much better job. My motto is first shape with your fingers, then tweak and refine your shape with your tools. If you do this every time you work with wire, you will come to know the wire better and use your tools less and less. Many times tools become a crutch, preventing you from achieving a flowing quality in your designs.

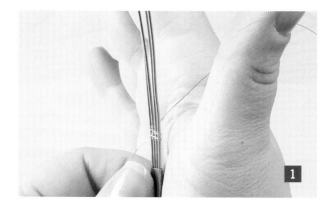

The act of wire weaving is done with the fingers, and if you're not careful, can cause discomfort. How you handle wire is important to maximize the results while relieving stress on your hands. Remember to take breaks frequently and stretch those hands.

Holding Fine Gauge Wires

Our natural tendency is to pinch the fine gauge wire between our thumb and forefinger to guide it as you weave. This is fine, but you will find that your hand will cramp up over time. This can make weaving unpleasant. I use an alternative method inspired by needlecrafts. Just like hooks or needles in crocheting and knitting, there are many ways to hold and handle wire to create tension and make weaving more comfortable. I will be teaching my method, but feel free to modify and alter it to accommodate your needs.

Run a length of wire across your palm underneath the pinky and across your ring and middle finger. Allow the wire to run through your fingers while you guide it with your middle finger. Your hand can be open or loosely closed in a fist, but the most important thing is that you're not clenching the muscles in your hand *(Figures 1–3)*.

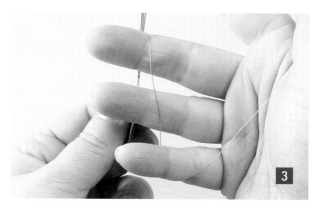

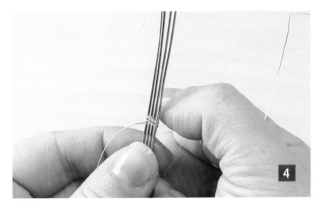

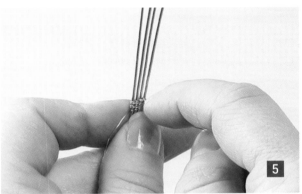

In the beginning, holding the wire this way may feel awkward, so I want you to first focus on learning the weave and getting it right. Hold the wire in a way that is natural to you. Then, once you are comfortable with the weave, come back and work on how you hold your wire. This will make it more manageable to learn, and soon you will find that it has become second nature.

Protecting Your Fingers

Letting the fine gauge wire run along your fingers as described can cause chaffing. Fabric medical tape is a great way to protect your fingers, creating a buffer between you and the wire. It is pliable and does not restrict movement in your hands. Use the tape anywhere that the wire is bothering you.

Reducing Hand Fatigue

As your dominant hand weaves your wire, your non-dominant hand holding the base wires can also become fatigued and cramp. A ring clamp is a wonderful tool that grips the wire without marring it and fits comfortably in your hands. Readjust your clamp frequently so that no more than ½" (1.3 cm) of the weave is above the jaws of the clamp. If too much weave is exposed, when you stop and compress the weave, there is not enough support and the woven strip will buckle under the compression.

Another benefit to holding wire this way is that you can use your fingers to tap the fine gauge wire as you're weaving. This gives the right amount of tension to wrap the wire tightly around the base wires as you weave. Using the pad of your fingers while the wire is towards the back of your work, tap with your thumb *(Figure 4)*. As you move to the front of the work, use your forefinger to tap *(Figure 5)*.

When pulling the wire to tighten, which uses your arm muscles making it difficult to control the force you're putting on the wire, you will find your wire is more likely to break. By tapping with your fingers as shown, you are using much less force which should dramatically cut back on wire breakage. However, if you find you are still breaking the weaving wire using this method, you're probably using your nails to tap the wire down. The harder surface of your nails can cause the weaving wire to break; the key is to use the pads of your fingers.

For an added layer of security and to further reduce hand fatigue, I use painter's tape to keep base wires secure and in the right position when I begin my weave. The tape gives you a wider surface to grip whether using a ring clamp or holding the base wire with your hand. It doesn't leave a sticky residue like many other tapes and is easy to remove.

Straightening Wire

Nylon-jaw pliers can be used to straighten wire, but they also compress the wire, work hardening it and slightly flattening it. I prefer to use my fingers instead. Draw the wire between your thumb and index finger with the thumb pushing against the wire and the index slightly above the thumb position guiding the wire. This will cause the wire to arc slightly. Draw the wire through your fingers again, this time pushing with your index finger, with the thumb slightly above guiding the wire, to arc the wire in the opposite direction. Continue to draw the wire between the thumb and index finger, alternating the finger positions each time. The process is finished when the wire feels smooth between your fingers. Draw it one more time, this time pressing evenly between both fingers; this will straighten it out of the arc. A polishing cloth can be used to protect your fingers, creating a buffer between you and the wire as you are drawing. For stubborn kinks, use flat-nose or chain-nose pliers.

TIP **PREVENTING KINKS**

Be mindful of the wire. If you see the wire looping onto itself, take the time to stop and unloop it to prevent kinks before they happen.

Managing Wire

The last thing you want to do is spend more time untangling and removing kinks from your fine gauge wire than weaving. Plus, preventing kinks helps eliminate potential weak points in your wire. These weak points are where your wire will most likely break, and we want to minimize this from happening.

Bobbins

Bobbins come in several sizes and are traditionally used to make kumihimo. They can be found at most bead stores and online. I personally like the small 1⅞" (4.8 cm) bobbins as this size fits nicely in the palm of my hand. Bobbins are inexpensive and are the best way to prevent your wire from tangling or forming kinks. Starting at the end, wind a length of wire onto the bobbin and snap it shut. The closed bobbin has enough tension to hold your wire so it won't unravel, but still allows you to pull out a foot at a time while you are weaving.

When I am weaving around curves or long lengths of wire, I like to work from the center out. To do this, use two bobbins and wind both ends to the center of the small gauged wire. For example, if 30' (9.1 m) of wire is called for, then 15' (4.6m) would be wound on each bobbin to meet at the center *(Figure 6)*. One bobbin becomes your tail and the other is what you are pulling from. When you have finished one side, flip it over and use the wire on the other bobbin to weave the other half. The leftover wire on the spool can be used for smaller projects, so little is wasted or ends up in the recycle jar.

Working from a Spool

Working with wire directly off a spool is more difficult than working with bobbins, but it can be managed. The wire will uncoil off the spool faster than you can work with it, causing it to tangle. You can prevent this by putting the spool on the floor; this stretches the uncoiled wire so it does not tangle on itself. Another option is to find a container just wide enough to hold the spool upright so the spool will spin freely as you work and will not uncoil. This can also be done with multiple spools in one container, and is how I store and work from my spools.

> **NOTE** *If your wire arrives in a coil, take the time to wrap it around a spool or bobbin before working on a project.*

Storing Unfinished Projects

Wire weaving takes patience, and some pieces will require more than one sitting to complete. How you store your unfinished work can help prevent frustrating tangles or broken wires. Personally, I like to prepare my base wires and spool the fine gauged wire onto bobbins before I begin. This way as I weave and layer, the wires are ready to incorporate into the design. When I am done for the night, the fine gauge wire is wound on a bobbin and the unfinished work with all the loose wires for the project are put into a resealable bag to be stored in a designated container. By putting components in a resealable bag, I can store multiple projects together in the same container without tangles, and the bobbins keep the fine gauge wire kink-free.

Wire Techniques

I like to think of techniques as design elements. How you shape, hammer, torch, and file add little details to a design that together complete it. Here I show my most frequently used techniques and how to elevate your design for a more professional look.

Shaped Elements

Enhancing dimensional wire jewelry will have you forming both V shapes and curves.

CREATING V SHAPES

1 Mark the wire with a permanent marker where you want the bend.

2 With your flat-nose pliers, gently grip the wire so you just see the mark on the left-hand side of your pliers. Rest your thumb on the side of the flat-nose pliers and directly on top of the wire at the mark *(Figure 7)*.

3 With your thumb, push the wire away from you and against the pliers at the mark, forming a right angle.

> **NOTE** *If you are finding the arm of the V that was folded over with your fingers is still soft and relatively rounded, your thumb was further away from the pliers, causing the bend to start happening away from the pliers instead of right by the edge of the pliers.*

4 Flip the V so that the arm that was being held by the pliers is now the arm to be pushed against the pliers. Gently squeeze the arm in the pliers to further straighten the arm *(Figure 8)*.

5 Continue to decrease the angle of the V, keeping each arm straight by gently squeezing with flat-nose pliers. Frequently switch from arm to arm as you work to get a tighter angle. This will create symmetry in the shaping of the V.

6 If the tip of your flat-nose pliers is too thick to make a crisply pointed V shape, switch to chain-nose pliers *(Figure 9)*.

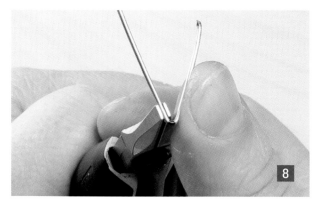

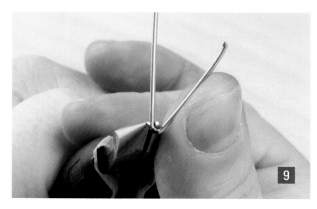

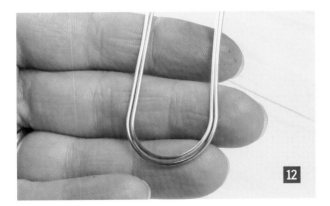

CURVED SHAPES

I use my ring mandrel more for shaping curves than I do to make rings. Dowels, bail pliers, permanent markers, highlighters, crochet hooks, and knitting needles also work well to create curved forms. Using the same tool repeatedly will help you get consistency in your shapes.

1 For larger curves mark the center of where you want the curve to be on your wire.

2 Hold the wire against a mandrel the approximate size of your finished curve. With your thumb positioned over the center mark to keep the wire in place, use your fingers to mold and shape the wire around the ring mandrel from the center out. Only shape one quarter of the way around the mandrel on both sides, creating a U shape *(Figure 10)*.

3 Stop and make sure the mark is still centered. If it is not, tug the wire on the shorter side while holding the curved wire to the mandrel with your fingers. This will reposition the wire without disfiguring the curve *(Figure 11)*.

4 Continue to shape around the mandrel, making sure to alternate between the two sides until you have reached your desired curvature.

5 Take your shaped wire and place it onto your bench block. With a rawhide or nylon mallet, tap the curve of the U to remove any waves that might have happened while shaping.

HOW TO NEST CURVES

The Aries Pendant (page 128) requires you to shape and nestle several wires together. These wires need to be shaped before weaving. If you wove the wire together first before shaping, you would end up with a curved woven wall instead of a flat woven curve.

I have found that when I use my ring mandrel if I put 3 sizes between each bend, I get curves that nest perfectly. For example if the first wire is shaped around size 10, I shape the second wire around size 13 on my mandrel *(Figure 12)*.

LOOPS

1 Gently grip the end of the wire with your round-nose pliers.

2 Rotate the pliers as you press the wire up against the pliers with your thumb. The idea is that your thumb is doing the work and shaping the wire as the pliers are rotating *(Figure 13)*.

3 Remove the pliers and use flush cutters to trim the tip of the loop and remove the flatter, tool-marked end. This gives you a beautiful, open, circular loop.

4 For a closed loop chain-nose pliers and, with a loose grip, use your fingers to shape the wire around the pliers until the loop is closed *(Figure 14)*.

FREE-FORM SHAPING

The best way to create flowing free-form shapes is to move the wire from the end; this can be done with your fingers or your pliers. Shaping from the end of the wire lets you guide or lead the wire in the direction you want while still maintaining smooth flowing lines. This also allows for a more organic natural movement to occur, creating subtle nuances in the form that aren't achieved when forcing the wire in place with tools or fingers. Forming from the end allows for more smoothly flowing curvatures.

When I free-form shape, I let the wire choose how it wants to bend and move. I am controlling it to a degree, but if it does bend in a different manner than expected, I let it and don't try to change the shape too much.

With practice you'll find that you have more control over how the wire is shaped by manipulating the end in different directions. The Tidal Wave Ring (page 54) is a good design to practice this technique *(Figure 15)*.

13

14

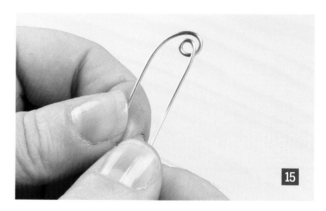

15

Hammered Elements

Knowing how and when to hammer adds greatly to your design. Going from a round wire to a gently flared, flattened ribbon invites the eyes to follow the flow and movements of the wire. It adds an elegant touch, and when coupled with beveling techniques, gives the finished piece an artistic flair.

1 To hammer, bring the head down flat onto the wire then stroke the wire in the direction that you want the wire to spread. This motion should be fluid with the stroking motion both helping the wire spread in the desired direction and smoothing the wire. Remember, you don't need to flatten the wire all at once; as you continue to bring the head down, radiate your strokes out. This helps prevent the wire from overspreading in one direction.

2 Flipping the hammered wire over every couple of strokes can also help create a consistent spreading of the wire. If you are experiencing tool marks, then your head is not coming down parallel to the wire, and the edge of the head is hitting the wire and causing the dents.

16

PADDLED ENDS

Paddled ends are a great way to finish your base wires. It does not require using a torch and adds a subtle dimension to the design. When paddling, the idea is to create a flared tip.

1 File the wire end flat before hammering; this will cut back on any filing that might be needed afterwards. Keep the wire straight or you can gently curve the end just a touch with your round-nose pliers. This will give a softer, more flowing finished design that I find melds perfectly with the swoops and swirls that I have in the design.

2 Using a chasing hammer, bring the head of the hammer down flat onto the end of the wire and draw the hammer towards the end of the wire in a stroking motion. Continue to hammer, radiating the strokes out to uniformly flare the tip of the wire. If needed, flip the wire to the opposite side to ensure even hammering on all sides. File to smooth the edge round *(Figure 16)*.

FLATTENING V ENDS

Flattening the tips of a V shape gives it crispness. When flattening the wire, you want to prevent it from spreading too much. The stroking motion should run the length of the end instead of radiating out from the wire. This will flatten the wire without too much of a flare in one direction.

FLATTENING CURVED WIRE

When hammering a curve, you want the wire to gradually spread or flare out more around the curve. This can be the whole curve, or when flattening a loop, just a section.

1 With your chasing hammer, begin hammering the curved section of the wire element, radiating the strokes outward from the wire. As your wire begins to flatten, focus more of the hammered strokes around the areas that you want to flare out more dramatically.

> **NOTE** *It is easy to misshape your curve as you are hammering. This happens when you spend too much time hammering in one section of the curve before the rest of the curved wire has been flattened.*

FOLDING HAMMERED WIRE

Folding your hammered wire is a great way to add another subtle touch of dimension to your design. In the Scribble Earrings (page 88), folding the hammered wire is what gives the design a WOW factor. This can be done without annealing, but then you must use more force, which can result in more tool marks. Additionally, if your wire becomes too brittle, you risk breakage.

1 Hammer your wire to the desired thickness. With a torch, anneal your wire to soften it. Quench in water to cool the wire.

2 With flat-nose pliers, grip the point where the base of the V will be. Holding onto one arm of the V, use your thumb to shape the other arm to form the angle *(Figure 17)*.

3 Rotate the wire so that the flat-nose pliers now grip the side that was shaped by your thumb. Shape the other side so that it is folded nicely against the nose of the pliers. Keep shaping until you get the desired angle, rotating the wire frequently to guarantee that the wire is evenly and symmetrically shaped.

Filing Different Shaped Elements

Filing is the last step in shaping wire. It is subtle but does make a difference in the final product. For me it is easier to use needle files or an emery board, as they allow me to get into smaller spaces. These filing techniques can be used anytime you hammer, even if not specified in a project.

BEVELING FLATTENED WIRE

Holding your file at a 45-degree angle, file along the edge of your flattened wire. This will create a nice bevel along the edge. I particularly like doing this around flared-out loops and flattened V shapes.

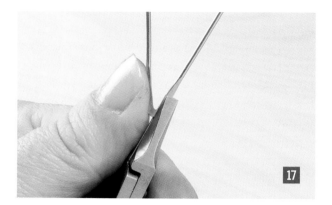

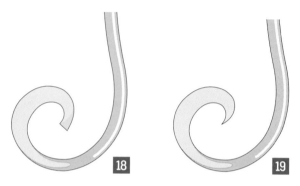

POINTED SWIRLS

1 To create pointed swirls, first loop the end of the wire, then hammer flat.

2 Take a permanent marker and block out the tip that you want to remove *(Figure 18)*.

3 Trim off most of the marked wire with your wire cutters. You should already see your pointed swirl emerging.

4 Use a file to remove the rest of your marked wire. Step back and inspect your work. Continue to file along the outer curve until the edge is smooth and seamlessly comes to a point *(Figure 19)*.

> **NOTE** *Use the beveling technique to finish the swirl for even more depth.*

FILING FOLDED WIRE

Files can be used to file folded wire into a more rounded shape by smoothing the edges. This is done by first beveling the outer edge and then filing smooth the edge created by the beveling. This will give a smooth sloping shape to the outer edge that pairs well with hammered swirls and paddled curved tails.

> **NOTE** *I avoid filing the inside edges of my shaped wire as it is harder to get into the tight areas. The only exception would be if you want to bevel the inside edge of a folded V shape. After folding the hammered V, place the file directly onto the inside edge and remove it.*

FILING HAMMERED ENDS

After creating paddle ends of wire, use your files to round the outer edge. This is both aesthetically pleasing and brings uniformity to your work. The technique is the same one used in other filing situations. Hold your file at a 45-degree angle to the wire and remove excess material until the desired edge shape is achieved.

REMOVING FILE MARKS

You will quickly find that needle files leave your wire with a rough brushed nickel look. After you finish shaping and beveling with your files, use sandpaper in graduated grits to remove the tool marks until you are left with a velvety satin finish. In class I give my students 800, 1000, 1500, and 2000 grit sandpaper. You can use sandpaper from the hardware store or actual jeweler's sandpaper, which comes in even finer grits. Trust me; you won't regret this added step. Finish with a Pro-Polish pad; this will give you a high polish and help you see any remaining tool marks that need to be removed. If you still see tool marks, start from the beginning with your 800 grit sandpaper and repeat the process.

If you have a flex shaft, then you can use silicone wheels to achieve the same results in less time. Pay attention to what you are doing and use a light touch. It is very easy to remove too much material when using a flex shaft. You can always go back and remove more, but once it is gone, it is gone.

Torched Elements

The hottest part of a torch is just in front of the blue flame. To see the blue flame better, dim the lights. Always use a heat shield underneath your torch and have a bowl of water ready to cool down your wire and tweezers. Locking tweezers are a must, and I prefer working with the longer tipped tweezers.

ANNEALING WIRE

Annealing is done when wire has been work hardened, becoming brittle, but still needs to be further shaped. By heating the wire, it softens and becomes more malleable again. I find I often need to anneal wire after hammering it flat. Annealing can be done on a charcoal block, firebrick, or with your locking tweezers holding the wire.

1 Gently heat the length of the wire with your torch, being careful not to stay in one spot long enough to begin melting the wire.

2 When the wire surface develops a matte finish and the wire begins to glow, the wire has been softened.

> **NOTE** *If you are annealing a woven strip, be careful of 28-gauge wire. It will want to melt before the base wire has fully annealed. Another way to determine when your wire has reached the appropriate temperature is to mark the wire with a permanent marker. When the mark disappears, the wire is annealed.*

3 Allow the wire to air cool for a minute before quenching the wire in water.

DRAWING A BEAD

A bead drawn on the end of a piece of wire can add a beautiful detail to your finished work. It isn't a difficult technique, but takes a bit of practice to control the size of the bead. If you allow it to get too big, the weight of the metal will cause it to drop off the end of the wire.

1 Hold the tip of the wire perpendicular to the flame. As the wire melts, the melted material will begin to move up the wire, forming a ball. When you have reached the desired ball size, remove it from the flame.

2 Let it air cool for a second before dropping the wire into water. Any fast movements made while the ball is still liquid will misshape the ball.

THE DOUBLE HELIX EARRINGS (PAGE 48) FEATURE BEAUTIFUL BEADED WIRE ENDS.

PICKLING

Sterling silver and copper develop what is called fire scale when heated. Fire scale darkens the wire and can't be removed by polishing so you need an added step to bring back the shine. This is called pickling.

Commercial pickling solutions are readily available but highly corrosive, even when stored in a sealed container. I noticed even my tools stored near the container were rusting. This was a major deciding factor for me to work with fine silver instead.

However, sometimes I still use sterling silver or copper and need to anneal it. After much research, I decided to go with a slower but more natural approach to pickling. I use a cup of white vinegar with a tablespoon of salt to clean fire scale. This natural solution can be heated but also works when cold, though it then takes a little longer to clean. Just like the commercial solution it can be stored, but unlike it, my tools near the container no longer rust.

When the white vinegar solution no longer works, then it is time to dispose of it. Due to the heavy metal content, it is not safe to dump down the drain and needs to be dropped off at your local disposal station.

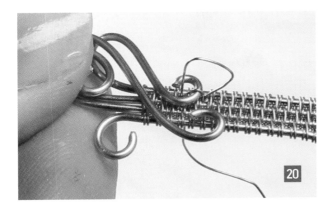

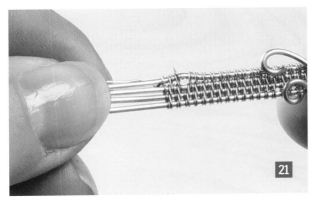

Finishing Touches

The final stage in making your jewelry is one that I see many rush through. At the end of the project, one can get sloppy in the haste to cross the finish line. In this section I show you how to make your designs structurally strong, as well as how to embellish them. Any time you're securing wires or beads, it is critical to make sure your connections are precise, tight, and secure.

Adding Beads

Embellishing with beads can add a pop of color to your work. In some cases, they'll be woven into the design as you go, but in other cases they're added to the work after the weaving is done.

PUNCTURING THE WEAVE

A beading awl is used to puncture a finished weave between the base wires. This will give you an opening to sew beads or wire to the weave and creates many design possibilities.

As you puncture the weave, you want a small hole just big enough to slip 28-gauge wire through two or three times **(Figure 20)**.

If you push the beading awl too far in, then you end up breaking the weave **(Figure 21)**.

SECURING BEADS

When adding beads to a design, it is important to always wrap twice around the base wire before going back through the bead. Wrapping twice locks the bead in place and prevents the 28-gauge wire holding the bead from loosening **(Figure 22)**.

Securing Shaped Base Wires

LASHING

Those who know me know that I like to tack everything down. I don't want my shaped wires to become undone by a snagged scarf. I also want to give my jewelry as much structural strength as possible. Sewing all the shaped wires together ensures this, and whenever possible I secure shaped wires directly onto the woven strip.

1 To secure shaped base wires, begin by puncturing a hole in the woven strip as you would to add a bead. Secure the base wires by wrapping two wires together 2–3 times.

2 Use beads as a way to get from one point to the next point when multiple wires need to be secured.

Coiling is a great way to get from point A to point B to secure the wires together. When coiling, wrap tightly and frequently compress the coil with your fingers. It is really easy to overlap the coils or create uneven spacing, which gives the coil a sloppy look. Slow down and be aware of what is happening, so if a mistake does happen you can easily go back and fix it.

Securing the Sewing Wire

The 28-gauge wire used to add beads or to secure base wires will itself need to be secured before trimming off the excess. To do this, wrap the wire around a base wire 2–3 times or until you come to a balled end. The smaller the base wire, the better; too large of a base wire, such as 14-gauge, will not secure 28-gauge wire and over time it will unwind *(Figure 23)*.

If you have attached a bead with 28-gauge wire, then the best place to secure it is around the 28-gauge wire that holds the bead in place. After securing the wire, trim it in the back; this way it is tucked out of the way and not seen.

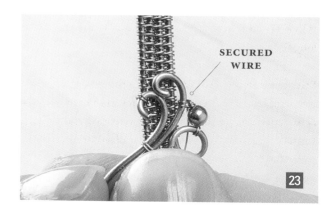

SECURED WIRE

23

Patina

I always patina my jewelry; it brings out the details. Just like a coloring picture looks flat when all you see is the outline, the same picture is transformed when you add shadows and highlights, making it jump out from the page. Antiquing your jewelry will have the same effect. The shadows and highlights that result from adding patina to your finished jewelry draw the eyes and showcase the depth this style of jewelry is known for. Patina will make the texture of your wire weaving pop as well as creating contrast to your smooth hammered wire elements.

Using Liver of Sulfur

There are many chemicals out there to create a patina finish. Since I use fine silver or copper wire, my preference is liver of sulfur in the gel form. It is easy to use and lasts a long time.

Liver of sulfur has a strong smell and should be used in a well-ventilated area. It works the quickest in hot water; the cooler the water, the longer it takes to oxidize and patina the wire. Mix a small amount of liver of sulfur into hot water and stir with a wooden pick or jewelry tongs. While wearing gloves and using tongs, place your jewelry into the solution.

NOTE *If the solution gets on your hands, then anything you touch that is silver or copper will start to oxidize.*

To get a deep patina, leave your jewelry in the solution until it has turned a uniform charcoal gray color. When you have reached a deep charcoal finish, remove the jewelry and soak it in cold water with a couple of teaspoons of baking soda mixed in. This will neutralize the liver of sulfur.

NOTE *For fine silver this may take longer; fine silver oxidizes in a rainbow of colors before reaching the charcoal color. While these colors are beautiful, I have found when polishing the jewelry that they make the crevices look dirty instead of antiqued.*

To neutralize liver of sulfur, place it on a windowsill in a sealed jar or in a spot that gets a lot of sun. The sun will break down the solution; when it has lost its color, it is neutralized and safe to dispose of. This can be done in the sink, toilet, or even in your garden or lawn as a fertilizer. Mixing baking soda into the solution is another way to neutralize liver of sulfur; again, it is neutralized when it has lost its color.

Polishing

Once your jewelry has been oxidized, you have several options for how to polish the finished piece. As a first step to any method, I recommend scouring the piece with 0000 super fine steel wool. Steel wool makes polishing simple and easy.

Tear off a small amount of steel wool. Working over a sink, wet the steel wool and work a little bit of dish soap into it. Begin to scrub the jewelry. Rinse the soap off the jewelry frequently while scrubbing to ensure that you aren't missing any areas. The goal is to remove the patina off the high points while leaving the recesses dark.

I wet my steel wool for two reasons: the first is that steel wool when used dry will flake and leave steel particles in the air. This is not healthy to breathe in. By wetting it, the steel particles are trapped in the water and fall into the sink instead of the air, becoming harmless. Second, by adding dish soap to the steel wool, you increase productivity and the patina comes off easier where you are scrubbing.

When you are done polishing, take a soft brass bristle brush or toothbrush and scrub the jewelry all over. This will remove any steel wool that may be caught in the jewelry. Rinse the jewelry one more time and dry.

Creating a Mirror Finish

You can leave the jewelry as is after removing patina from the high points for a satin finish, or choose to add one more step to give the jewelry a high-shine, mirror finish. There are two simple ways that I achieve this finish.

TUMBLER

The easiest way to give your jewelry a beautiful mirrored finish is with a tumbler. A three-pound tumbler with a pound of steel shot and a drop of dish soap is all that is needed. The steel shot acts like tiny little hammers and smoothens the wire surface.

Jewelry can be tumbled for 30 minutes to several hours with no damage to the jewelry. Because the steel shot is smoothing the surface of the wire, it also does a great job blending the transitions from light to dark within your jewelry.

> **NOTE** *Be careful what stones and crystal you put in the tumbler. They should have a hardness of at least 7 on the Mohs scale. I choose not to tumble any stones, gems, crystals, or pearls. I add all my embellishments after the jewelry has been tumbled. Also avoid tumbling chain; otherwise you end up with a tangled mess.*

SOFT BRASS BRISTLE BRUSH

Scrubbing a jeweler's soft, brass bristle brush over your jewelry also gives it a higher polish than steel wool alone. It is not as good as the tumbler, but if a tumbler is not practical for you, this is an excellent option. Be sure to use a jeweler's grade brass brush; hardware store options are not as soft and will scratch the surface instead of polishing it. Simply scrub the jewelry with the brass brush until you achieve your desired level of shine.

TUMBLER

Fixing and Hiding Mistakes

It would be a shame after spending hours on a piece to have it ruined by a mistake or two. Mistakes happen to all of us, and it doesn't have to mean a destroyed design. There are many ways to fix, hide, or embrace those flaws.

COILING BASE WIRE

In the beginning I had a lot of tool marks. I was struggling with the tools and couldn't get the shaping down, so the wire was reworked over and over. This really mangled the wire. I found the best way to cover up the imperfections was by using 28-gauge wire to coil over exposed base wires. This gives a nice textured touch to the design as well as hiding imperfections. As my skills progressed, I got to the point that now I only coil for aesthetic purposes.

TOOL MARKS

The best ways to avoid tool marks is to use tools as little as possible. However, when tools are needed and marks are made, one way to fix them is with your needle files. If the mark is shallow, then a light filing is all that is needed. This gives the wire a brushed look. Fine grit jeweler's sandpaper can be used to remove the brushed look if desired. For deeper grooves, filing the wire to give it a flattened look is the way to go. Whatever you do, remember to do the same on the other side to keep your symmetry.

GO WITH THE FLOW

When a mistake is not tool marks but happens in the shaping or assembling of the wires, or not having the proper wire length needed, then it is time to go with the flow. Instead of fighting the wire into submission, modify the design and work around the mistake. This can end up dramatically altering the design, which is okay. Be creative, maybe adding another layer of shaped wire to balance the mistake or sculpting and molding the woven form differently to make it work. The modification can be as simple as embellishing with more or different beads to bring the piece together.

MISTAKES BECOME NEW DESIGNS

Some of my favorite designs were complete failures that took a new direction. It is an opportunity to step back, think outside the box, and get very creative. I find I become more adventurous in my designs when mistakes happen. The piece is already possibly ruined, so why not go extreme and see what becomes of it? The worst that could happen is that I have to start anew; the best is that I can end up with an amazing design. For me that possibility is worth it. And at the very least it is an opportunity to learn and grow.

weaving

I LOVE THAT I CAN achieve wondrous designs, full of depth, movement, and details, with wire alone. Wire weaving is what makes this possible. It is what pulls everything together, giving your project structural strength while also creating a foundation to work upon.

Wire weaving is rather ornate wirework. I find that consistent, uniform textures compliment my designs better. I limit my work to only 3 types of weaves for this reason, but I encourage you to explore other weaves as you find what works best for your style. Each of the weaves I use serves a specific purpose and allows me to work with the wires in different ways.

In the beginning, go slow and make sure the weaving wire wraps each base wire tightly before continuing on. This is very important; if you don't, you will end up with loose sloppy stitches. I have found that the best way to do this is to stop every time you are perpendicular to the base wires and gently tighten the weaving wire before continuing on to wrap the next base wire. Yes, this will slow you down, but it is worth it. The more you practice, the faster you will become, and you will quickly see your weaves improve.

There is one more technique I use for a tight weave, which is compression. After approximately 3 rows to ¼" (6 mm) of weaving, stop and compress the weave with the pads of your fingertips (see Handling Wire, page 20). This serves two purposes, consistency and rest. The overall band of woven wire will be more consistent when you take a moment to compress the weave as you go. The goal is not to compress the weave to the point where you can't see the base; that's not possible. Instead you're trying to make sure the texture is consistent and even from left to right and from top and bottom. Even if your wire springs up, it will be more consistent if you compress it. This is also an opportunity to rest your hands and give them a stretch, which dramatically cuts back on hand fatigue.

For the base wires that become the foundation around which you'll weave fine gauge wires, I prefer mixing 20- to 14-gauge wires. It's easier to manipulate and shape 20-gauge wire when woven, while 16-gauge and 14-gauge wires create a sturdy backbone to a woven strip. By mixing different wire gauges, you can achieve an array of looks and functionality for your design. Weave the base wires together with either 28-gauge or 30-gauge wire. By weaving your base wires with these more delicate gauges, you create a finely textured and compact weave that lends itself well to more feminine, dainty jewelry.

It can help to preoxidize your base wires when you are first learning to wire weave. This will give you a contrast between the base wires and the weaving wire, allowing you to better see where the wires are traveling. Before you begin any weaving, make sure your wires are shaped properly. Once you start, it will be harder to make adjustments.

Basic Figure 8 Weave

This weave is a good one to start out with when first learning to wire weave. It is simple and looks good with tight consistent stitches. If the stitches are loose and sloppy, it is transformed into a rustic organic style that is pleasing as well. This makes the weave very forgiving to work with as you learn to handle smaller gauge wire and make your weave nice and tidy.

This weave creates grooves or channels between each base wire. These grooves are left dark when patina is applied, accentuating the movement of the base wires. It can be woven in a strip then shaped and sculpted, giving the base wires underneath more movement, as you can see in the Lilium Bracelet (page 78). This weave has a more organic quality to it, making it my go-to weave when I am looking for more ebb and flow to my design or when I want to work free-form.

The Basic Figure 8 Weave is also looser, making it easier to pierce to create openings to sew embellishments onto the base. The weave has the added appeal of being able to easily transition when increasing or decreasing the base wires anywhere in the design.

> **NOTE** *When working from the center to an outer edge rather than edge to edge, as in the Aries Pendant (page 128), start at step 3.*

1 Straighten 16" (40.5 cm) of 18-gauge practice wire and cut four 4" (10 cm) lengths. Tape the 4 wires together at the bottom, leaving a fingernail's distance between each wire. These are the base wires. Cut 5' (152.5 cm) of 28-gauge practice wire; this is the wire used for weaving. The first row is the starter row. It's different from the rest of the weave because it attaches the base wires together. It also stabilizes and positions the base wires. I will refer to the base wires by number, starting on the left with Wire 1, followed by 2, 3, and 4.

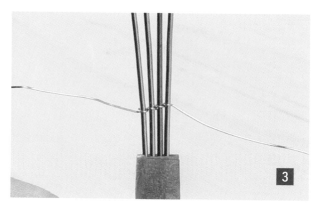

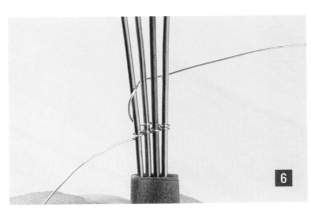

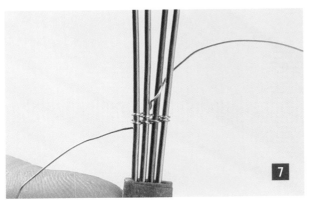

2 Leaving a 6" (15 cm) tail, bring the rest of the 28-gauge wire to the back of the base wires. Thread the 28-gauge wire between Wires 1 and 2, and then wrap it around Wire 1, toward the back *(Figure 1)*. Thread the 28-gauge wire between Wires 2 and 3, and then wrap it around Wire 2, toward the back *(Figure 2)*. Thread the 28-gauge wire between Wires 3 and 4, and then wrap it around Wire 3, toward the back. Bring the 28-gauge wire across the back of Wire 3 and Wire 4, and then wrap it around Wire 4, toward the back *(Figure 3)*. Push this starter row down to the base of your thumb. This secures the base wires to each other.

3 It's time to begin weaving. The 28-gauge wire will now be used to weave in and out of the base wires. Starting on the right side, from the back, bring the 28-gauge wire across the back of Wire 4 and wrap it around Wire 4, toward the back. The 28-gauge wire should now be in the back between Wires 3 and 4 *(Figure 4)*. Bring the 28-gauge wire across the back of Wire 3 and thread it between Wires 2 and 3, toward the front. Take the 28-gauge wire over the front of Wire 2 and thread it between Wires 1 and 2 *(Figure 5)*. You have reached the end of the row and should be back on the left side of the weave, with the 28-gauge wire in the back.

4 Bring the 28-gauge wire around the outside of Wire 1, toward the front. Thread the 28-gauge wire between Wires 1 and 2, across the back of Wire 2, and then thread it between Wires 2 and 3 *(Figure 6)*. Bring the wire over the front of Wire 3, thread it between Wires 3 and 4, and then across the back of Wire 4 *(Figure 7)*. Bring the 28-gauge wire around the outside of Wire 4, and then thread it between Wires 3 and 4, toward the back. Continue the weave pattern until you reach the left side of the weave, as in step 3.

5 Repeat the previous steps to continue the weave. As you weave, make sure your 28-gauge wire remains tight, particularly on the ends.

Variation

Wrap the base wire on the end twice before continuing on with the weave. This creates a smoother, more polished line on the edge of the weave, while also thickening the base wire being wrapped. This is a subtle way of drawing your eyes without being too obvious *(Figure 8)*.

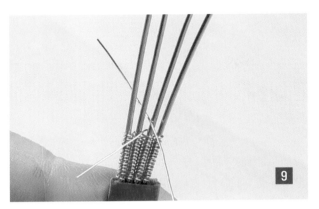

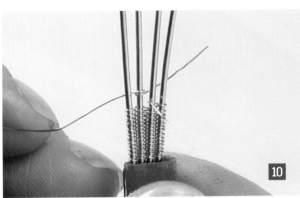

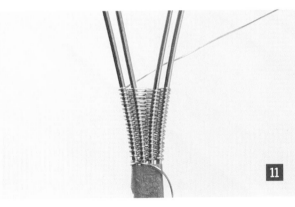

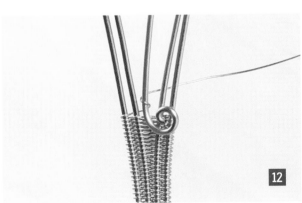

Adding a New Weaving Wire

Breaks happen. When they do, it doesn't mean that you have to start over. Look at where your break happened. If it is on an outside base wire, undo the weave until you are in the inside of the weave between two base wires. You should end up with a little tail.

Take your new length of 28-gauge wire and insert the tip into the opposite direction of the existing tail. You now have two tails facing opposite directions between the same base wires. Leave enough of a tail to hold down with your thumb *(Figure 9)*.

Wrap once around the base wire before continuing on with your weave in the same direction you were weaving before *(Figure 10)*.

After you have woven your strip, trim the tails flush then use your flat-nose pliers to tuck the trimmed ends into the weave.

Adding a Base Wire

To add a base wire into the weave, spread the existing wires apart where the new wire should be inserted. Continuing weaving until you have enough space to comfortably fit the new wire between the existing base wires *(Figure 11)*.

Weaving left to right, stop when you reach the new wire. Coming from the back, completely wrap around the new base wire once before continuing the weave. This secures the new wire to the base *(Figure 12)*.

Modified Soumak Weave

This is my favorite weave. It can be woven into a strip and shaped. Once formed, it holds its shape well. It also works great when weaving shaped wires together. When weaving, the goal is to have the base wires as close together as possible. Modified Soumak itself creates a tight, uniform texture that does not detract from the overall design. Although it's more complicated than the Basic Figure 8 weave, it is repetitive. However, since the weave is tighter, puncturing the weave when adding an embellishment does take a little more strength.

The Modified Soumak weave has a tendency to zigzag. Compress frequently to keep the rows straight. A row is weaving left to right, and then right to left, finishing at the starting point. It consists of one row of short wraps and one row of longer wraps. You can use two wires or more for the base. The more wires you add, the less compact it becomes.

1 Straighten 16" (40.5 cm) of 18-gauge practice wire and cut four 4" (10 cm) lengths. Tape the 4 wires close together at the bottom. These are the base wires. Cut 5' (152.5 cm) of 28-gauge practice wire; this is the wire used for weaving.

Left to Right: Back Row

Start by weaving left to right. The base wires are numbered starting on the left with Wire 1, followed by 2, 3, and 4.

2 Leaving a 6" (15 cm) tail, bring the rest of the 28-gauge wire to the back of the base wires, thread it between Wires 1 and 2, toward the front, and then wrap it around Wire 1 in a clockwise direction toward the back *(Figure 1)* .

3 Bring the 28-gauge wire across the back of Wire 2 and thread it between Wires 2 and 3. Wrap the 28-gauge wire around Wire 2 in a clockwise direction, ending with the 28-gauge wire in the back *(Figure 2)*.

4 Bring the 28-gauge wire across the back of Wire 3 and thread it between Wires 3 and 4. Wrap the 28-gauge wire around Wire 3 in a clockwise direction, ending with the 28-gauge wire in the back.

5 Bring the 28-gauge wire across the back of Wire 4 and then wrap it around Wire 4 in a clockwise direction, ending with the 28-gauge wire in the back *(Figure 3)*.

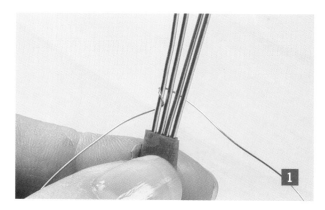

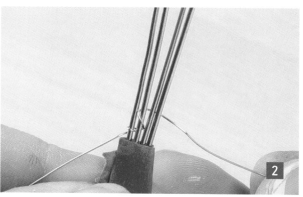

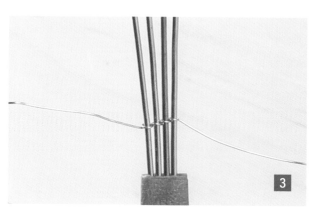

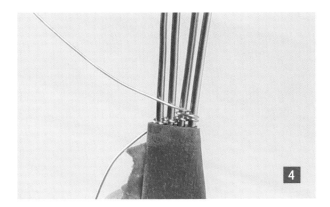

Right to Left: Front Row

You will now be weaving back across the front, right to left. The 28-gauge wire should be in the back, between Wires 3 and 4.

6 Bring the 28-gauge wire across the back of Wire 4 and around the outside of Wire 4 toward the front.

7 Bring the 28-gauge wire over the front of Wires 4 and 3, and then thread it between Wires 2 and 3, toward the back *(Figure 4)*. Wrap the 28-gauge wire around Wire 3 going clockwise, ending on the front, on the right side of Wire 3.

8 Bring the 28-gauge wire over the front of Wires 3 and 2, and then thread it between Wires 1 and 2, toward the back. Wrap the 28-gauge wire around Wire 2 going clockwise, ending on the front, on the right side of Wire 2 *(Figure 5)*.

9 Bring the 28-gauge wire over the front of Wires 2 and 1, and then wrap it around Wire 1 going clockwise. The 28-gauge wire should now be in the front and on the right side of Wire 1 *(Figure 6)*.

10 You have completed the first row. You should have a row of four short wraps followed by a row of three long wraps. These two rows equal one completed row. Repeat the weave pattern as you did in the beginning, weaving from left to right *(Figure 7)*.

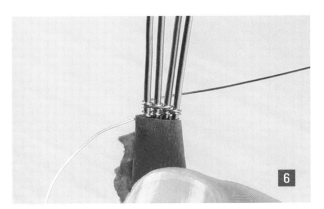

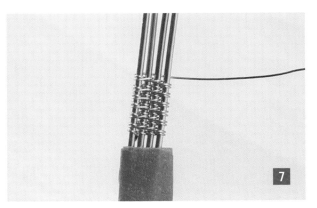

Adding a New Weaving Wire

If the weaving wire breaks, back out of the weave so you are somewhere in the middle of the weave. Insert the new wire between the same two base wires as the broken tail. (The new tail should be going in the opposite direction as the broken tail.) Hold down the tail with your thumb and continue your weave *(Figures 8 and 9)*. Trim the tails after you finish the weave.

When this weave is done properly, the base wires are only a 28-gauge wire distance apart, so the new 28-gauge wire stays tucked between the base wires without the need for an additional wrap. And as you compress the weave, it further secures the new 28-gauge wire. If there is too much space between the base wires, it will not hold. If this is the case, wrap around the base wires once before continuing the weave.

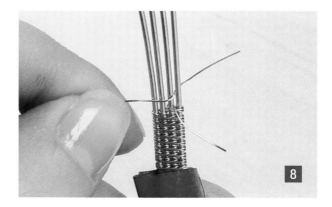

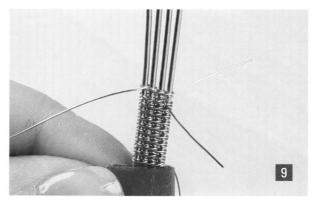

Lashing Weave

Lashing can be incorporated into a two-base-wire weave by alternating coiling with lashing, creating a pleasing pattern. It has the added appeal of being a quick weave, and is my go-to weave when I need to weave around an enclosed shape like the links in the Interlace Bracelet (page 70).

1 Straighten 8" (20.5 cm) of 18-gauge practice wire and cut two 4" (10 cm) lengths. Tape the 2 wires close together at the bottom; these are the base wires. Cut 3' (91.5 cm) of 28-gauge practice wire; this is the wire used for weaving.

> **NOTE** *The left wire will be Wire 1, followed by Wire 2.*

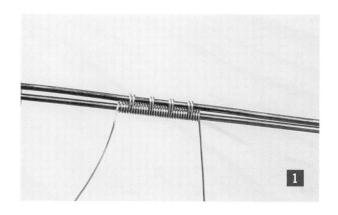

2 Leaving a 6" (15 cm) tail, bring the rest of the 28-gauge wire to the back of the base wires. Coil the 28-gauge wire around Wire 1 twice, making sure that the coils are tight. At the next turn, coil around Wires 1 and 2 two times to lash them together. Coil Wire 2 six times and then lash Wires 1 and 2 twice. Continue the pattern until you reach the desired length *(Figure 1)*.

> **NOTE** *Always coil around one wire before lashing two wires together. This creates a 28-gauge buffer between the base wires.*

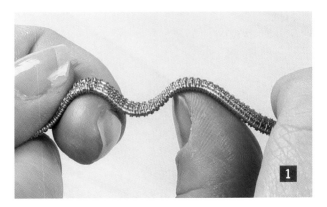

Sculpting Woven Strips

Forming woven wire strips is an easy way to add dimension and depth to jewelry. You can choose to go subtle or extreme, altering the design and its size. Forming is usually the last thing I do. When possible, I create my woven forms flat because it's easier to achieve symmetry.

A straight woven strip can be shaped in a variety of ways. For an organic look, use your hands to bend, twist, or gently curve the weave *(Figure 1)*. For more uniform shaping, use a mandrel. If your fingers are not strong enough to shape the strip against the mandrel, use a rawhide mallet.

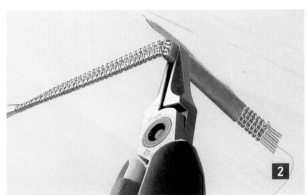

Sometimes when forming your woven wire, you will need to use more force, whether it is with a mallet or pliers. However, the small-gauged wire is delicate and must be handled properly. The last things you want to do are flatten or break the weave. To prevent damaging the weave, cover your weave with painter's tape or use nylon-jaw pliers *(Figure 2)*.

sculpting

One of the aspects that drew me to wire was its ability to be sculpted and shaped. In this section, we will explore a variety of ways to sculpt jewelry and the subtle ways sculpting your wire evokes a different feel in the finished jewelry. Don't discount the power of subtly shaping. The slightest doming in a design can breathe life to the jewelry and help draw the eyes to the focal point of your work.

double helix

EARRINGS

These earrings are a good introduction to using your fingers to sculpt a woven strip. While we weave these earrings flat, they transform by adding a little twist.

EARRING LENGTH
2½" (6.5 cm) , not includ-ing the French ear wires

MATERIALS
4½" (11.5 cm) of fine silver 14-gauge wire

25" (63.5 cm) of fine silver 20-gauge wire

12' (3.7 m) of fine silver 28-gauge wire

Two ear wires

TOOLS
Wire cutters

Needle files

Chasing hammer

Bench block

1.25 mm hole punch pliers

Butane micro torch

Cross-lock tweezers

Tile or rimmed cookie sheet

Quenching bowl

Permanent marker

Painter's tape

Chain-nose pliers

Nylon-jaw pliers (optional)

Liver of sulfur

0000 Steel wool

Brass bristle brush

1 Cut 2¼" (5.5 cm) of 14-gauge wire. File one end flat and paddle ¼" (6 mm) of one end to ⅛" (3 mm) wide. Punch a 1.25 mm hole in the center of the paddled wire and round the end with your files.

2 With the butane torch and cross-lock tweezers, grasp the wire at the paddle end and draw a bead on the opposite end of the wire. Quench in water. Once cool, mark the center with the permanent marker *(Figure 1)*.

3 Cut two of each length of 20-gauge wire: 2" (5 cm), 1¾" (4.5 cm), and 1½" (3.8 cm). Again using the butane torch and cross-lock tweezers, draw a bead at each end of all six wires. Quench in water to cool.

4 With the chasing hammer, lightly flatten the balled end to a disc.

5 Line up the six 20-gauge wires on either side of your 14-gauge wire going from the longest to the shortest, with the balls graduating directly above the balled end of the 14-gauge wire *(Figure 2)*. I will refer to the base wires by number, starting on the far left with Wire 1, followed by 2, 3, 4, 5, 6, and 7.

6 Tape the seven wires together at the center mark of the 14-gauge wire, positioning the hammered paddles so they're perpendicular to the tape. Cut a 6' (1.8 m) section of 28-gauge wire. Position the center of the 28-gauge wire between Wires 1 and 2. Using the Modified Soumak weave (see Modified Soumak Weave, page 42), weave Wires 1, 2, and 3 for the first row *(Figure 3)*.

Fig 1

Fig 2

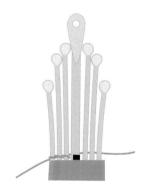

Fig 3

Fig 4

Fig 5

Fig 6

7 Slip the 28-gauge wire between Wires 3 and 4, to bring the 28-gauge wire to the front of the work *(Figure 4)*. Cross the 28-gauge wire over Wire 4, the 14-gauge wire, and between Wires 4 and 5 *(Figure 5)*.

> **NOTE** *As you weave, you'll notice you're essentially switching to the Basic Figure 8 weave (see Basic Figure 8 Weave, page 38) when you reach the center 14-gauge base wire. Having a looser weave around the 14-gauge wire will allow you to twist the woven strip with more ease when you're done weaving. You will switch to this weave every time you come to the center 14-gauge wire as you weave.*

8 Return to weaving Modified Soumak weave across Wires 5, 6, and 7. Bring the 28-gauge wire around to the front to continue the weave, making sure that you switch to the Basic Figure 8 weave when you come to the 14-gauge wire *(Figure 6)*.

9 Decrease the weave as you reach each paddled end *(Figure 7)*. Coil around the last 20-gauge wire three times to secure the 28-gauge wire, then trim off the excess wire *(Figure 8)*.

10 Remove the tape, flip the woven form over, and use the remaining 28-gauge wire to finish weaving the second half of the woven strip following steps 6–9 *(Figure 9)*.

11 Hold the top of the woven form with your thumb and forefinger of one hand and the bottom of the woven strip with the thumb and forefinger of your other hand. Twist your hands in the opposite direction. Your woven strip will start to twist and rotate around the 14-gauge wire *(Figures 10 and 11)*.

12 With chain-nose pliers rotate the paddled balls so that they sit flush along the edge of the weave.

13 Repeat steps 1–12 for the second earring component. In step 11, twist your woven strip in the opposite direction to make the second earring a mirror image of the first.

14 Attach an ear wire to each component through the hole in the 14-gauge wire.

Finishing

15 Oxidize with liver of sulfur, then polish with 0000 super fine steel wool. Use a jeweler's brass bristle brush to remove the steel wool caught in the weave.

Fig 7

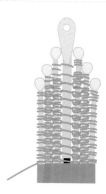

Fig 8

Fig 9

Fig 10

Fig 11

tidal wave

RING

Normally designs are woven flat then sculpted to add dimension. In this ring, you'll weave and sculpt at the same time. The end result is a beautiful, undulating, organic ring. Have fun curving and shaping the wire. The idea is to relax and let the wire speak to you.

RING SIZE
1" (2.5 cm), ring
size is variable

MATERIALS
8" (20.5 cm) of sterling
silver 16-gauge wire

20" (51 cm) of fine
silver 20-gauge wire

13' (4 m) of fine silver
28-gauge wire

5 mm pearl or bead

TOOLS
Ruler

Wire cutters

Permanent marker

Round-nose pliers

Mallet

Ring mandrel

Chain-nose pliers

Liver of sulfur

0000 Steel wool

Brass bristle brush

Preparations

1 Cut an 8" (20.5 cm) length of 16-gauge wire; mark the center. Center the mark to the back of your round-nose pliers. With your fingers, form the wire around the pliers until the arms are parallel in a U shape.

2 With your fingers, bring the two arms together an inch above the curve, keeping the arms parallel. With your mallet, shape the curved section around a ring mandrel at your desired ring size *(Figure 1)*.

3 Cut two 10" (25.5 cm) lengths of 20-gauge wire; mark the center of each wire. Center the mark of one wire just below the tip of your round-nose pliers. With your fingers, form the wire around the jaw of the pliers until the arms are parallel in a U shape. Repeat for the second wire.

4 Slip both U-shaped 20-gauge wires onto the 16-gauge wire so that they are resting in the bottom of the curve of the 16-gauge wire. Shift the arms of the 20-gauge wires so that they are parallel and the arms are alternating between each other *(Figure 2)*.

5 Working from a 13' (4 m) length of 28-gauge wire, weave the four 20-gauge base wires together using the Basic Figure 8 weave (see Basic Figure 8 Weave, page 38). Compress the weave as you work and push it as close as possible to the 16-gauge wire. Weave until you have woven the distance between the two arms of the 16-gauge wire *(Figure 3)*.

TIP MANAGING WIRES

Due to the complexity of the design, it can be difficult to remember which wire is which as you work. To remember the wire numbers, use your permanent marker to create small dots on the end that correlate with the number. For example, Wire 1 would have one mark or dot on the end while Wire 4 has four marks or dots.

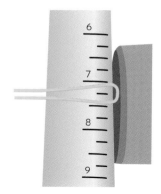

Fig 1

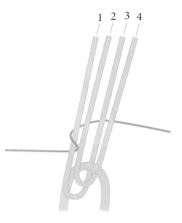

Fig 2

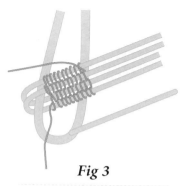

Fig 3

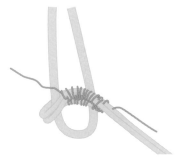

Fig 4

Fig 5

Fig 6

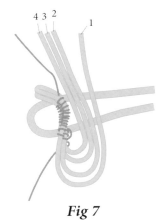

Fig 7

Free-Form Shaping

6 With your fingers, curve the woven section. Rotate the weave so that the end of the weave rests perpendicular to the 16-gauge arm on the right.

> **NOTE** *It is important that you maintain an opening between the curved section of the 16-gauge wire and the curved section of the weave* **(Figure 4)**.

7 Weave for two more rows, then secure the woven strip to the 16-gauge wire to the right side with your weave, making a total of five base wires.

> **NOTE** *It is important to make sure you are wrapping tightly around the 16-gauge wire as you weave. This will connect the woven strip to the ring* **(Figure 5)**.

8 Hold the end of Wire 4 with your fingers and curve it across the 16-gauge base wires. Tug on the wire to shrink the curve **(Figure 6)**.

9 Shape the remaining 20-gauge wires in the same manner as step 8. Allow for some space between the wires as they curve. Let the wires stack on each other at a sloped angle. This is what will make the woven strip more dimensional **(Figure 7)**.

10 Continue to weave across Wires 1, 2, 3, and 4. Wrap around the outer 20-gauge wire, Wire 1, four times every time you come to it in your weave.

> **NOTE** *Extra wraps around the outside edge of nestled curves like this are to compensate for the largest circumference. Depending on your curvature you may find that you need more or fewer wraps. As you weave around your curve, compress the weave every row to keep it as tight as possible.*

11 When you have woven around the curved area, stop adding the extra wraps around the outer wire and continue to weave until you have reached the 16-gauge base wire on the left *(Figure 8)*. Adjust the shape of the curved weave, then secure the 20-gauge base wire to the 16-gauge wire as you did in step 7.

12 Repeat step 8, again curving the 20-gauge wire to the right so that it travels back across the 16-gauge base wires. Then shape the remaining 20-gauge wire as you did in step 9 *(Figure 9)*.

13 Continue weaving in the Basic Figure 8 pattern. Stop when the weaving wire reaches the right 16-gauge base wire. With your fingers, rotate and twist the weave so that it's perpendicular to the 16-gauge base wires.

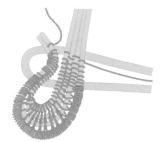

Fig 8

Fig 9

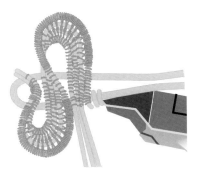

Fig 10

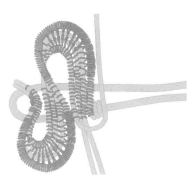

Fig 11

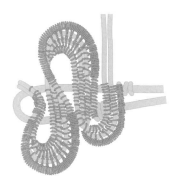

Fig 12

14 Tightly wrap the 20-gauge wire closest to the 16-gauge base wire (Wire 1) around the base wire twice. Trim excess wire *(Figure 10)*. Compress the wrapped 20-gauge wire with your chain-nose pliers.

> **NOTE** *The wrapped 20-gauge wire is what will secure the woven strip to the 16-gauge wire. If the wrap is not tight, the weave will slide back and forth on the ring.*

15 Wrap Wire 4 across the 16-gauge base wires leading it to the left arm *(Figure 11)*. Curve the remaining two 20-gauge wires as you have for previous curves, leading each into position next to Wire 4.

16 Continue weaving around the curve, adding extra wraps as needed to the outer area of the curve. Weave until you reach the 16-gauge base wire on the left.

17 Repeat step 14, and tightly wrap the 20-gauge wire furthest right around the 16-gauge base wire. Trim excess wire *(Figure 12)*. Compress the wraps around the base wire with your chain-nose pliers. Curve the last two remaining 20-gauge wires to cross over the 16-gauge base wires again.

18 Weave around the curve adding extra wraps on the outer curved 20-gauge wire. Switch back to weaving normally as you come out of the curve. Weave until you reach the 16-gauge wire on the right.

19 Wrap the 20-gauge wire on the left around the 16-gauge base wire, trim excess wire and compress the wraps with your chain-nose pliers. Curve the remaining 20-gauge wire across to the 16-gauge base wires.

20 Coil the 28-gauge weaving wire around the remaining 20-gauge wire. Wrap the 20-gauge wire around the 16-gauge base wire, trim excess wire, and compress the wrapped wire with your chain-nose pliers *(Figure 13)*.

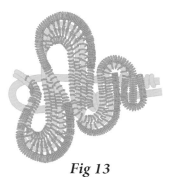

Fig 13

Finishing

21 Shape the 16-gauge base wires around the ring mandrel at the desired ring size so that the ends are touching the curve of the 16-gauge wire. Trim the 16-gauge wire to ¼" (6 mm) past the starting U in the 16-gauge wire. Slip the cut ends through the opening between the curved 16-gauge wire and the weave.

22 With chain-nose pliers, pull the 16-gauge arms tight and fold over to lock in the ring size *(Figure 14)*. Trim and tuck the ends in. Do not trim the 28-gauge tail wire from the beginning of the weave.

23 Oxidize with liver of sulfur and polish with 0000 super fine steel wool. Use a jeweler's soft brass bristle brush to remove any steel wool caught in the weave.

24 Use the tail wire from the beginning of the weave to sew in the 5 mm pearl (see Finishing Touches, page 31). Trim excess 28-gauge wire.

Fig 14

VARIATIONS

Instead of trimming all of the 20-gauge wires, use one or two to come back up after securing to swirl on top of the weave.

tempest

CLASP

Even though this is a clasp, I love wearing it in front of a necklace. It is just too pretty to hide in the back. I suggest making your first Tempest Clasp as an asymmetrical necklace. Then, take it a step further for a more challenging symmetrical design by creating a second mirror image of the clasp. The two components connect just as easily as one.

CLASP LENGTH
2½" × 1" (6.5 cm × 2.5 cm)

MATERIALS
7.5" (19 cm) of fine
silver 14-gauge wire

5" (12.5 cm) of fine
silver 16-gauge wire

12" (30.5 cm) of fine
silver 18-gauge wire

7' (2.1 m) of fine
silver 28-gauge wire

Bead of your choice
for the dangle

TOOLS
Wire cutters

Ruler

Permanent marker

Flat-nose pliers

Butane micro torch

Cross-lock tweezers

Tile or rimmed
cookie sheet

Quenching bowl

Round-nose pliers

Chasing hammer

Bench block

Needle files

Sandpaper in
graduated grits

1.25 mm hole
punch pliers

Pro-Polish pads

5 mm dowel

Liver of sulfur

0000 Steel wool

Brass bristle brush

Wire 1

1 Mark a 4½" (11.5 cm) length of 14-gauge wire 2" (5 cm) from one end. With flat-nose pliers bend the wire at the mark. Squeeze the bend to bring the arms as close as possible at the bend.

2 With the butane torch draw a bead on the wire at the bend.

3 Trim the ends to 1½" (3.8 cm) and 2" (5 cm) from the tip of the balled end. Spread the two arms apart directly above the ball letting them gently curve out as they're spread.

4 With round-nose pliers, form an open loop at the end of the 2" (5 cm) length of wire. Swirl the loop towards the balled end. With chasing hammer and bench block, flatten the loop and balled end. Following the pointed swirl instructions (see Wire Techniques, page 28) shape the open loop to a pointed swirl. Use your needle files to further shape the pointed loop, rounding and beveling the outer edge *(Figure 1)*.

5 With permanent marker block out the edges of the hammered ball to form a point or arrowhead shape. Remove the blocked-out sections with wire cutters. With needle files, bevel the outer edge to create a facet along the straight edges just cut *(Figure 2)*. Remove all file marks with sandpaper in graduated grits.

6 Bend the 1½" (3.8 cm) arm towards the balled end, keeping the arm past the bend straight. Mark the arm ¾" (2 cm) in from the cut end. With the swirled arm oriented at the bottom, use flat-nose pliers to form a 90-degree angle in the wire at the ¾" (2 cm) mark. With chasing hammer and bench block, flatten the arm to the bend just formed. The end should be no wider than 3mm. Round the cut end with needle files *(Figure 3)*. This will be referred to as Wire 1.

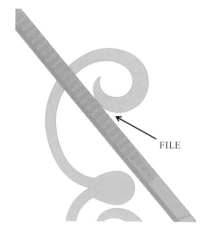

FILE

Fig 1

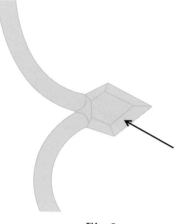

Fig 2

Fig 3

Fig 4

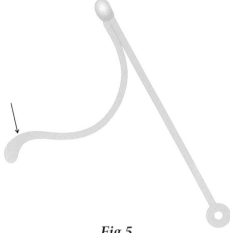

Fig 5

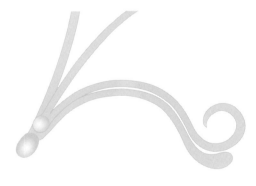

Fig 6

Wire 2

7 Repeat steps 1–2 with a 5" (12.5 cm) length of 16-gauge wire, placing the bending mark 2"(5 cm) from one end.

8 Trim the arms at 1⅝" (4.1 cm) and 2" (5 cm) from the balled end. Draw a bead on the cut end of the 2" (5 cm) arm.

> **NOTE** *The bead drawn should be small and the finished length of the balled wire should be no less than 1⅞" (4.8 cm)*

9 Form the shorter arm to the outside of the swirled arm on Wire 1, with the balled V point of the 16-gauge wire touching the curved bend in Wire 1 *(Figure 4)*.

10 With round-nose pliers, curve the end of the arm just formed into a tail. With the chasing hammer and bench block, flatten the tail. Round the hammered end with needle files. With chasing hammer and bench block, flatten your balled end on the longer arm to a 3 mm width. Punch a hole through the center of the hammered ball with 1.25 mm hole punch pliers. Remove any burs with needle files. This will be referred to as Wire 2 *(Figure 5)*.

Wire 3

11 Repeat steps 1–2 with a 6" (15 cm) length of 18-gauge wire, placing the bending mark 2½"(6.5 cm) from one end. The bead drawn should be smaller than the bead made in the same fashion on Wire 2. Cut the shorter arm to 2" (5 cm) from the balled end.

12 Spread the arms apart approximately ¼" (6 mm). With round-nose pliers, form a small loop on the end of the 2" (5 cm) arm. With chasing hammer and bench block, flatten the loop, trim, and file the outer edge of the loop to create a beveled pointed swirl. Polish with graduated sandpaper and a Pro-Polish pad to remove the file marks.

13 Place the balled end of the 18-gauge wire directly above the balled V of Wire 2. Form the looped arm to the top edge of the smaller arm of Wire 2 *(Figure 6)*. This wire will be referred to as Wire 3.

Wire 4

14 Draw a bead on the end of a 6" (15 cm) length of 18-gauge wire. Mark the wire at ¼" (6 mm) and ¾" (2 cm) from the balled end.

15 Form the balled end to the inside curve of the pointed swirled arm on Wire 1 aligning the ¾" (2 cm) mark just below the arrowhead of Wire 1 *(Figure 7)*. This wire will be referred to as Wire 4.

Weaving

16 Working with a 7' (2.1 m) length of 28-gauge wire and leaving a 12" (30.5 cm) tail, weave Wires 4 and 1 together starting at the ¾" (2 cm) mark on Wire 4 using the Modified Soumak weave (see Modified Soumak Weave, page 42). Weave for five complete rows. Push the weave as close to the arrowhead as possible while still keeping the ¾" (2 cm) mark on Wire 4 from shifting *(Figure 8)*.

17 Add Wire 2 to the outer edge of the swirled arm of Wire 1, with the balled end of the V point touching the curved bend in Wire 1. Weave the three wires together for 3 rows *(Figure 9)*.

18 Place the balled V point of Wire 3 behind the balled V point of Wire 2 with the looped arm of Wire 3 running along the top edge of Wire 2. Weave all four wires together to the ¼" (6 mm) mark on Wire 4.

TIP. ORIENTING THE FORM

At this point, I like to orient my form with the swirls on the right-hand side.

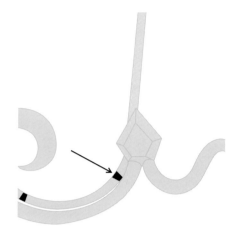

Fig 7

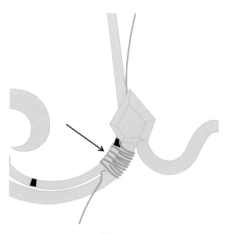

Fig 8

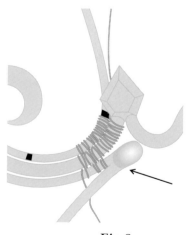

Fig 9

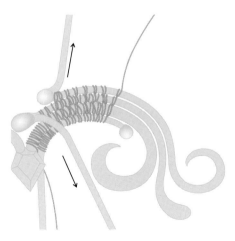

Fig 10

19 Push the long arm of Wire 3 up away from the form. Mark the arm ⅝"(1.5 cm) from the balled V point. Bend the long arm of Wire 2 down across the woven form *(Figure 10)*.

20 Place the 5 mm dowel between the long arm of Wire 3 and the weave. Shape Wire 3 over the dowel into a wave. Bend up at the ⅝" (1.5 cm) mark; adjust the curve by pulling out at the bend so that the mark at the bend lines up with the end of the weave and sits above the short arm of Wire 3 *(Figure 11)*.

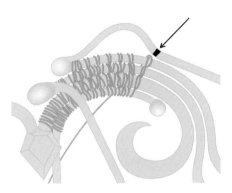

Fig 11

21 Weave all five wires together for three complete rows. Use the tip of your round-nose pliers to form Wire 3 into a simple loop over the three rows of weaving.

> **NOTE** *Do not cut the long arm of Wire 3 after forming the simple loop. The tail should travel behind the work.*

Weave Wires 1, 2, and 3 together until you reach the balled end of Wire 4. Decrease the weave, weaving only Wires 2 and 3 together for another three rows *(Figure 12)*.

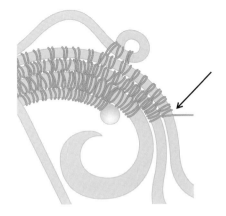

Fig 12

Shaping & Positioning Wire Ends

22 Mark Wire 4 at ⅝" (1.5 cm) from the start of the weave near the arrowhead. Bend Wire 4 to the back of the work and form a curve hiding it behind Wire 1. Bend Wire 4 at the ⅝" (1.5 cm) mark to flow back towards the weaving. Using the 12" (30.5 cm) tail of 28-gauge wire, coil the length of Wire 4 from the weaving to the point it crosses the arm of Wire 1. Lash Wire 4 to Wire 1 three times where they cross (see Lashing Weave, page 44). Thread the 28-gauge wire through the lashing twice and trim off the excess 28-gauge wire. Curve Wire 4 in a wide arc so that it runs parallel to the short arm of Wire 3 *(Figure 13)*. Returning to the front of the work, lash Wire 4 to the short arm of Wire 3 with three wraps.

23 Serpentine the long arm of Wire 2 over the front of the form, bending towards the loop in Wire 3 and then out across the pointed swirls of Wire 1.

24 Place a 5 mm dowel above the lashes on Wire 4. Bend Wire 4 around the 5 mm dowel *(Figure 14)*. With your fingers, bend Wire 4 so that the tail travels up between the loop in Wire 3 and the wave formed in step 20. Trim Wire 4 to ¼" (6 mm) beyond the highest point of the wave in Wire 3. Mark ⅜" (1 cm) in from the end just cut *(Figure 15)*. Bend Wire 4 at a 90-degree angle, bending towards the back. Tuck the bent wire inside the wave of Wire 3 and wrap it against the back of the work.

25 Working on the back of the work, shape the long arm of Wire 3 to curve along the pointed swirl of Wire 1. Rest a 5 mm dowel against the swirl of Wire 1 and the shaped end of Wire 2. Form Wire 3 around the dowel to form a U shape. Trim Wire 3 just before the lashes made to Wires 3 and 4. Bring the long arm of Wire 2 through the loop you just made *(Figure 16)*. With the 28-gauge wire, coil down the short arm of Wire 3 for about ¼" (6 mm). Lash Wire 3 to Wire 4 near the pointed swirl of Wire 3.

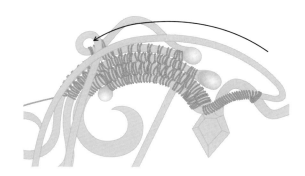

Fig 13 - Back View

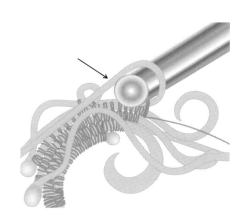

Fig 14

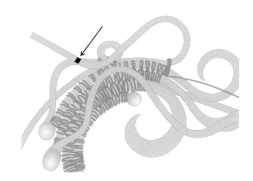

Fig 15

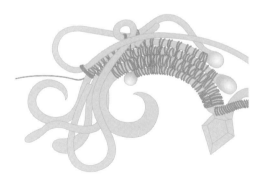

Fig 16- Back View

Fig 17

Fig 18

26 Continue to coil Wire 3 until it's possible to lash Wire 2 to Wire 3.

> **NOTE** *If the hole in the hammered ball of Wire 2 faces the front of the work, rotate it 90 degrees.*

Lash the two wires together three times. Thread your 28-gauge wire through the lashings in the back twice. Trim off the excess 28-gauge wire.

27 Measure and mark ⅜" (1 cm) from the hammered end of Wire 1. With round-nose pliers placed over the mark, fold the end to the front and over the pliers. Bend the end up. This is the hook of the clasp. Adjust the hook to barely slip a 14-gauge wire through *(Figure 17)*.

Finishing

28 Using a 3" (7.5 cm) length of 14-gauge wire and round-nose pliers, form a simple loop at one end and shape into a pointed swirl. Polish your swirl with graduated sandpaper and a Pro-Polish pad. Continue to swirl the 14-gauge wire around in a larger spiral. Bend the unformed end of wire to a 90-degree angle from the swirl. With chasing hammer and bench block, flatten the straight end to 3 mm wide and punch a 1.25 mm hole in the center of the paddle. Round the edge with your files *(Figure 18)*.

29 Attach a dangle to the hole punched in the straight end of the swirl. Use jump rings or wire-wrapped links to attach chain through the hole in the hammered ball of Wire 2 on the woven form and to the spiral made in step 28.

30 Oxidize with liver of sulfur and polish with 0000 super fine steel wool. Scrub with a jeweler's brass bristle brush to remove any steel wool caught in the weave.

interlace

BRACELET

This bracelet looks deceptively hard, but combining the two woven strips is simpler than it looks. You'll begin by weaving the outer frame of rings before lacing a woven strip through. When finished, others will marvel at how the piece was created.

BRACELET SIZE
6¼" (16 cm) with 1"
(2.5 cm) extension chain

MATERIALS
56" (142 cm) of sterling
silver 16-gauge wire

18" (45.5 cm) of sterling
silver 18-gauge wire

16' (4.9 m) of fine
silver 26-gauge wire

20' (6.1 m) of fine
silver 28-gauge wire

1" (2.5 cm) of 2–3 mm
chain (for extension)

TOOLS
Ruler

Wire cutters

8 mm dowel

Flush cutters

Chasing hammer

Bench block

2 pairs of chain-
nose pliers

Permanent marker

Round-nose pliers

Flat-nose pliers

Painter's tape

Bracelet mandrel

Files

Liver of sulfur

0000 Steel wool

Brass bristle brush

Eyelet Strip

1 Cut a 20" (51 cm) length of 16-gauge wire. Coil the 16-gauge wire around an 8 mm dowel. With flush cutters, cut the coil to form jump rings.

> **NOTE** *You will use 12 jump rings for a 6 ¼" (16 cm) bracelet. If you need to adjust the size of the bracelet, you will need to add or decrease the jump rings in groups of two. This will change the bracelet in 1" (2.5 cm) segments.*

2 With the ball-peen end of your chasing hammer, flatten the cut ends of each jump ring *(Figure 1)*. With chain-nose pliers, open all the jump rings after hammering them.

3 Cut an 18" (45.5 cm) length of 18-gauge wire; mark the center. Cut a 16' (4.9 m) length of 26-gauge wire and find the center. Lining up the center of the 26-gauge wire at the center mark of the 18-gauge wire, wrap the 18-gauge wire four times with the 26-gauge wire. Lash (see Lashing Weave, page 44) an open jump ring to the 18-gauge wire twice *(Figure 2)*.

4 Form the 18-gauge wire on the jump ring to the right of the lashing *(Figure 3).* Continue coiling around the 18-gauge wire for a total of 4 wraps before lashing the jump ring twice to the 18-gauge wire. Alternate this pattern of 4 coils, 2 lashes until you come around to the paddled end. Bend the 18-gauge wire out away from the jump ring after the last lashing and coil 8 times around the 18-gauge wire. Repeat on the other side. Close the jump ring. *(Figure 4)*.

TIP JUMP RINGS

Before closing my jump ring, I like to take my chain-nose pliers and grip one paddled end and rotate the jump ring to see if I can fit another set of coils and lashes to the jump ring.

Fig 1

Fig 2

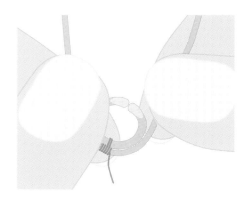

Fig 3

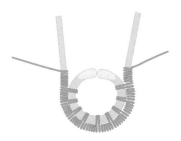

Fig 4

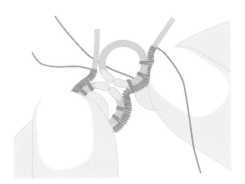

Fig 5

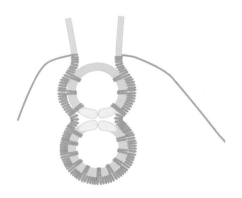

Fig 6

Fig 7

5 Lash the next jump ring to the base. Orient the jump ring so that the paddled ends are facing the previous ring. Coil 7 times. Make sure your coils are compact. Form the 18-gauge wire to your jump ring. Lash twice around the jump ring, coil 7 times, and then lash two more times. Bend the 18-gauge wire out away from the jump ring and coil 8 times. You should have three sets of lashes *(Figure 5)*.

TIP CURVED SHAPES

Curved shapes are notorious for shifting and rotating as you are weaving. Use that to your advantage here. Rotate your jump ring with the paddles to the side for better access to weave around, then spin your jump ring around to face down after you close your ring before starting the next step.

6 Close the second jump ring. Repeat the coiling and lashing on the other side, but this time you will have to thread your 26-gauge wire through the jump ring every time you lash *(Figure 6)*.

7 Continue lashing jump rings to the 18-gauge outer wire, shaping it to the rings as you weave. With each new jump ring, adjust the orientation of the paddled ends to alternate, keeping paddled sides together *(Figure 7)*.

> **NOTE** *You may notice that the jump rings will be touching when the paddled ends are facing each other and will be further apart when they are not. This is normal. If you are having a hard time fitting a jump ring in between the 18-gauge wires, then spread them further apart. This will also drop the jump ring so they are closer together.*

8 When 12 jump rings are lashed to the 18-gauge wire, coil the weaving wire around the 18-gauge wire 6 times on either side. Trim excess 26-gauge wire. Set aside.

> **NOTE** *As you add your jump rings, pay attention to how they are stacking on top of each other to maintain a straight line. It is very easy for the eyelet strip to begin to curve as you add each new jump ring.*

Woven Strip

9 Cut two 16" (40.5 cm) lengths of 16-gauge wire; mark the centers. Take one 16" (40.5 cm) length and line up the center mark to your round-nose pliers. Form a U in the 16-gauge wire around the base of your pliers. The two arms should be parallel and about 3 mm apart. Mark the two arms ¼" (6 mm) from the bottom of the U. Slip the 1" (2.5 cm) extension chain onto the wire.

10 Take the remaining 16" (40.5 cm) length and fold it at the center mark with your flat-nose pliers. This wire should nestle within the first 16" (40.5 cm) length of 16-gauge wire, with the arms running parallel and having a 28-gauge distance between each arm **(Figure 8)**.

11 With 20' (6.1 m) of 28-gauge wire, begin weaving the four 16-gauge wires together with Modified Soumak weave (see Modified Soumak Weave, page 42). Compress and adjust the first row of weaving to line up with the ¼" (6 mm) mark on the base wires. Pull the two inner wires flush to the weave to create an opening. Wrap your tail around the inside 16-gauge wire two times and trim flush **(Figure 9)**.

TIP MAINTAINING SPACE

It is important to maintain the space between the outer 16-gauge wire and the inner 16-gauge wire. As you compress the weave, you can end up pushing them closer together until there is no space left. To prevent this, cut a 6" (15 cm) length of painter's tape and roll it up along the length of the tape. Stick this tape in between the two wires as a buffer. You can also use a 3 mm dowel.

12 Continue weaving in Modified Soumak weave until the woven strip is the same length as the eyelet strip. Set aside.

> **NOTE** *It is important that you maintain a tight, consistent weave along the length of the strip. If your woven strip starts to spread in width, it may not fit between the jump rings of the eyelet strip.*

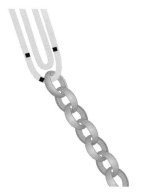

Fig 8

Fig 9

Fig 10

Fig 11

Forming

13 Form the eyelet strip by bending the strip accordion-style between each jump ring *(Figure 10)*. Orientate the strip so that the open ends of the jump rings are on the bottom; this is the back of the bracelet.

14 Thread the woven strip through the jump rings of the eyelet strip, leading the extension chain through the finished end of the eyelet strip first *(Figure 11)*.

15 Wrap the 18-gauge wires from the eyelet strip around the outer 16-gauge wire at the opening in the first woven strip, going from the inside out. Wrap twice, and then trim off the excess 18-gauge wire *(Figure 12)*.

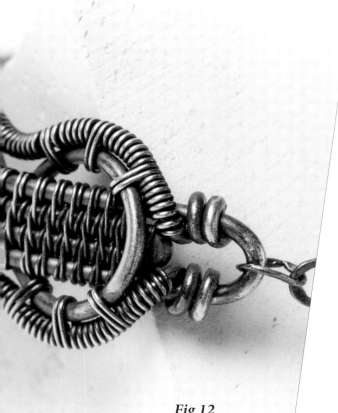

The woven and eyelet strips are married into a single piece in step 15.

Fig 12

16 Starting on the end with the chain, form the two strips together by bending the combined strips in the opposite direction of the original bends made in the eyelet strip in step 13. This will straighten the eyelet strip while at the same time sculpting the woven strip to conform around the eyelet strip. Overexaggerate the bends to give more depth to the woven strip *(Figure 13)*.

TIP BUNCHING

As you work your way across the bracelet, don't let the eyelet strip bunch up. Continually push the eyelet strip along the woven strip to stretch it back out.

Fig 13

Finishing

17 Bend the four 16-gauge wires of the woven strip left unfinished at a 90-degree angle to the bracelet and trim off the excess, leaving a ¼" (6 mm) tail. With your chain-nose pliers, bend the wires to the back of the bracelet. Cover the ends with painter's tape and pinch the wire ends with flat-nose pliers further to tuck them in *(Figure 14)*.

18 Form the bracelet around a bracelet mandrel. Set aside.

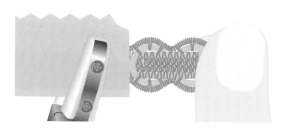

Fig 14

19 Make a clasp; cut a 3" (7.5 cm) length of 16-gauge wire. File one end smooth. Form a simple loop at one end of the wire with round-nose pliers. Bend the loop at a 90-degree angle to the wire. Mark the wire 1" (2.5 cm) from the loop. Center the mark in the base of your round-nose pliers, with the loop running parallel to the jaws. Form the wire over towards the loop. Curve the wire out just before the loop and bend the loop 90 degrees from the hook. Trim the excess wire beyond the curve and file the cut end smooth. With your chasing hammer and bench block, hammer the curves of the clasp and flare out the cut end, then round the flared end with your files.

20 Attach clasp hook to the end of the bracelet without the extension chain.

21 Oxidize with liver of sulfur, and then polish with 0000 super fine steel wool and a jeweler's brass bristle brush.

lilium
BRACELET

Don't hesitate to overexaggerate the edges when forming this bracelet. This is what gives it character and emphasizes the organic nature of the design. If your fingers are having a difficult time shaping, use your nylon-jaw flat-nose pliers.

BRACELET DIAMETER
6 ¾" (17 cm)

MATERIALS
70" (1.8 m) of fine silver 18-gauge wire

17" (43 cm) of sterling silver 16-gauge wire

12" (30.5 cm) of fine silver 26-gauge wire

42' (12.8 m) of fine silver 30-gauge wire

2 mm, 3 mm, or 4 mm metal beads to embellish

TOOLS
Ruler

Wire cutters

Permanent marker

Round-nose pliers

Painter's tape

Bobbin

Ring clamp (optional)

Flat-nose pliers

Beading awl

Bracelet mandrel

Chasing hammer

Bench block

Files

Liver of sulfur

0000 Steel wool

Brass bristle brush

Preparation

1 Cut one 7½" (19 cm) length of 16-gauge wire. Mark the wire at 2, 3, 3¾, 4, and 4½" (6.5, 7.5, 9.5, 10, and 11.5 cm) along the length. Cut one 6½" (16.5 cm) length of 16-gauge wire; mark the center.

2 Cut four 6½" (16.5 cm) lengths of 18-gauge wire; mark the center.

3 Cut one 5" (12.5 cm) length of 18-gauge wire and four 3½" (9 cm) lengths of 18-gauge wire. With round-nose pliers, form a loop at one end of each wire and continue to curl, giving the loops a slight swirl *(Figure 1)*.

4 Arrange the wires for weaving, aligning the center marks; place two 6½" (16.5 cm) 18-gauge wires on either side of the 16-gauge wires. While holding the wires together, mark the longest wire 1" (2.5 cm) from the end and mark the 5 shorter wires ½" (1.3 cm) from the ends. These marks will all align. Tape the wires together at this mark. I will refer to these as Wire 1, 2, 3, 4, 5, and 6, from left to right.

> **NOTE** *I recommend using marker to label the wires to maintain the order.*

5 Cut 40' (12.2 m) of 30-gauge wire and wind it on a bobbin.

Fig 1

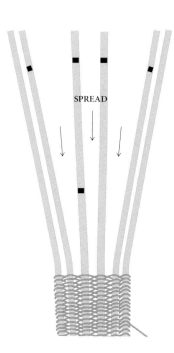

Fig 2

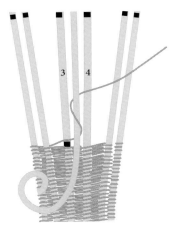

Fig 3

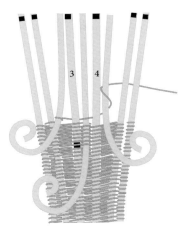

Fig 4

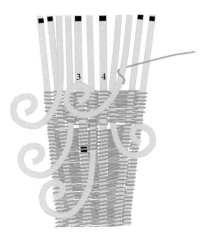

Fig 5

Weaving

TIP. RING CLAMP

This bracelet has a lot of weaving; use a ring clamp to reduce hand fatigue.

6 Leaving an 8" (20.5 cm) tail, begin weaving the 6 wires together with Basic Figure 8 weave (see Basic Figure 8 Weave, page 38). Stop weaving at the 2½" (6.5 cm) mark on Wire 3.

7 Spread the base wires apart between Wires 2 and 3, 3 and 4, and 4 and 5. The goal is to have enough room at the 3" (7.5 cm) mark to add in additional base wires between the spread wires *(Figure 2)*. Continue to weave the spread wires together, stopping between Wires 2 and 3 at the 3" (7.5 cm) mark on Wire 3.

8 Add the 5" (12.5 cm) 18-gauge wire between Wires 3 and 4 with the swirl on top of the woven area. Working from back to front, wrap the weaving wire around the new wire before continuing to weave. This secures the new wire to the weave and is done every time we introduce a new wire into the weave. Adjust Wires 3 and 4 so that they are running parallel to the new 18-gauge wire *(Figure 3)*.

9 Continue to Basic Figure 8 weave, joining new 18-gauge wire swirls between Wires 2 and 3, and Wires 4 and 5 about ¼" (6 mm) after adding the first 5" (12.5 cm) length of 18-gauge wire *(Figure 4)*.

TIP SWIRLS

You might have noticed that I have not mentioned how to orientate the swirls. This will happen before we decrease. Keep your focus on weaving precisely, not on the placement of the swirled wire.

10 Allow the base wires to continue to spread apart to make room for two additional base wires to be added. One is added to the left side between Wire 2 and the 18-gauge wire added in step 9, and one on the right in the mirror position next to Wire 5 *(Figure 5)*.

11 Once secured, adjust the eleven base wires so they are parallel. Continue Basic Figure 8 weave passing the center marks and stop at the 4" (10 cm) mark on Wire 3 *(Figure 6)*.

12 With round-nose pliers, adjust the swirls into a pleasing arrangement *(Figure 7)*.

TIP.

Because this weave is a looser weave, you can also pull the swirls out further from the weave if you want more exposed base wires, or push the swirls further into the weave by tugging the ends.

13 Bend the 4th wire from the left and the 4th wire from the right to a 90-degree angle, perpendicular to the weave. Trim to ⅛" (3 mm) *(Figure 8)*.

14 Adjust the base wires to close the gap left by the wires just cut. Continue weaving Basic Figure 8 weave (see Basic Figure 8 Weave, page 38) until all the base wires have converged and are running parallel to each other, approximately ¼" (6 mm) past the cut wires.

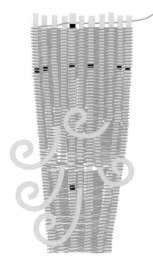

Fig 6

Fig 7

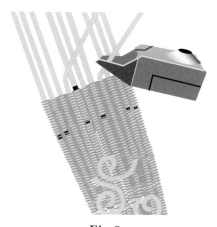

Fig 8

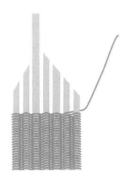

Fig 9

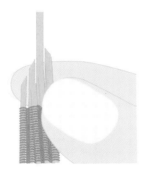

Fig 10

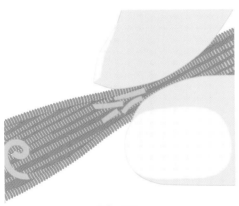

Fig 11

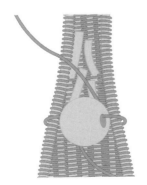

Fig 12

15 Repeat step 13 with the 3rd wire from the left and the 3rd wire from the right. Repeat step 14, realigning the base wires and weaving until 1" (2.5 cm) from the end of the longest 16-gauge wire. Cut the 30-gauge wire leaving an 8" (20.5 cm) tail.

> **TIP**
>
> If steps 13–15 are done correctly, you will have decreased by four wires before reaching the 4½" (11.5 cm) mark on Wire 3.

Forming

16 With the cutters, trim the ends of your wire at an angle. Do not cut the longest 16-gauge wire *(Figure 9)*. Repeat on opposite end.

17 Use flat-nose or nylon-jaw pliers to press the protruding 18-gauge wires that were cut in steps 13 and 15 so they are flush against the weave.

18 Fold the edges of the end of the weave together *(Figure 10)*. Continue forming the strip into a fold directly over the cut ends, where the weave was decreased. With your fingers, pinch the edges of the weave to hide the cut ends of wire *(Figure 11)*.

19 With the beading awl, pierce the weave on both sides just before the concealed cut wires. Thread one end of a 12" (30.5 cm) length of 26-gauge wire through the punctured weave on the left. Leave a 3" (7.5 cm) tail on the inside of your folded weave.

20 Add a 4 mm bead to the 26-gauge wire. Cross over to the right side of the weave and thread the 26-gauge wire through the hole punctured in step 19, making sure that you are coming from the outside and going into the center *(Figure 12)*.

21 Pierce your weave on both sides ahead of the 4 mm bead and over the concealed wires, about the space of your next bead. Thread the 26-gauge wire from the inside of the fold through the hole on the right to the outside of the weave.

22 Add a 3 mm bead to the 26-gauge wire and thread the 26-gauge wire over the weave to pass through the opposite hole from the outside to the inside. Continue adding beads of decreasing size until you can no longer see the cut wire ends. Secure the 26-gauge wire through a final piercing of the weave large enough to pass the 26-gauge wire through twice. Thread the 26-gauge wire through without any beads, lashing the two woven sides together with two wraps (see Lashing Weave, page 44). Coil the 26-gauge wire around the lashings and trim off the excess. Coil the original tail around the wire going through the 4 mm bead twice and trim *(Figure 13)*.

> **NOTE** *The wire in Figure 13 has been darkened for easier viewing.*

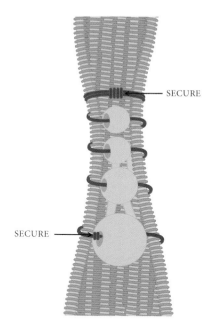

Fig 13

Fig 14

Add End Caps

23 Cut two 12" (30.5 cm) lengths of 18-gauge wire. Leaving a 3" (7.5 cm) tail, position one of the lengths of 18-gauge wire over the folded end of the bracelet approximately ¼" (6 mm) before the weave ends. Hold down the tail with your thumb and begin to coil the 18-gauge wire over the folded end. Continue to coil compactly and neatly, covering the angled ends until you reach the long 16-gauge wire. Wrap tightly around the 16-gauge wire once and trim off the excess 18-gauge wire.

24 Wrap the 3" (7.5 cm) tail once around the folded weave. With round-nose pliers, loop and swirl the end of the tail. Bend the 16-gauge wire at a 90-degree angle and form a large loop with the round-nose pliers *(Figure 14)*.

25 Create a hole with your beading awl that will allow you to pass 30-gauge wire through three times. With the 30-gauge tail, lash the swirled end of the cap to the weave.

> **NOTE** *I like to lash in two spots for added strength. Secure the 30-gauge wire by threading through your lashings twice before trimming.*

26 Repeat steps 23–25 on the other end of the bracelet, first forming a fold in the weave for the cap to wrap.

Finishing

27 Form the woven strip over a bracelet mandrel.

28 Use a 2' (61 cm) length of the 30-gauge wire to secure the swirled wires to the base weave. Utilize beads as a way to jump from one spot to the next as you lash the swirls down *(Figure 15)*.

29 Make a clasp: Cut a 3" (7.5 cm) length of 16-gauge wire. File one end. At the base of your round-nose pliers, create a large loop on the filed end. Bend the loop to a 90-degree angle to the wire. Mark the wire 1" (2.5 cm) from the loop. Center the mark in the base of the round-nose pliers, with the loop running parallel to the jaws. Form the wire over towards the loop. Curve the wire out just before the loop and bend the loop 90 degrees from the hook. Trim the excess wire above the curve, and file the cut end flush.

30 With chasing hammer and bench block, hammer the curves and flare out the cut end of the clasp; round the flared end with files. Attach the clasp to the loop end of the bracelet. With your flat-nose pliers, rotate the other looped end of the bracelet to slip the hook through the loop.

31 You can add more movement to the outer edges of your weave by rippling or sculpting the edges with your fingers, or using your nylon-jaw pliers to bend and shape the edges for added dimension.

32 Oxidize with liver of sulfur, then polish with 0000 super fine steel wool and a jeweler's brass bristle brush.

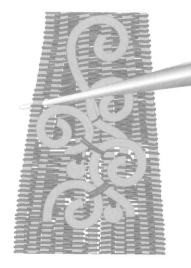

Fig 15

VARIATIONS

There are a variety of ways to make this design your own. Ideas include:

— Hammer the swirls or draw a bead on the end of the 18-gauge wire before adding them into your weave.

— Instead of trimming all your decreased wires, leave one or two untrimmed. Form swirls in the long ends after decreasing and bend them back on the weave.

— Cut random lengths of 18-gauge wire from ½" (1.3 mm) to 1 ¼" (3.2 cm). Draw beads on both ends. Use these balled wires to add into your weave instead of the four 3½" (9 cm) lengths of 18-gauge wire.

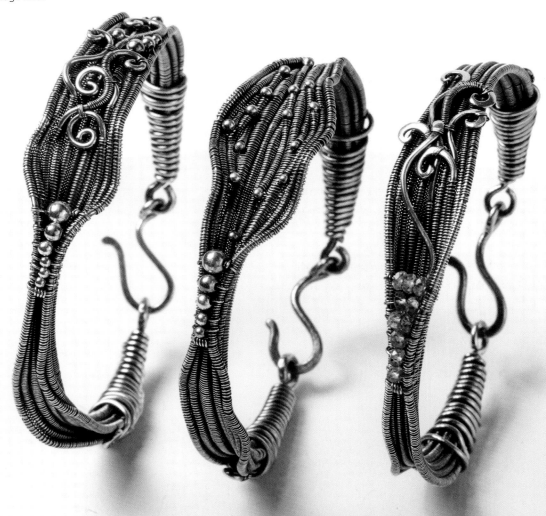

scribble

EARRINGS

MATERIALS
15" (38 cm) of sterling
silver 14-gauge wire

18" (45.5 cm) of fine
silver 18-gauge wire

12" (30.5 cm) of sterling
silver 20-gauge wire

6" (15 cm) of fine
silver 24-gauge wire

14' (4.3 m) of fine
silver 28-gauge wire

Two 2 mm sterling
silver round beads

Two beads or gems
of your choice
for the dangle

TOOLS
Ruler

Wire cutters

Needle files

Permanent marker

Flat-nose pliers

Round-nose pliers

Chasing hammer

Bench block

1.25 mm hole
punch pliers

Pickle solution

Charcoal block

Butane micro torch

Cross-lock tweezers

Tile or rimmed
cookie sheet

Quenching bowl

Ring mandrel

Liver of sulfur

0000 Steel wool

Brass bristle brush

My students have been begging me to turn these earrings into a class since their inception in 2012. They are a perfect example of subtly sculpting, but instead of sculpting your weave, we will be sculpting flattened wire. This technique is one that I love to employ in my master designs and is a great way to draw the eyes to the movement of the shaped wire.

Scribble Shape

The instructions are for one earring. Due to the complexity of the shaping, I recommend you make both earrings side by side for each step. When making earrings, the second earring needs to be a mirror image, or flipped when working on the steps. Slow down to ensure that you don't make any mistakes.

1 Cut a 7½" (19 cm) length of 14-gauge wire; file the end flat. Mark the wire at 2", 3½", 4¾", 5¾", 6½", 7", and 7¼" (5, 9, 12, 14.5, 16.5, 18, and 18.5 cm) from one end.

2 With your flat-nose pliers, bend the 14-gauge wire at the 2" (5 cm) mark, bending completely around the tip of the pliers. At the next mark, bend completely around the tip of the flat-nose pliers in the opposite direction of the first bend. Continue to bend at each mark, alternating the direction of the bends until you reach the last mark. Bend the last bit of wire straight down *(Figure 1)*.

3 With round-nose pliers, create a large open loop with the 2" (5 cm) length of wire that begins your scribble shape. Give the top arm a slight curve as you create your loop *(Figure 2)*.

4 Place the round-nose pliers in the first bend of the scribble and plump, or widen, it slightly. With round-nose pliers still within the bend, grip the next bend with your fingers and push it towards the wire above. This will give the second arm of the scribble a slight curve to match the top curved arm with the loop. Repeat this process with each bend except for the last bend *(Figure 3)*.

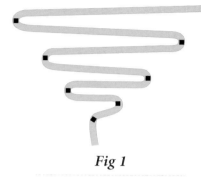

Fig 1

Fig 2

Fig 3

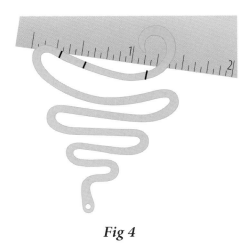

Fig 4

Fig 5

Fig 6

5 With chasing hammer and bench block, flatten the 14-gauge wire. Hammer the bends to give them more of a flared-out look. Paddle the bottom ¼" (6 mm) to a 3 mm width.

> **NOTE** *Do not overflatten the wire. You will also notice that your scribble has stretched out; this is normal.*

6 Create a pointed swirl on your loop at the top of the scribble (see Wire Techniques, page 28) and punch a 1.25 mm hole in the center of the bottom paddle. Round the edge of your paddle with your files. Anneal the scribble and pickle to remove fire scale.

7 Mark the top arm from the scribbles at ¼" (6 mm), ½" (1.3 mm), and 1⅛" (2.9 cm) *(Figure 4)*.

8 With flat-nose pliers, add a fold to the bends of the scribble in alternating directions in an accordion style *(Figure 5)*. Grip the last ¼" (6 mm) of the scribble and rotate 90 degrees so the outer edge is facing the front. With your round-nose pliers, curve the last ¼" (6 mm) into a serpentine shape *(Figure 6)*. Set aside.

> **NOTE** *I will be referring to this wire as Wire 1.*

Shaped Elements

NOTE *It may be helpful to label each wire made in the following steps.*

9 Draw a bead on one end of a 5" (12.5 cm) piece of 18-gauge wire. Measuring from the tip of the ball, trim the wire to 4¾" (12 cm). Create a small open loop with a slight swirl on the trimmed end. Hammer the loop. Turn the loop into a pointed swirl with your cutters and files. (See Wire Techniques, page 28).

10 Place the pointed swirl above the swirl of Wire 1. Form the 18-gauge wire to the underside of your top arm, letting the extra length cross Wire 1 at the first bend. Transfer the marks from Wire 1 to the 18-gauge wire *(Figure 7)*. This will be referred to as Wire 2. Set aside.

11 Draw a bead on one end of a 6" (15 cm) piece of 20-gauge wire. Place the wire on the underside of Wire 2, with the ball on the left and just past the mark on the far left. Form the 20-gauge wire to Wire 2. This will be referred to as Wire 3.

12 Draw a bead on both ends of a 2" (5 cm) length of 18-gauge wire. Create an open loop using the center of your round-nose pliers. Continue to swirl the wire around for one turn. With round-nose pliers turn the other end up, curving it in the opposite direction. It should look like a question mark *(Figure 8)*.

13 Nest the swirled wire on top of Wire 1 between the ½" (1.3 mm) and 1⅛" (2.9 cm) marks, with the larger end of the 18-gauge wire on the left. This will be referred to as Wire 4.

14 Draw a bead on one end of a 2" (5 cm) length of 18-gauge wire. Trim to 1¾" (4.5 cm). Create a small pointed swirl on the trimmed end. Curve the balled end in a wide curve with your round-nose pliers. Your balled end should be about the same height as your pointed swirl. This will be referred to as Wire 5.

NOTE *Wire 5 is not shown individually. However, it can be seen in Fig. 15 on page 95.*

Fig 7

Fig 8

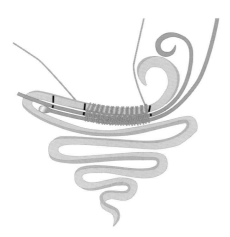

Fig 9

Fig 10

Fig 11

Weaving

15 Place Wire 2 below the top arm of Wire 1, lining up the marks. Place Wire 3 below Wire 2, with the balled end on the left side of the far-left mark on Wire 2. Using a 7' (2.1 m) length of 28-gauge wire and leaving a 12" (30.5 cm) tail, weave all three wires together starting at the ½" (1.3 cm) mark on Wire 1, using the Modified Soumak weave (see Modified Soumak Weave, page 42) until you reach the 1⅛" (2.9 cm) mark *(Figure 9)*.

NOTE *Do not trim excess wires.*

16 Place your ring mandrel on top of Wire 1, on the left side of the weave. Form Wire 2 around the ring mandrel at the size 3 mark. With your round-nose pliers, curve the balled end of Wire 2 to curve over the 1⅛" (2.8 cm) mark on Wire 1. The balled end of Wire 2 should fit inside the pointed swirl of Wire 1. Adjust the curve as needed *(Figure 10)*.

17 Place Wire 4 above Wire 1 with the swirl positioned over the ½" (1.3 cm) mark. Position the curved end above the curved end of Wire 2. With the 12" (30.5 cm) tail, continue to weave the left side incorporating Wire 4 where it rests against Wire 1 for two complete rows. Weave Wires 1, 2, and 3 together for another complete row *(Figure 11)*.

TIP. ROTATING FORM

I like to rotate my form around for this step. For me, it is easier to weave. I also like to push the shaped section of Wire 2 to the back, splitting it open like a jump ring, so that I can get between the wires better. No matter what, I go slowly to make sure I am weaving correctly and tightly, since all the wire ends are going in different directions.

18 Continue to weave Wires 2 and 3 together with your tail. Stop weaving as you come to the balled end of Wire 3 and coil around Wire 3 to the ball. Trim off the excess 28-gauge wire.

19 With the 28-gauge weaving wire on the right side, weave all five wires (Wires 1, 2, 3, the curved end of Wire 2, and Wire 4) together for three complete rows, or until you reach the ball of Wire 4. Decrease and weave the four wires together for several rows. Decrease again weaving Wires 1, 2, and 3 together for a couple of rows before decreasing one last time and weaving Wires 2 and 3 together. Stop your weave when the two wires are no longer running parallel to each other *(Figure 12)*.

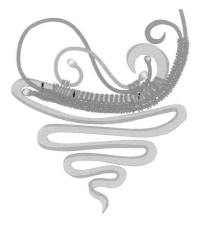

Fig 12

20 Curve Wire 3 around in a wide arc with your fingers. With the 28-gauge weaving wire, coil around Wire 3 until you have enough space to add a 2 mm bead between the pointed swirl of Wire 2 and Wire 3. Thread a 2 mm bead onto your 28-gauge wire. Cross over to the pointed swirl of Wire 2. Wrap your 28-gauge wire twice around Wire 2 before threading the 28-gauge wire back through the bead *(Figure 13)*.

21 Place Wire 5 inside the wide arc of Wire 2, with the pointed swirl above and to the left. Make sure that Wire 5 touches Wire 3, Wire 2 at the pointed swirl, Wire 4 where it crosses over Wire 2, and also touches the large loop in Wire 2. Adjust the shape until it touches all 4 points. Mark Wire 3 where it touches Wire 5 *(Figure 14)*.

Fig 13

22 Continue to coil Wire 3 to the mark, being careful not to misshape the arc as you coil. Weave Wire 5 to Wire 3 at the mark for two complete rows of Modified Soumak weave. Stop on a short stitch row. With your 28-gauge wire in the back, bring it down and between the two wires.

> **NOTE** *This will position the 28-gauge wire so that it is ready to coil around the bottom of Wire 5.*

Fig 14

Fig 15

Fig 16

23 Begin to coil down the length of Wire 5. Lash Wire 5 (see Lashing Weave, page 44) to the pointed swirl of Wire 2 where they touch. Continue to coil down Wire 5. Lash Wire 5 to Wire 4 where they touch. Coil around Wire 5 a few more times before lashing Wire 5 to the large loop in Wire 2 three times. Secure the 28-gauge wire by coiling around Wire 5 to the ball or by going through the lashing twice. Trim off the excess wire *(Figure 15)*.

24 Curve the end of Wire 3, continuing the arc until the end of Wire 3 is crossing over the first bend in Wire 1. Trim the wire flush at the bottom arm of the first bend. File the end smooth, rounding the edges *(Figure 16)*.

25 Grip the end of Wire 3 with the tip of your flat-nose pliers. Bend the tip to the back. This will create a hook that will connect to the first bend of Wire 1, closing off your earring.

26 Draw a bead at one end of a 3" (7.5 cm) piece of 24-gauge wire. Thread a bead onto the 24-gauge wire and attach through the hole in the bottom of Wire 1.

Finishing

27 Oxidize with liver of sulfur, then polish with 0000 super fine steel wool. Use a jeweler's brass bristle brush to remove any steel wool caught in the weave.

symmetry

I love symmetry, but my experience teaching has shown that while it may seem a simple concept, perfecting symmetry is not easy for most. You have to train your eye to pick up slight nuances in a design. Taking the time to slow down and adjust your work as you go leads to amazing results. .

Techniques for Mastering Symmetry

Half of the projects in this book are devoted to symmetry. Symmetry is something everyone struggles with, but with practice, patience, and a few helpful tips you'll find that your symmetry techniques will continue to improve with each piece. Remember it is a journey; the more you work with symmetry the better you will become.

It is important to slow down and take your time. It is hard to achieve a symmetrical design when you are rushing. Step back frequently, look at the whole piece, and see if it is spaced the same on all sides. Break down the shaping so that what you do on one side you immediately do to the other side before continuing on. If you are getting frustrated, take a break. Things always look and work much better with a fresh perspective and a rejuvenated spirit.

Referencing the Center

Having a point of reference can help you pinpoint where your symmetry is off. Use your permanent marker to draw a line down the center axis of the design. The mark is not permanent and can be removed when finishing the jewelry. This line will help you visually see if all the shaped and woven wires are centered. If they are not, adjust and shape the wires until they are.

Measure

One of the easiest ways to ruin the symmetry is to get your measurements off. Even being ¹⁄₁₆" (1.6 mm) off can skew the symmetry in your jewelry. Keep a ruler handy and frequently measure how far elements are from the center reference line.

Consistent Spacing

Dowels are a great way to achieve even spacing as you shape your wire. Be sure you're using the same dowel when shaping elements on either side of center. You can also use dowels to spread the wire to consistent distances before further shaping.

Pliers can also greatly aid in achieving consistent shapes. It is important when using pliers to shape an element that you mark the point where you plan to grip the wire. Pliers, whether round-nose, flat-nose, or chain-nose, all taper. This tapering gives versatility but it can throw your symmetry off if you're not shaping the wire around the same point on the pliers. You can mark the pliers with a permanent marker or with a little bit of painter's tape *(Figure 1)*.

Create a Square

I have a reference square permanently attached to the top of my workstation so that I can check my symmetry at each stage. I find it incredibly helpful to place the piece I'm working on within the square to further visualize where symmetry might be negatively affected.

To create the square on my work surface, I use two different colors of tape. Take a square or ruler and line it up to the edge of your workstation. Lay down 6" (15 cm) of the darker tape along your ruler.

Line the ruler perpendicular and in the center of the tape you just placed down. Lay down 6" (15 cm) of this new tape along the length of the ruler. I like it to be lighter in color so I can see the tape below *(Figure 2)*.

You now have two axes that you can use to quickly line up your work as you go to verify that you are truly centered and keeping the wirework symmetrical *(Figure 3)*.

Fig 1

Fig 2

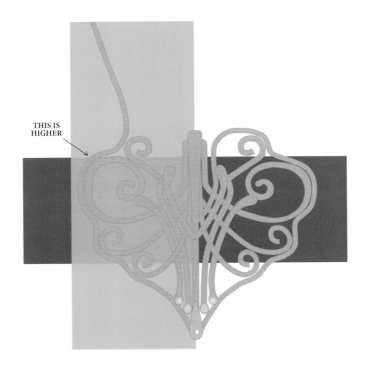

THIS IS
HIGHER

Fig 3

Graph Paper

If I find I still can't pinpoint the lack of symmetry or I am dealing with a highly intricate shape, then I pull out my graph paper and use this method to fine-tune a design.

Using ¼" (6 mm) graph paper, with a colored pencil, pen, or fine-tipped marker draw a vertical line down the center of the graph paper with a ruler, making sure to line up with the existing grid lines. Pick a second color and draw a horizontal line in the center of the graph paper with the ruler, again making sure to also line up with the existing grid lines *(Figure 4)*.

These lines are your reference points to quickly line up your project along the center axis, and then check each square from left to right as it radiates out from the center to guarantee that the wires are in a mirror image along the center line *(Figure 5)*.

Tracing

To further insure symmetry, you can trace components to see that they are identical. I use this method when I am shaping an intricate structure with the wire, such as the Aries Pendant (page 128). This method allows me to verify that each curve is symmetrical from side to side. It also helps when I hammer this more intricate shape so that I can check that I truly did flair out the curves evenly.

Take a scrap piece of paper. Lay your shaped wire on top of the paper. Trace the outer edge of one side of the shaped wire with a pen. Stop at the center reference line of the component.

Flip the shaped wire over and line it up with your traced outline. With a different colored pen trace the outer edge. If the shaped wire is symmetrical, the two pen marks will line up on top of each other. You will be able to see very clearly where you need to adjust the shape.

After making your adjustments, repeat the process until you are happy with your symmetry.

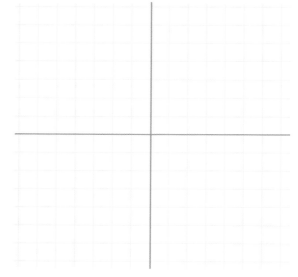

Fig 4

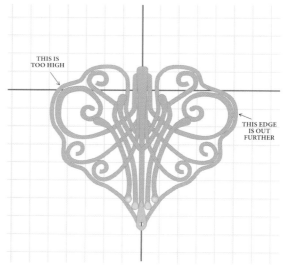

THIS IS
TOO HIGH

THIS EDGE
IS OUT
FURTHER

Fig 5

Check the Back

Sometimes no matter what I do in the front, I can't seem to figure out what is causing the lack of symmetry. I know I measured correctly, and my shaped wire is consistent, but something is still off. When this happens, it is time to inspect the back. It is just as important for the back to be symmetrical as it is for the front. Flipping the piece over, I usually find that a wire is bulging or shaped radically different from what it should be, using up more wire and creating the inconsistency in the front.

VARIATION

This variation of the Flora Pendant (page 112) is a beautiful example of the importance of symmetry. The marquise-shaped focal bead sits perfectly in the center of the design with mirror-image looped arms fanning out around it.

lorelei
PENDANT

At first glance, it may look like there is nothing symmetrical about this pendant, but there are two small sections of weaving hidden on the backside of the pendant offering the perfect chance to practice making things balanced and even. This is also a wonderful project to practice your finishing techniques. Perfect your pointed swirls, take the time to bevel your hammered wires, and then use graduated sandpaper or a flex shaft to polish your beveling to a fine luster. You'll see how these extra steps take the design to a whole new level.

MATERIALS

7" (18 cm) of fine
silver 14-gauge wire

7¼" (18.5 cm) of fine
silver 16-gauge wire

10⅛" (10.7 cm) of fine
silver 18-gauge wire

3' (91.5 cm) of fine
silver 26-gauge wire

10' (3 m) of fine
silver 28-gauge wire

2 sterling silver 2 mm
beads, holes need to be
larger than 0.8 mm

2 sterling silver
3 mm beads

1 sterling silver
4 mm bead

1 Swarovski
crystal 20 mm
square pendant

TOOLS

Ruler

Wire cutters

Permanent marker

Flat-nose pliers

Chasing hammer

Bench block

Needle files

Fine grit sandpaper

Butane micro torch

Cross-lock tweezers

Tile or rimmed
cookie sheet

Quenching bowl

Round-nose pliers

Beading awl

Liver of sulfur

0000 Steel wool

Brass bristle brush

Component 1

1 Cut a 3" (7.5 cm) length of 14-gauge wire; file the ends flat. Mark the wire at ¾" (2 cm), 1½ (3.8 cm), and 2¼ (5.5 cm). Grip the wire with your flat-nose pliers at the 1½-inch (3.8 cm) mark. Bend at a 90-degree angle.

> **NOTE** *The mark should be on the left and just on the outside of the jaws.*

2 Move the flat-nose pliers to the ¾" (2 cm) mark. This time grip the wire with the mark on the left and inside of your jaws. Bend at a 90-degree angle. Move the jaws to the 2¼" (5.5 cm) mark. This time grip the wire with the mark on the right inside of your jaws. Bend at a 90-degree angle. The finished shape is a square.

3 Place the 20 mm Swarovski crystal on top of the shaped square wire; the wire should frame the outer edge of the crystal *(Figure 1)*. Make any adjustments needed for a better fit. With chasing hammer and bench block, hammer the shaped wire flat and slightly flair out the cut ends.

4 With files, bevel the outside edge of the flattened wire and round the hammered ends (see Wire Techniques, page 28–29). Use graduated sandpaper or a flex shaft with silicone wheel attachments in graduated grits to smooth out the file marks. Set aside.

> **NOTE** *Sandpaper will leave a satin finish unless you are also using super fine grit jewelers sandpaper. I prefer to use standard grits from the hardware store and finish the final mirror polishing in the tumbler.*

Component 2

5 Draw a small bead on both ends of a 2⅛" (5.4 cm) and 2⅞" (7.3 cm) length of 18-gauge wire. Once quenched in water to cool, mark the center of the short wire. Make a 20-degree bend at the mark. Gently flair out the balled ends of the wire. Mark 1" (2.5 cm) in from one balled end on the longer wire. Make a 20-degree bend at the mark. Fit the two wires together with the longer wire below the shorter, with the long arm on the right *(Figure 2)*.

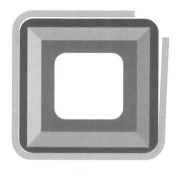

Fig 1

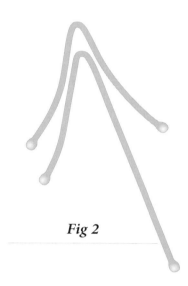

Fig 2

> **NOTE** *You need the small opening between the two points later on in the project. If you don't have this opening, adjust the angles until you do.*

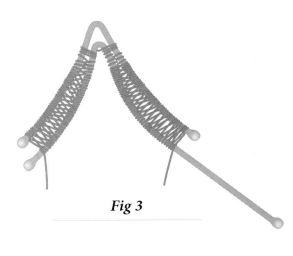

Fig 3

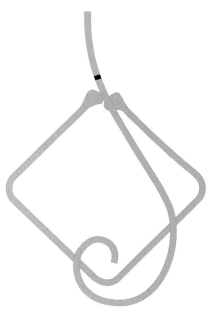

Fig 4

6 Working from a 6' (1.8 m) length of 28-gauge wire, lash the two arms on the left of component 2 together. Starting at the bend, lash three times leaving a 2' (61 cm) tail to the left (see Lashing Weave, page 44). Cross to the right side and lash the two arms together on the right three times. Adjust the arms so that they are no further than 2 mm apart at the end of the first balled wire.

7 Component 2 is now secure and ready to weave. Starting on the left side with the 2' (61 cm) tail wire, weave 3 rows of Basic Figure 8 weave (see Basic Figure 8 Weave, page 38). Continue to weave, wrapping the base wire twice before crossing over to the other side.

> **NOTE** *It is important to wrap twice. If you don't, your base wires will shift underneath the weave. Stop weaving when the balled end of the outside base wire is reached. Cross to the inner base wire, wrap once, and do not trim the excess wire.*

8 Repeat step 7 on the right side of component 2. Set aside *(Figure 3)*.

Component 3

9 File both ends of a 4" (10 cm) length of 14-gauge wire. With the round-nose pliers create an open loop on one end. Swirl the loop a half turn. Place the swirl on top of component 1 with the swirl on the bottom right. Curve the 14-gauge wire above the swirl so that the 14-gauge wire runs over the center of the top of component 1 *(Figure 4)*.

10 Mark the other end of the 14-gauge wire 1" (2.5 cm) from the end. With chasing hammer and bench block, flatten the swirl and the straight end.

> **NOTE** *When hammering the straight end, do not pass the 1" (2.5 cm) mark.*

Connecting Components 1, 2, & 3

11 Following the pointed swirl technique (see Wire Techniques, page 28), shape the swirl end of the wire and bevel the edge. Finish with graduated sandpaper to remove the file marks. Place component 2 on top of component 3. Align the 1" (2.5 cm) mark on component 3 to the top point in component 2. Where the weaving ended in step 8, lash components 2 and 3 with three wraps *(Figure 5)*.

12 Position component 1 behind components 2 and 3. The swirl of component 3 should align with the bottom point of component 1. Lash component 1 to the inside arms of component 2 three times. Set aside *(Figure 6)*.

> **NOTE** *If needed, adjust the arms of component 2 so that they're symmetrical on either side of component 1.*

Component 4

13 Draw a bead on one end of a 3¼" (8.5 cm) length of 16-gauge wire. File the other end flat and mark the wire 1½" (3.8 cm) in from the filed end. With chain-nose pliers, bend an angle in the wire at the mark slightly narrower than the angle in component 2.

14 Form a small open loop on the filed end, with the loop going out and towards the left-hand side. With chasing hammer and bench block, hammer the loop and the bent angle. Following the pointed swirl technique (see Wire Techniques, page 28), cut, file, and bevel the open loop. Finish with graduated sandpaper to remove the file marks.

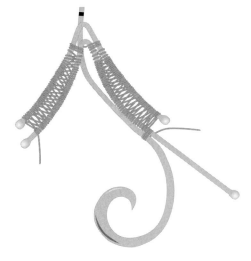

Fig 5

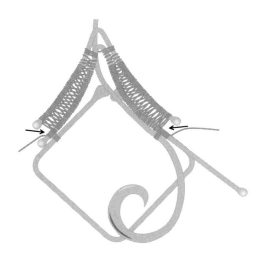

Fig 6

15 Lash the swirl end of component 4 to the bottom balled end of the left arm of component 2. Secure the 28-gauge wire by either wrapping around the 18-gauge wire until you reach the ball or threading the 28-gauge wire through the lashing twice then trim off the excess 28-gauge wire. With a 12" (30.5 cm) length of 28-gauge wire and leaving a 6" (15 cm) tail, lash for two wraps component 4 to component 2 just below the peak of the top angles of the components *(Figure 7)*.

16 Flip your form over to the back. Cross the lashing wire over the arm of component 3 and lash components 2 and 4 together, mirroring the opposite side. Wrap the lashing wire around component 3 and through the opening in component 2 *(Figure 8)*.

17 Repeat step 16 two more times, ending with a total of 4 lashings, two sets of 2 lashings, on both sides of component 4, and component 3 should be fitted tight against the back of component 2.

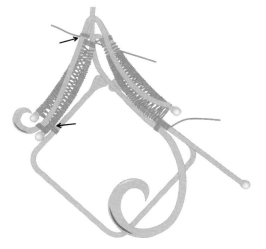

Fig 7

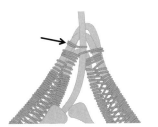

Fig 8 - Back View

Embellishing

18 Returning to the front of the work, thread both 28-gauge tail wires to the front left side of component 2. Slip a 2 mm, 3 mm, 4 mm, 3 mm, and 2 mm round metal bead onto both tails. Thread both 28-gauge wires through the weave on the right-hand side of component 2, about halfway down. Pull tight to make sure the beads are snug *(Figure 9)*.

> **NOTE** *Use a beading awl to create an opening in the weave, if needed.*

19 Bring one piece of the 28-gauge wire to the front of the work and thread it back through as many beads as possible and pull tight. Trim excess wire tight to the last bead passed through. Secure the remaining 28-gauge wire by bringing it to the front of the work, wrap twice around the wires holding the beads in place, and then trim excess wire *(Figure 10)*.

20 With round-nose pliers, form a simple loop with the flattened end of component 3, rolling the wire towards the front of the pendant. Leave a little bit of space between the loop and component 4. This is the bail of the pendant.

Component 5

21 File one end flat of a 4" (10 cm) length of 16-gauge wire. Curve the filed end slightly with round-nose pliers. With chasing hammer and bench block, flatten the curved end. Round the flattened end with files, bevel, and finish with graduated sandpaper.

22 Position the hammered curve of component 5 above and to the right of the large swirl of component 3. Lash component 5 to the inner base wire of component 2 *(Figure 11)*.

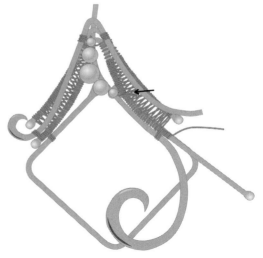

Fig 9

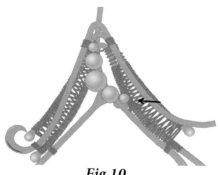

Fig 10

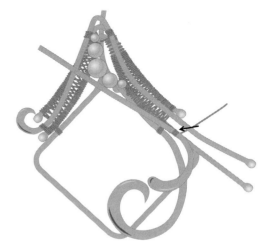

Fig 11

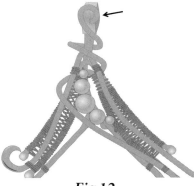

Fig 12

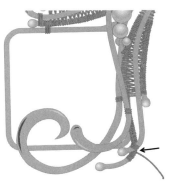

Fig 13

Fig 14

23 Spiral the straight end of component 5 around the top of the pendant tightening the spiral just below the bail, then stop wrapping in the front of the work. With round-nose pliers, form a simple loop at the end of component 5 and position the loop over the bail *(Figure 12)*.

> **NOTE** *Because we all draw different size beads on our wires at slightly different lengths, shape differently, or line up components in slightly different spots, you may find that wire ends in the following instructions don't line up exactly as mine do. It's okay! Shape the wires as instructed and find alternative anchor points to suit your piece.*

24 Curve the inner base wire of component 2 inward so it rests over component 3. Curve the balled end of component 4 over the long arm of component 2. Coil the 28-gauge wire down the long arm of component 2. Lash component 4 to component 2 three times where they cross *(Figure 13)*.

25 Continue to coil component 2, and stop just before the balled end. With the round-nose pliers, bend the ball away from the work. Lash component 2 to component 3 three times *(Figure 14)*.

Component 6

26 Draw a bead on one end of a 5" (12.5 cm) length of 18-gauge wire. Curve the balled end slightly. Position the balled end under the tail of component 5 and on top of component 1.

27 Following a similar path as component 5, spiral the straight length of component 6 around the top of the pendant. Wrap tightly just below the bail and trim excess wire *(Figure 15)*.

28 Coil the 28-gauge tail wire around component 1 approximately five times. Lash component 6 to component 1 with three wraps. Coil the 28-gauge wire around component 6 until the ball end. Trim excess wire.

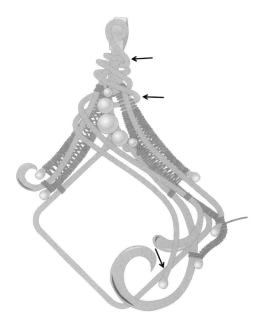

Fig 15

Finishing

29 Using a 2' (61 cm) length of 28-gauge wire, lash your crystal to the top left of component 1, wrapping three times and leaving a 12" (30.5 cm) tail. Flip the form to the back of the work and secure the lashing by wrapping the tail wire around the lashings three times. Trim off the excess tail wire. Wrap the working wire to the right side of the crystal and lash to component 1 with three wraps. Repeat step to secure the lashing on the back of the work *(Figure 16)*.

> **NOTE** *The crystal may fit behind, not inside the square.*

30 Oxidize with liver of sulfur, and polish with 0000 super fine steel wool and a jeweler's brass bristle brush.

> **NOTE** *Adding patina and polishing can be done prior to adding the crystal in step 29 to avoid damaging the finish on the crystal. Simply perform the lashing with preoxidized wire once the base pendant is complete.*

Fig 16 - Back View

VARIATIONS

— Add a subtle detail and visual interest by embellishing the bare side of component 1 with 2 mm or 3 mm beads while leaving out the center crystal.

— Another unique option to make this pendant your own is to string a single pearl in the center of the pendant from a handmade headpin.

flora
PENDANT

PENDANT SIZE

2" × 1⅞" long
(5 cm × 4.8 cm)

MATERIALS

1 ¾" (4.5 cm) of fine
silver 14-gauge wire

3' (91.5 cm) of fine
silver 16-gauge wire

17" (43 cm) of fine
silver 18-gauge wire

4" (10 cm) of fine
silver 22-gauge wire

4" (10 cm) of fine
silver 26-gauge wire

26' (7.9 m) of fine
silver 28-gauge wire

1 Swarovski 5 mm
pearl round

1 Swarovski 12 mm
coin pearl

TOOLS

Ruler

Wire cutters

Files, needle files

Permanent marker

Chasing hammer

Bench block

1.25 mm hole
punch pliers

Butane micro torch

Cross-lock tweezers

Tile or rimmed
cookie sheet

Quenching bowl

Round-nose pliers

Flat-nose pliers

Ring mandrel

Mallet

Painter's tape

3 mm dowel

Beading awl

Liver of sulfur

0000 Steel wool

Brass bristle brush

This is a great pendant to develop your symmetry skills. While there is layering involved, it is broken up into two parts, making it easier to integrate the layers while also maintaining the symmetry.

Component 1

1 File the ends of a 1¾" (4.5 cm) length of 14-gauge wire flush. Mark the wire at ¼", ¾", and 1" (6 mm, 2 cm, and 2.5 cm). With chasing hammer and bench block, flatten both ends to a 3 mm width making sure not to go beyond the ¼" (6 mm) and 1" (2.5 cm) marks.

> **NOTE** *It can be difficult to flatten longer lengths of wire. I suggest practicing on copper wire first. Even if your hammering is not perfect, it can be fixed by filing the edges to create straight walls.*

2 Punch a 1.25 mm hole in the center of the paddle at the end marked with ¼" (6 mm). With files, remove any burs and round the edges of both paddles.

3 Draw a bead on one end of each of two 1½" (3.8 cm) lengths of 16-gauge wire. Trim the wires to 1⅛" (2.9 cm) from the balled end. With round-nose pliers, gently curve the cut ends.

> **NOTE** *Remember this is a symmetrical design; take the time to ensure the two wires are shaped identically.*

4 With chasing hammer and bench block, flatten the curved ends and round the edges with files. Draw a bead on one end of each of two 2½" (6.5 cm) lengths of 18-gauge wire.

5 Mark the center of a 2" (5 cm) length of 18-gauge wire. With flat-nose pliers, bend a 45-degree angle at the mark. Trim the ends ¾" (2 cm) from the angle. Shape the ends around the tip of your ring mandrel. Use a rawhide mallet to shape, if needed *(Figure 1)*. Hammer the curved ends and the angle flat. Use files to round the curved ends of flattened wire.

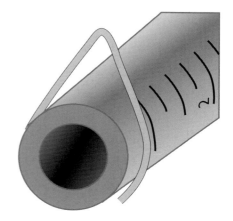

Fig 1

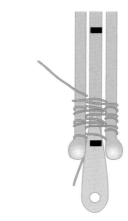

Fig 2

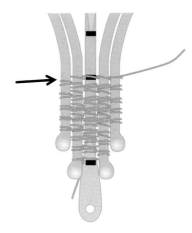

Fig 3

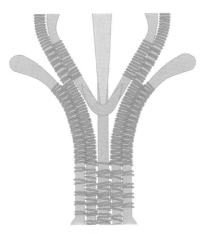

Fig 4

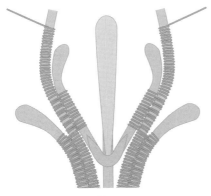

Fig 5

6 Align the two pieces of 18-gauge wire with balled ends on either side of the ¼" (6 mm) mark on the 14-gauge wire with the balled ends and punched hole all pointing down. Cut a 7' (2.1 m) section of 28-gauge wire. Take the 14-gauge wire and orient it so that the hole is facing down. Leaving a 3' (91.5 cm) tail in a 7' (2.1 m) length of 28-gauge wire, start weaving Modified Soumak weave (see Modified Soumak Weave, page 42) at the ¼" (6 mm) mark to weave the three wires together for three complete rows **(Figure 2)**.

7 Add the 16-gauge wires on either side of the 18-gauge wires above the balled ends of the 18-gauge wires. The ends of the 16-gauge wires curve away from the center of the component. Weave all five wires together to the ¾" (2 cm) mark on your 14-gauge wire **(Figure 3)**.

8 Mark both 18-gauge wires ½" (1.3 cm) above the weave. Curve the 18-gauge wires so that they run parallel to the 16-gauge wires. Weave the 18-gauge and 16-gauge wire together on the right. Stop weaving when you have reached the ½" (1.3 mm) mark **(Figure 4)**.

9 Use the 3' (91.5 cm) tail wire to come up from the back to weave the 18-gauge and 16-gauge wire on the left together to the mark.

10 Place the V-shaped wire between the two woven arms, with the point down. Align the bottom point of the V with your 1" (2.5 cm) mark on the center wire.

> **NOTE** *If needed, adjust the arms to ensure a proper fit.*

Weave the V to the 18-gauge wires for ¼" (6 mm). Continue to coil around the 18-gauge wire until you are even with the paddled ends of the V. Set aside **(Figure 5)**.

Component 2

11 Cut four 7" (18 cm) lengths of 16-gauge wire. Mark the wires at 3" and 4" (7.5 and 10 cm) from one end. Place all four wires next to each other with the marks aligned; tape the wires together at the 3" (7.5 cm) mark. With a 7' (2.1 m) length of 28-gauge wire and leaving an 18" (45.5 cm) tail wire, weave the four wires between the 3" and 4" marks with Modified Soumak weave.

12 Remove the tape and mark the center of the woven section. Form the woven section around a 3 mm dowel at the center mark. This is the bail of the pendant. Pinch the woven strip with your fingers to bring the woven ends closer together *(Figure 6)*.

13 Starting with the two outer wires in the back, bend the base wires into a fan, alternating the base wires from the front to the back. The two center base wires should be from the front. I will refer to these wires as Wire 1 through Wire 8 from left to right *(Figure 7)*.

14 Trim Wires 1 and 8 to 1" (2.5 cm); trim Wires 2 and 7 to 2¼" (5.5 cm); trim Wires 3, 4, 5, and 6 to 1½" (3.8 cm) from the weave.

15 Use round-nose pliers to create a large loop on the end of Wires 1, 2, 3, 6, 7, and 8, looping them out and up from the center. I like to leave the loops slightly open, just enough to allow a 28-gauge wire to easily pass through. Spiral the loops of Wires 2 and 7 for a half turn *(Figure 8)*.

> **NOTE** *Do not loop Wires 4 and 5.*

16 Adjust loops and wires as needed until symmetrical. With chasing hammer and bench block, flatten the spiraled outer edge of Wires 2 and 7. Readjust for symmetry as needed.

Fig 6

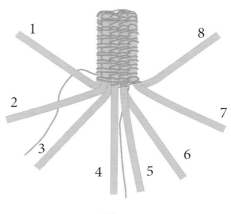

Fig 7

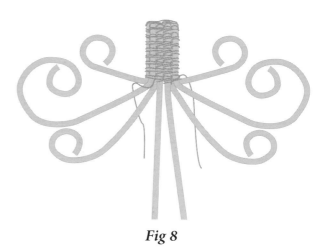

Fig 8

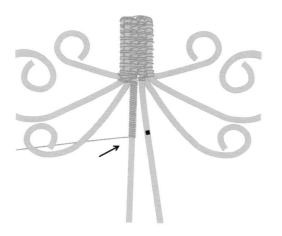

Fig 9

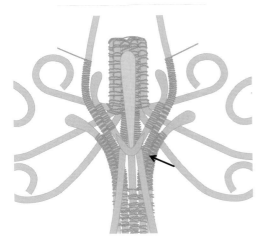

Fig 10

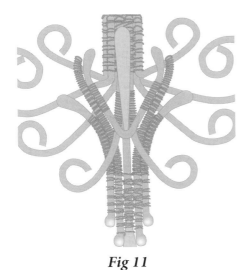

Fig 11

17 Mark Wires 4 and 5 at ⅜" (1 cm) from the bail weave. Weave the 28-gauge wire tails so that there is one tail around Wire 4 and one around Wire 5. Coil the tail wires down Wires 4 and 5 to the ⅜" (1 cm) mark *(Figure 9)*.

Connecting Components 1 & 2

18 To merge component 1 over component 2, slip Wires 4 and 5 between the V and on either side of the 14-gauge wire of component 1 from back to front. Push through until the V point is butting up against the coils of Wires 4 and 5 *(Figure 10)*.

> **TIP. ANGLING**
>
> I find that it is easier to come in at an angle when joining these two components. If you are still having problems slipping Wires 4 and 5 through, then use your beading awl to lift the point of the V up.

19 Wrap the 18-gauge wires from component 1 around Wires 1 and 8 of component 2. Trim the 18-gauge wires in the back and tuck the ends in. Trim off all your 28-gauge tails.

20 Use round-nose pliers to form a large loop at the end of Wires 4 and 5 of component 2 *(Figure 11)*.

BACK OF PENDANT

Edging

21 Mark the center of a 10" (25.5 cm) length of 18-gauge wire. With the flat-nose pliers, bend a 90-degree angle at the mark. Mark both arms ⅝" (1.5 cm) from the angle. Using a 12' (3.7 m) length of 28-gauge wire, coil the 18-gauge wire between the two marks, starting from the center and working out.

22 Place the coiled 18-gauge wire below the loops of Wires 4 and 5 and behind component 1. Using Modified Soumak weave, (see Modified Soumak weave, page 42) weave the arms of the 18-gauge wire to the loops for two rows on both sides. This will anchor the 18-gauge wire to the form so it can be further shaped in the following steps *(Figure 12)*.

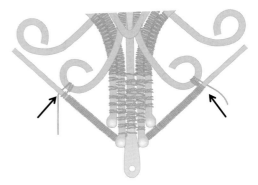

Fig 12

23 Focusing first on the right-hand side, form the 18-gauge wire to the outside of the loop on Wire 5. With your fingers bend the 18-gauge wire away from the work directly above the loop so that the wire is resting below the loop of Wire 6. Continue weaving Modified Soumak weave around the loop of Wire 5. Switch to coiling the 18-gauge wire as it begins to shape away from the loop. Stop coiling where the 18-gauge wire touches the next loop, Wire 6, and weave Wire 6 to the 18-gauge wire for two rows *(Figure 13)*.

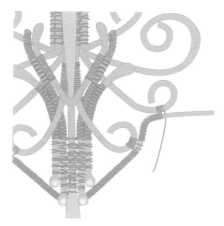

Fig 13

TIP. SYMMETRY

For the best symmetry results, work up both sides of the edging at the same time.

24 Shape the 18-gauge wire to the loop of Wire 6 in the same manner as the previous loop. Continue to work your way around the outside edge of the pendant using Modified Soumak weave to connect the 18-gauge wire to the loops where the two wires run parallel to each other. Adjust the positions of your loops as needed to get the spacing you desire *(Figure 14)*.

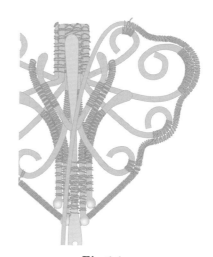

Fig 14

TIP. WEAVING

If you are having a hard time weaving around a loop, open the loop like a jump ring as you are weaving around it, and then close it when you are done.

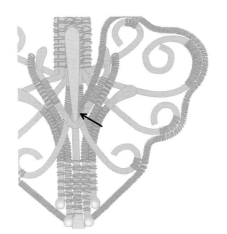

Fig 15

Fig 16

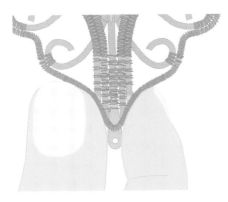

Fig 17 - Back View

25 After weaving the loop of Wire 8 to the 18-gauge wire, coil around the 18-gauge wire. As you coil, shape the 18-gauge wire to the inside curvature of the V section of component 1. Stop coiling just before reaching the point of the V. Trim the 18-gauge wire ¼" (6 mm) from the coils. With chain-nose pliers, bend the 18-gauge wire inwards towards the pendant. Slip the end of the 18-gauge wire between Wire 5 and the 14-gauge wire, just above the point of the V *(Figure 15)*.

> **NOTE** *You may need to use a beading awl to make room between the wires to slip the 18-gauge wire through.*

26 Pull the 18-gauge wire tight from the back, and then tuck the end around Wire 5 in the back. Trim off your 28-gauge wire. If working the right and left edges independently, repeat steps 23–25 on the left-hand side of the pendant *(Figure 16)*.

> **TIP. FLIPPING**
>
> I flip my pendant over when I work on the left-hand side. This will change the position to the right so that I can weave in the same direction as before. Then I flip it back over to the front to finish coiling and tucking the ends in.

Finishing

27 Tighten the loops of component 2 with round-nose pliers, giving them a slight swirl. Working from the back of the pendant, pinch the 90-degree bend in the edge wire, bringing the wires closer together *(Figure 17)*.

28 Using a 4" (10 cm) length of 26-gauge wire, attach a 5 mm bead between Wires 4 and 5 of component 2, just below the V of component 1.

29 Draw a bead on one end of a 4" (10 cm) length of 22-gauge wire to make a headpin. Add the 12 mm coin pearl to the headpin and attach it to the hole in the 14-gauge wire.

30 Oxidize the pendant in liver of sulfur and polish with 0000 super fine steel wool. Use a jeweler's brass bristle brush to remove any steel wool caught in the weave.

lauren

EARRINGS

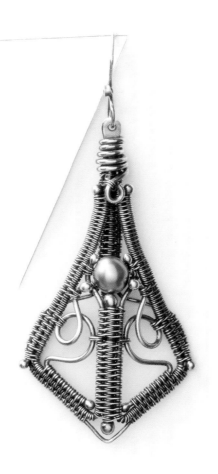

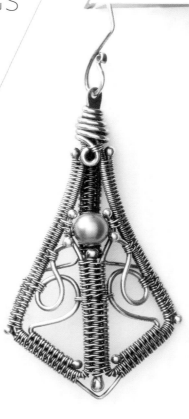

Not only are these earrings symmetrical in design, but they also showcase another way to sculpt with weaving. In this instance, we will be making a box or prism with the weave. This is also a great project to practice using graph paper to check your symmetry.

EARRING LENGTH
3⅛" (8 cm) including
the French ear wires

MATERIALS
6" (15 cm) of fine
silver 14-gauge wire

18½" (47 cm) of fine
silver 18-gauge wire

16" (40.5 cm) of fine
silver 20-gauge wire

12" (30.5 cm) of fine
silver 26-gauge wire

32' (9.8 m) of fine
silver 28-gauge wire

Two 8 mm pearls

French ear wires
or posts

TOOLS
Ruler

Wire cutters

Butane micro torch

Cross-lock tweezers

Tile or rimmed
cookie sheet

Quenching bowl

Permanent marker

Flat-nose pliers

8 mm dowel

Round-nose pliers

Beading awl

Chasing hammer

Bench block

1.25 mm hole
punch pliers

Files

Liver of sulfur

0000 Steel wool

Brass bristle brush

Center Wall

NOTE *While the instructions are for one earring, for the best results make both earrings at the same time. Since it is a symmetrical design there is no need to worry about making them in a mirror image.*

Also, it may be helpful to mark each wire with its identifying number as you work through the instructions.

1 Draw a bead on both ends of a 1¼" (3.2 cm) length of 14-gauge wire. Mark the center between the ball ends.

2 Draw a bead on one end of each of two 5" (12.5 cm) lengths of 18-gauge wire. Mark each piece of wire ⅞" (2.2 cm) from the balled ends. These will be referred to as Wire 1 (right and left).

3 Place the 18-gauge wires on either side of the 14-gauge wire, with the balled ends of 18-gauge wires pointing up. Align the marks of all three wires. Starting at the aligned marks and approximately 2' (61 cm) from the end of an 8' (2.4 m) length of 28-gauge wire, weave the three wires together with the Modified Soumak weave (see Modified Soumak Weave, page 42) using the 2' length. End the weave on the right side *(Figure 1)*.

4 Rotate the form over and use the 6' (1.8 m) tail of 28-gauge wire to weave three wires together as in step 3. Stop the weave when reaching the balled end of the 14-gauge wire. Rotate the form back to position the three balled ends of wire towards the top of the work. End the bottom section of weaving on the right.

5 Bend both 18-gauge wires to a 45-degree angle to the woven center. Mark the wires ⅝" (1.5 cm) from the bend. Bend the wires at the ⅝" (1.5 cm) mark at a 90-degree angle. The 18-gauge wires should be touching their balled ends at the top of the work. With your fingers, curve the 18-gauge wires above the balled ends so that they are parallel to each other *(Figure 2)*.

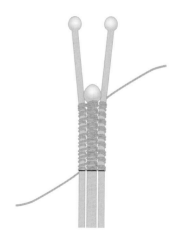

Fig 1

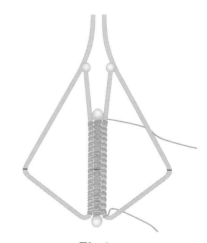

Fig 2

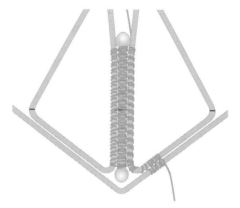

Fig 3

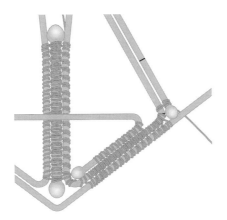

Fig 4

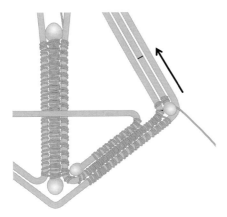

Fig 5

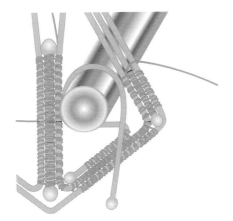

Fig 6

6 Draw a bead at both ends of each of two 2½" (6.5 cm) lengths of 18-gauge wire. Mark each wire ½" (1.3 cm) from one end. With flat-nose pliers, form a 45-degree angle in each wire at the mark. These will be referred to as Wire 2 (right and left).

7 Mark the center of an 8" (20.5 cm) length of 20-gauge wire. With flat-nose pliers, form a 90-degree angle at the mark. This will be referred to as Wire 3.

8 Place Wire 3 below the woven form so that the arms of Wire 3 are running parallel to the arms of Wires 1. The angle in Wire 3 is directly below the balled end of the 14-gauge wire. Adjust the angle, if needed. Using the 28-gauge tail on the bottom right of the weave, coil around Wire 1 (right) until you reach the point where Wire 1 and Wire 3 are touching. Weave them together for three complete rows of Modified Soumak weave *(Figure 3)*.

9 Add one Wire 2 to the inside of Wire 1 on the bottom right of the form with the ball touching the center woven wall. Weave the three wires together until you reach the bend in Wire 2. Decrease your weave, weaving Wires 1 and 3 together until you reach the bend in Wire 1 *(Figure 4)*.

Sidewall

10 Draw a bead on both ends of each of two 1¾" (4.4 cm) lengths of 18-gauge wire. Mark each wire ⅜" (1 cm) from one end. These will be referred to as Wire 4 (right and left).

11 Place one Wire 4 along the right edge of Wire 1 above the weave with the mark on Wire 4 orientated to the bottom. With the 28-gauge weaving wire on the bottom right corner of the form, weave Wire 1 and Wire 4 together for one complete row. Pull Wire 4 up so that the balled end at the bottom is flush to the weave. Form Wire 3 so that it runs parallel to Wire 4 *(Figure 5)*. Weave all three wires together until you reach the ⅜" (1cm) mark on Wire 4.

12 Nestle an 8 mm dowel between Wire 2 above the bend and Wire 1 along the side on the right. Form Wire 2 around the dowel *(Figure 6, page 123)*.

13 With your fingers, gently compress the loop just formed to give it a slight oval shape. This will also make it fit better inside your form. The loop needs to be touching Wire 1 just above the weave on the sidewall at the ⅜" (1 cm) mark. Adjust the shape as needed.

14 Weave the loop in Wire 2 to the sidewall for two complete rows, weaving four wires together.

> **NOTE** *If your 28-gauge wire is on a bobbin, it will need to be unspooled as you will have to thread your 28-gauge wire through the loop of Wire 2 to weave it to the sidewall.*

After weaving the four wires together, bend Wire 3 out away from the woven sidewall *(Figure 7)*.

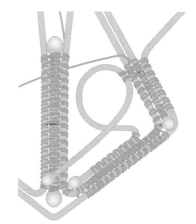

Fig 7

15 With your fingers or round-nose pliers, continue to loop Wire 2 around to form a smaller loop next to the sidewall. With your round-nose pliers curve the balled end in towards the center of the component. Weave Wires 1 and 4 together until you reach the point where the curved balled end of Wire 2 touches Wire 1. Weave the three wires together for two rows *(Figure 8)*.

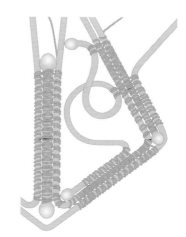

Fig 8

16 Curve the balled end of the ⅞" (2.2 cm) length of Wire 1 from the center wall on the right, curving in. Position the curved end so that it touches Wire 1 on the right-side wall and above the balled end of Wire 2 that was just woven into the sidewall.

17 Continue to weave Wires 1 and 4 together, adding the curved balled end of Wire 1 to the weave for two rows. Continue the weave until the balled end of Wire 4 is reached. Coil Wire 1 until it passes the balled end of Wire 4. Trim the 28-gauge wire leaving a 6" (15 cm) tail *(Figure 9)*.

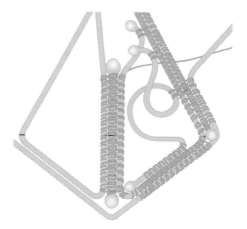

Fig 9

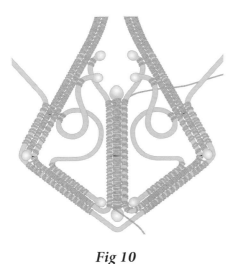

Fig 10

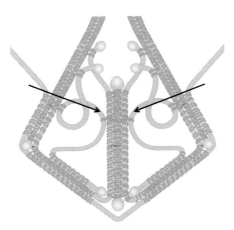

Fig 11

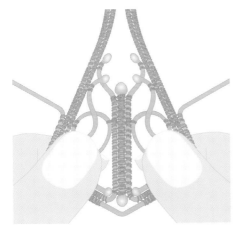

Fig 12

18 Repeat steps 8–17 on the left side of the component creating a mirror image of the right side using a 6' (1.8 m) length of 28-gauge wire *(Figure 10)*.

19 With your beading awl pierce the weave in the center wall where Wire 2 on the right touches the weave. The hole needs to be large enough to pass your 28-gauge wire through twice. Use your 28-gauge tail at the top of the center wall to come through the pierced hole from the back. Lash Wire 2 to the center wall twice (see Lashing Weave, page 44). With your beading awl pierce the left side where Wire 2 on the left touches the weave. Bring your 28-gauge wire over from the back to lash the left side to the weave in the same manner *(Figure 11)*. Secure the 28-gauge wire by threading through the lashing twice in the back. Trim the excess 28-gauge wire.

Back wall

20 Draw a bead on one end of a 1¾" (4.5 cm) length of 14-gauge wire. Trim the 14-gauge wire to 1½" (3.8 cm). With chasing hammer and bench block, flatten the cut end to a 3 mm width. Punch a 1.25 mm hole in the center of the flattened end. Round the edge with files. Mark the wire 1" (2.5 cm) from the balled end.

21 Position Wires 3 (left and right) to run vertically towards the top of the component. Mark the wires ⅜" (1 cm) from the weave. With flat-nose pliers, bend both Wires 3 away from the component.

22 With your fingers, bend the sidewalls towards the back. The center wall acts like a hinge that will allow the sidewalls to pivot at the sides *(Figure 12)*.

23 Push both Wires 3 to the back of the work, bending the wires directly above the weave. The wires should be perpendicular to the woven form with the arms running parallel to each other but not quite touching. Adjust the angles as needed *(Figure 13)*.

24 Place the 14-gauge wire made in step 20 between the arms of Wires 3 with the balled end just inside the bends closest to the component. With a 4' (11.2 m) length of 28-gauge wire, weave the three wires together. Stop weaving at the 1" (2.5 cm) mark on the 14-gauge wire *(Figure 14)*.

25 Push the back wall up so that the paddle of the 14-gauge wire sits between the arms of the front center wall and the end of the weave lines up with the end of the coils on the left arm of Wire 1 *(Figure 15)*.

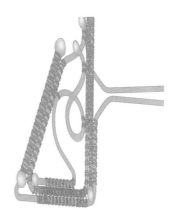

Fig 13 - Side View

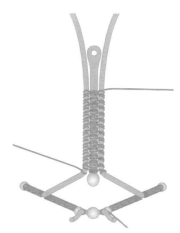

Fig 14 - Back View

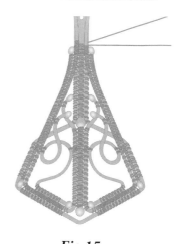

Fig 15

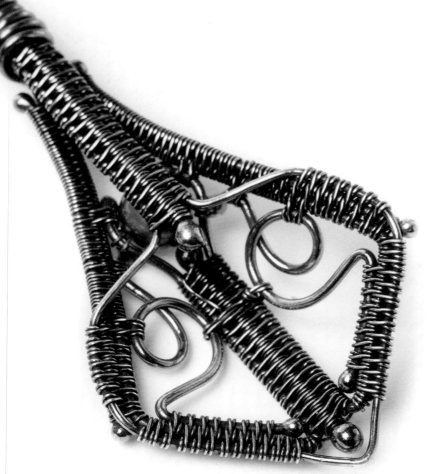

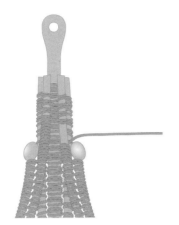

Fig 16

Fig 17

26 Weave the 28-gauge wire from the back wall around the four wires at the top of the component locking all the walls together. Weave for four rows. Coil around the 14-gauge wire three times and then trim off the excess wire. Trim all the base wires, except the 14-gauge wire, to ⅛" (3 mm) above the weave *(Figure 16).*

Finishing

27 Form a simple loop at one end of a 6" (15 cm) length of 18-gauge wire.

28 Position the loop over the right-side wall and below the balled end of Wire 4, with the loop swirling in towards the center of the component. Coil the 18-gauge wire around all the base wires towards the paddle of the 14-gauge wire till you reach the cut ends. Continue to coil around the 14-gauge wire twice. Trim the excess 18-gauge off in the back.

29 With the remaining 28-gauge tail on the right, lash the loop of the coiled cap just formed to the sidewall of the component on the right. Secure the 28-gauge wire by going through the lashings twice. Trim off the excess 28-gauge wire *(Figure 17).*

30 Using a 6" (15 cm) length of 26-gauge wire, add an 8 mm pearl to the center of the earring component. Place the pearl within the ⅞" (2.2 cm) curved arms of Wires 1, attaching the pearl to the wires on either side. Trim the excess wire.

31 Add a French ear wire or a post to the punched hole in the 14-gauge wire.

32 Oxidize with liver of sulfur, and then polish with 0000 super fine steel wool. Use a jeweler's brass bristle brush to remove any steel wool caught in the weave.

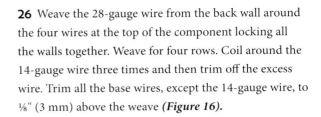

aries

PENDANT

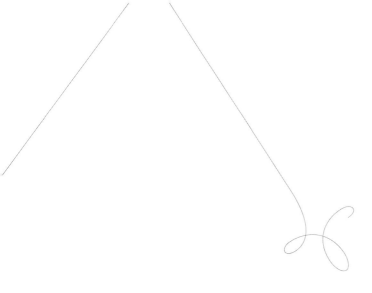

Practice your symmetry skills with this whimsical design. The trick will be shaping the 14-gauge wire. Check your symmetry after each new shaping, and then pay extra attention to how you are hammering to ensure that you stay symmetrical. Use the graph paper and tracing techniques for better symmetry.

PENDANT SIZE
2" × 2¼" (5 cm × 5.5 cm)

MATERIALS
4½" (11.5 cm) of fine silver 14-gauge wire

7" (18 cm) of fine silver 16-gauge wire

13" (33 cm) of fine silver 18-gauge wire

28" (71 cm) of sterling silver 24-gauge wire

6" (15 cm) of fine silver 26-gauge wire

22' (6.7 m) of fine silver 30-gauge wire

1 round 6 mm pearl

1 briolette 12 mm pearl

TOOLS
Ruler

Wire cutters

Permanent marker

Flat-nose pliers

Ring mandrel

Round-nose pliers

Chasing hammer

Bench block

Files, needle files

Sandpaper in graduated grits

Butane micro torch

Cross-lock tweezers

Tile or rimmed cookie sheet

Quenching bowl

3 mm dowel (optional)

10 mm dowel

Ring mandrel

Beading awl

Liver of sulfur

0000 Steel wool

Brass bristle brush

Component 1

Wire 1

1 Mark the center of a 4½" (11.5 cm) length of 14-gauge wire. With flat-nose pliers, bend a 45-degree angle at the mark.

> **NOTE** *It is better to have an angle slightly wider than to have your point less than 45 degrees.*

2 Mark each arm 1¼" (3.2 cm) from the bend. Form the arms around a ring mandrel, creating a leaf shape *(Figure 1)*.

> **NOTE** *Use the 1¼" (3.2 cm) marks to help achieve a symmetrical shape. When you are done shaping, the two marks should be parallel and touching.*

3 Spread the two arms apart. With round-nose pliers, form a simple loop with each end wire, turning the loop towards the center of the component. Holding the pointed end of the component in one hand and the right loop in the other hand, form the right arm over the ring mandrel at the size 4 mark *(Figure 2)*. Repeat on the left side.

4 With chasing hammer and bench block, flatten the shaped wire flaring out the curves and the loops. Trim the ends of the loops to a point with wire cutters and file into pointed spirals (see Wire Techniques, page 28). This wire will be referred to as Wire 1.

TIP. SANDING

Use fine grit sandpaper in graduated grits to remove file marks for a more polished result.

TIP. SYMMETRY

Use Techniques for Mastering Symmetry (see page 98) to perfect Wire 1. You'll find the tracing method is particularly useful for this wire.

Fig 1

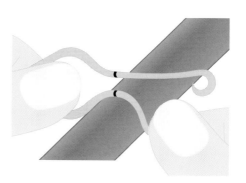

Fig 2

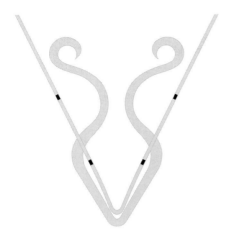

Fig 3

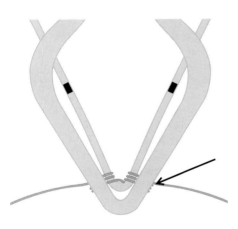

Fig 4

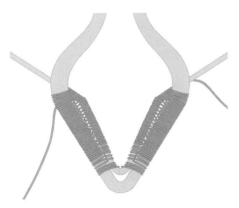

Fig 5

Wire 2

5 Mark the center of a 5" (12.5 cm) length of 18-gauge wire. With flat-nose pliers, fold the wire in half at the center mark. Trim the ends flush and then draw a bead on each end.

> **NOTE** *The beaded ends of wire should be the same length once balled.*

6 Mark both arms of the 18-gauge wire at ½" (1.3 cm) and 1⅛" (2.9 cm) from the bend. With your flat-nose pliers, open the arms up at the bend to form an angle that fits within the point of Wire 1 *(Figure 3)*. This will be referred to as Wire 2.

Weave

7 Place Wire 2 behind Wire 1 with the point of Wire 2 above the point of Wire 1. Working from the center of a 7' (2.1 m) length of 30-gauge wire, lash the two wires together on the left at the point (see Lashing Weave, page 44). Lash three times. Cross over to the other side and lash the right side three times *(Figure 4)*. Using the Basic Figure 8 weave (see Basic Figure 8 Weave, page 38), weave for two rows; stop and weave two rows on the other side with the tail wire.

> **NOTE** *This will help create even spacing from side to side before fully weaving the two wires together.*

8 Weave the two right wires together until reaching the ½" (1.3 cm) mark on Wire 2 using basic Figure 8 weave with double wraps around the base wires.

9 Bend Wire 2 out from the ½" (1.3 cm) mark, and then continue to weave the two wires together until reaching the spot where they cross.

10 Repeat steps 7–9 on the other side, using 3½' (1.1 m) tail wire to weave the left side *(Figure 5)*.

11 Starting on the right, coil around Wire 2 with 30-gauge wire until the 1⅛" (2.9 cm) mark. With flat-nose pliers, bend Wire 2 down and out at the mark. Place the base of your round-nose pliers or a 3 mm dowel between Wire 1 and the coiled section of Wire 2. With your fingers, form the coiled section around the jaw of the pliers *(Figure 6)*.

12 Repeat step 10 on the left side. This woven form is component 1 *(Figure 7)*.

Component 2
Wire 3
13 Mark the center of a 7" (18 cm) length of 16-gauge wire. Position the center mark over a ring mandrel at the size 4 mark. Evenly shape the wire around the ring mandrel from the center mark to create a U shape. Make sure the ends align with each other.

14 With round-nose pliers, form a large loop at the ends, looping inward. With chasing hammer and bench block, flatten the looped ends and the curved section. Trim the loops to a point then use your hand files for final shaping and rounding of the edges to form pointed spirals (see Wire Techniques, page 28). This wire will be referred to as Wire 3.

Wire 4
15 Draw a bead on both ends of a 4" (10 cm) length of 18-gauge wire. Once cooled, mark the center of the wire. Position the center mark over a ring mandrel at the size 1 mark. Evenly shape the wire around the ring mandrel from the center mark to create a U shape. Make sure the balled ends of wire align to each other. This wire will be referred to as Wire 4.

Wire 5
16 Repeat steps 13–14 on a 4" (10 cm) length of 18-gauge wire, forming small loops at the ends and forming the U shape around a 10 mm dowel. Mark the arms ½" (1.3 cm) from the bottom of the curve. This wire will be referred to as Wire 5.

Fig 6

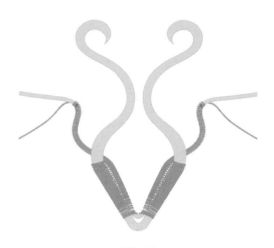

Fig 7

TIP **FILLING POINTS**

It can be more difficult filing the points of tinier loops. It helps to lift the swirl up as if you were opening a jump ring. This will give you better access with your files to round and smooth the edges. Push the point down when you are done.

Fig 8

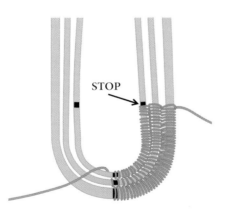

STOP

Fig 9

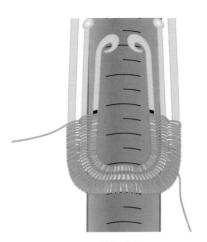

Fig 10

Weave

17 Nest Wires 3, 4, and 5, aligning the center marks *(Figure 8)*.

18 Working from the center of a 15' (4.6 m) length of 30-gauge wire, begin weaving the three wires together at the center mark using Basic Figure 8 weave. Wrap Wire 3 twice with each row. Continue weaving until reaching the straight portion of the base wires. As the wires straighten, stop wrapping Wire 3 twice. Weave the three wires until the ½" (1.3 cm) mark *(Figure 9)*.

19 Repeat step 18 on the left side using the 7½" (2.3 m) tail.

> **NOTE** *Any time you are weaving around curves, they like to shift and rotate. Before progressing to step 20, check the wire ends and make sure they are still even with each other. If not, gently tug on the shorter arm until they are once again even and symmetrical.*

20 Place the woven form over the ring mandrel with the bottom of the curve just below the size 3 mark and the arms going up towards the small end of the mandrel. With your fingers mold the form to the mandrel *(Figure 10)*.

21 Bend Wires 3 and 4 away from Wire 5 on both sides. Weave Wires 3 and 4 for three rows on both sides. This will be referred to as component 2.

Connecting Components 1 & 2

22 Place component 1 over component 2. Make any adjustments needed so that Wire 2, Wire 3, and Wire 4 are parallel.

23 Using the 30-gauge wire to weave component 2 on the right side, weave Wires 2, 3, and 4 together for about a ¼" (6 mm). Repeat on the other side. Use your fingers to curve the three wires so that they follow the curve of the pointed loop of Wire 1 *(Figure 11)*. Repeat on the left side.

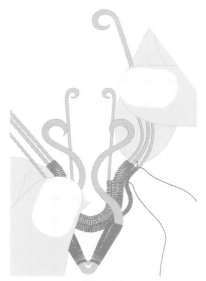

Fig 11

24 Returning to the right side, continue to weave Wires 2, 3, and 4 together until reaching the pointed spiral of Wire 1. Add the pointed spiral to your weave for three complete rows *(Figure 12)*. Repeat on the left side.

> **NOTE** *This will secure the spirals to the form; focus on achieving a tight weave to properly secure the spirals.*

25 Place a 10 mm dowel above the weave on the right. Wrap Wire 3 around the dowel, positioning the pointed spiral over the weave and below the pointed spiral of Wire 1. Swirl Wire 2 inside the large loop of Wire 3. Curve Wire 4 so that it runs parallel to Wire 3. Position the base of your round-nose pliers between Wires 1 and 5 and below the pointed spiral of Wire 1. Form Wire 5 over the jaw of the round-nose pliers so that the loop on Wire 5 touches Wire 4 above the loop of Wire 1 *(Figure 13)*. Repeat on the other side.

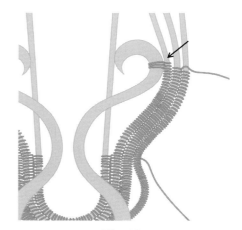

Fig 12

26 Weave Wires 3 and 4 together on the right until Wire 5 touches Wire 4. Add Wire 5 to the weave for three complete rows; this will secure the wire to the form *(Figure 14)*. Continue to weave Wires 3 and 4 together. Stop weaving just below the balled end of Wire 4. Push Wire 2 up against the balled end of Wire 4. Lash Wire 2 to Wire 4 three times *(Figure 15)*. Thread the 30-gauge wire through the lashing a couple of times to secure the 30-gauge wire. Trim excess lashing wire.

27 Repeat steps 25–26 on the left side of the pendant.

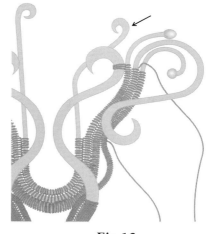

Fig 13

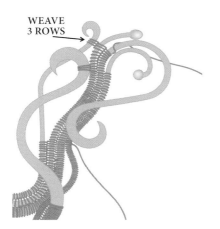

WEAVE
3 ROWS

Fig 14

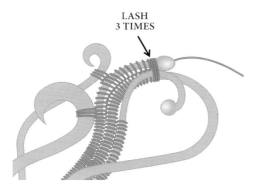

LASH
3 TIMES

Fig 15

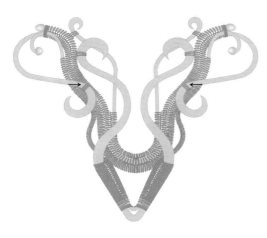

Fig 16

28 With the beading awl, puncture the weave and secure the pointed swirl of Wire 3 to the woven form. Make sure the hole is large enough to pass through 3 times with your 30-gauge wire. Lash the pointed swirl to the woven form and secure the end of the 30-gauge wire. Trim excess lashing wire.

29 Repeat step 28 on the left side. All wires are now secure and 30-gauge weaving wires have been trimmed *(Figure 16)*.

Finishing

30 Using a 4" (10 cm) length of 26-gauge wires, add a 6 mm pearl between the arms of Wire 5. Draw a bead on the end of a 4" (10 cm) length of 24-gauge wire. Quench to cool. Use the wire just made as a headpin to add a briolette dangle to the bottom V of the Aries Pendant.

31 Oxidize with liver of sulfur and polish with 0000 super fine steel wool. Brush out any steel wool caught in the weave with a jeweler's brass bristle brush. The Aries Pendant can be attached to a chain by connecting to the large loop of Wire 4. The sample shown uses graduated pearls with wrapped loops to hold the pendant.

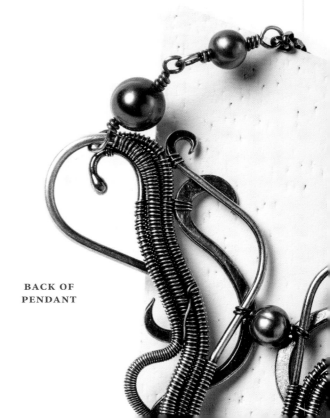

**BACK OF
PENDANT**

unravel

BRACELET

This bracelet took me a year and a half to figure out. No matter what I did, I kept breaking the weave as I shaped and opened the splits. The key is to use small nylon-jaw flat-nose pliers. I love how you get a lovely twist with the weave by offsetting where you start when you split, a great example of a happy accident.

BRACELET SIZE
7½" (19 cm)

MATERIALS
5' (1.5 m) of sterling silver 16-gauge wire

12" (30.5 cm) of fine silver 24-gauge wire

50' (15.2 m) of fine silver 28-gauge wire

4 Swarovski pearl 5 mm rounds

8 Swarovski pearl 4 mm rounds

16 Swarovski pearl 3 mm rounds

1" (2.5 cm) of sterling silver or copper 3 mm chain

TOOLS
Ruler

Wire cutters

Permanent marker

Chasing hammer

Bench block

Butane micro torch

Cross-lock tweezers

Tile or rimmed cookie sheet

Quenching bowl

2 Bobbins

Beading awl

Nylon-jaw pliers

Chain-nose pliers

Round-nose pliers

Round bracelet mandrel

Files

Liver of sulfur

0000 Steel wool

Brass bristle brush

Preparations

1 Cut one 9" (23 cm) length of 16-gauge wire. Mark the center and mark ¾" (2 cm) from each end. With chasing hammer and bench block, flatten the ends to approximately ⅛" (3 mm) wide.

2 Cut six 8" (20.5 cm) lengths of 16-gauge wire. Working on a heatproof work surface with a butane torch and cross-lock tweezers, draw a bead on each end of all wires cut. Quench in water.

> **NOTE** *Try to keep the wire lengths the same.*

3 Mark the centers of all six wires. Segment the shortest length of 16-gauge wire with balled ends into 1¾" (4.5 cm) increments, marking from the center out. You should have 5 marks total when done.

4 Line up the center marks on all seven wires. Arrange the wires, placing the balled wire with the 5 marks on the left. The 9" (23 cm) length of wire should be the 3rd wire on the left. Base wires will be referred to as Wires 1 thru 7, starting with the wire on the left as Wire 1 *(Figure 1)*.

5 Cut a 50' (15.2 m) length of 28-gauge wire. Starting on one end, spool 25' (7.6 m) onto a bobbin; spool the remaining 25' (7.6 m) onto a second bobbin.

Tubular Weave

6 Working from one bobbin of 28-gauge wire, start the first row of the Modified Soumak weave (see Modified Soumak Weave, page 42) at the center marks of the 7 wires. Stop after wrapping around Wire 7 *(Figure 2)*. With your fingers, pinch the base wires to bring Wire 1 and Wire 7 together, creating a tube *(Figure 3)*.

> **NOTE** *The short wraps will be inside the tube and the long wraps on the outside of the tube.*

Fig 1

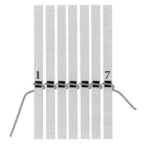

Fig 2

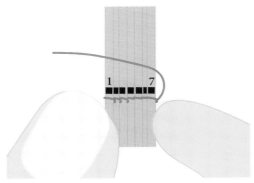

Fig 3

Fig 4

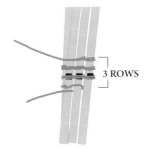

Fig 5

7 Wrap the 28-gauge wire around Wire 1. You have just finished the first row in the Tubular Modified Soumak Weave *(Figure 4)*. Continue to weave around the seven base wires until you have 3 rows. Stop the weave around Wire 1. Remember, Wire 1 is the wire with the 5 marks on it *(Figure 5)*.

8 Split the base wires apart between Wires 1 and 2. Insert a beading awl into the center of the tube. This will help plump out the tube and make it more circular. The beading awl can stay in as you weave or you can take it out.

Creating the Splits

9 Continue in standard Modified Soumak weave, weaving back and forth, with Wires 2 and 1 on the outer edges of the weave. Stop weaving when you reach the next mark on Wire 1. These flat woven sections will become the splits in your bracelet. Since these sections will later be shaped back into a tube, I try not to flatten the base wires. Instead keep it in a tubular or curved shape. *(Figure 6)*.

10 Place your nylon-jaw pliers near the center of your woven wall on the left and bend it inwards. This must be done with the nylon-jaw pliers. Anything else will break the weave *(Figure 7)*. Repeat on the right wall of the weave.

11 Bend the bare base wires beyond the weave back in place. Pinch Wires 1 and 2 together. To make a diagonal split between areas of flat weave, you will need to offset your new split with the previous one. Weave 3 rows of Tubular Modified Soumak weave, ending with the final wrap around Wire 7 (instead of Wire 1 as in step 7.) Create your new split by separating the base wires one wire to the right from the previous split, in this case, between Wire 1 and Wire 7 *(Figure 8)*. This will appear to move Wire 1 one position to the left.

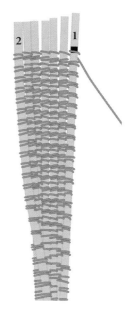

Fig 6

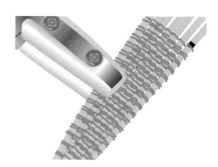

Fig 7

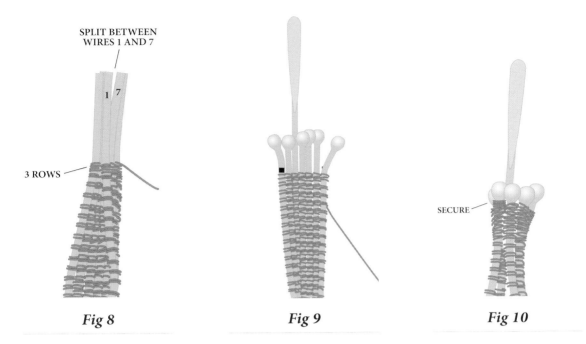

SPLIT BETWEEN WIRES 1 AND 7

1 7

3 ROWS

Fig 8

SECURE

Fig 9

SECURE

Fig 10

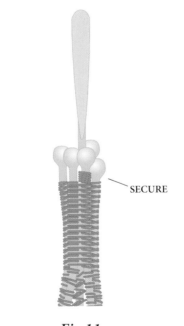

SECURE

Fig 11

12 Weave standard Modified Soumak weave, weaving back and forth, with Wire 1 and Wire 7 as the outside edges. Stop weaving at the next mark on Wire 1 *(Figure 9)*.

13 Repeat step 10 to shape the flat area of woven strip.

14 Bring the 7 base wires back into position and continue in Tubular Modified Soumak weave until reaching the balled ends of wire. Secure the 28-gauge wire by wrapping around a base wire several times. Trim off the excess 28-gauge wire *(Figure 10)*.

15 Repeat steps 6–13 on the opposite side of the bracelet. Remember to shift the position of the side edges in the sections of Modified Soumak weave when ending rows of Tubular Modified Soumak weave.

> **NOTE** *When working the opposite side, you begin with the Modified Soumak weave, not Tubular Modified Soumak weave. You need to end the weave about ⅛" (3 mm) before the end of your 1¾" (4.5 cm) segment before starting Tubular Modified Soumak weave.*

The distance between sections of Tubular Modified Soumak weave are approximately 1¾" (4.5 cm) *(Figure 11)*. End by repeating step 14 to close and secure the end of the bracelet.

Clasp

16 With chain-nose pliers, bend a 45-degree angle in each of the paddled ends of the wire.

17 Grip the center of your paddled wire with your round-nose pliers and form the end over the front of the jaw. Bend the tip up with your round-nose pliers. This is the hook side of the clasp *(Figure 12)*.

18 Trim the paddle at the opposite end of the bracelet to ½" (1.3 cm). With round-nose pliers, form a loop in the wire *(Figure 13)*.

19 Add 1" (2.5 cm) of 3 mm extension chain to the loop just formed. This will act as the catch for the hook portion of the clasp.

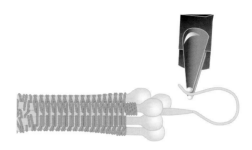

Fig 12

Finishing

20 Form the bracelet around the bracelet mandrel.

21 Oxidize your bracelet with liver of sulfur and polish with 0000 super fine steel wool. Remove any steel wool fibers with a jeweler's brass bristle brush.

22 Cut a 12" (30.5 cm) length of 24-gauge wire. Slip the wire through either tubular end of bracelet, leaving a 3" (7.5 cm) tail of wire. Wrap the tail wire around one of the base wires several times.

23 Slide Swarovski pearls onto the 24-gauge wire in the following order: 3 mm, 3 mm, 4 mm, 5 mm, 4 mm, 3 mm, 3 mm. Thread the 24-gauge wire through the next tubular section and pull tight to fit the beads within the split. Repeat all the way around the bracelet to the other end.

> **NOTE** *You may need to adjust the shape of your split to fit the pearls better.*

24 Pull the 24-gauge wire tight one last time and then wrap it around a base wire several times. Trim off excess 24-gauge wire.

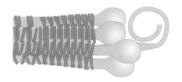

Fig 13

Try this bracelet with smaller sections and no pearls within the splits. This design looks just as beautiful with beads of a uniform size running through the tube as well.

transformation

THIS CHAPTER has been in the making for years. It has been my desire to show how to build more complex designs, while doing it in such a way that you are left with confidence and an open mind to the possibilities you can create. As you explore this chapter, you will see that we will be dismantling certain woven components found in earlier chapters, bringing them together in new and exciting ways to transform your work into a stunning masterpiece design.

To successfully achieve these finished designs, I suggest first making the components in their original projects. This will get you comfortable with the elements of the designs so that they can be combined together with more ease and less frustration on your part. The key is to go slow and walk away if you begin to get frustrated. Expect to take days to make these necklaces. I promise you, it will be worth it.

acantha

NECKLACE

This project is not for the faint of heart. While it is essentially just the Tempest Clasp (page 62) and component 1 from the Flora Pendant (page 112), this design has a lot of shifting in the beginning that can make it difficult to get the symmetry just right. Be patient, the end results are worth it. I can't stress enough how important it is to check your symmetry as you go for true success.

Component 1

1 Repeat steps 1–10 of the Flora Pendant (page 112) with the following adjustments: In step 6 cut a 9' (2.7 m) length of 28-gauge wire, with your tail 4' (1.2 m). In step 10, do not continue coiling the 18-gauge wire after weaving for ¼" (6 mm) on the V wire. Leave the 28-gauge wire. Trim the 18-gauge arms to 1⅛" (2.9 cm). With round-nose pliers, curve the ends of the 18-gauge wires in to form a small tail. With chasing hammer and bench block, hammer the curved ends, and then round the edges with files. Bevel the edges and finish with sandpaper in graduated grits *(Figure 1)*.

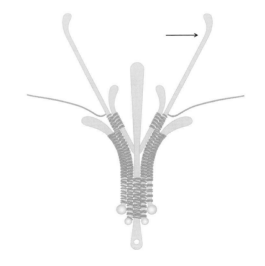

Fig 1

Component 2

2 Repeat steps 1–26 of the Tempest Clasp (page 62) with the following adjustments: In step 6, create a pointed swirl on the short arm of Wire 1. The swirl needs to be tighter and closer in towards the arrowhead. In step 16, leave a 18" (45.5 cm) tail. In step 22, do not coil Wire 4 along the length that travels behind Wire 1. When reaching step 26, stop short of coiling up to the pointed swirl. Instead, shorten the 28-gauge wrapping wire to 12" (30.5 cm) *(Figure 2)*.

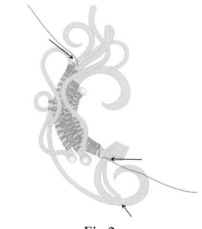

Fig 2

3 Create a second Tempest Clasp component with the same adjustments in mirror image to the first.

4 Place the two Tempest Clasp components side by side with the arcs of Wires 4 touching and the pointed swirls of Wire 1 pointing down. Using a 12" (30.5 cm) length of 28-gauge wire, weave the Wires 4 together where they touch for several rows using Modified Soumak weave (see Modified Soumak Weave, page 42) *(Figure 3)*. This will be referred to as Component 2.

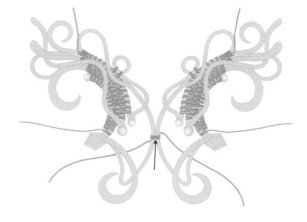

Fig 3

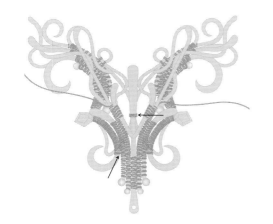

Fig 4

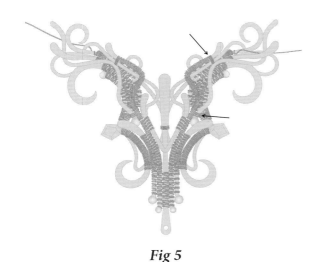

Fig 5

Assembling

5 Place component 1 on top of component 2 with the 14-gauge wire centered over the arc and the bottom pointed swirls of the clasp resting on the side of component 1. With the 28-gauge wire used to weave the Wires 4 together in step 4, lash component 2 and the 14-gauge wire of component 1 together three times (see Lashing Weave, page 44).

> **NOTE** *At this point there are ten tail wires to contend with. You will find that they're likely to tangle. Don't be tempted to cut or play with them. The more they're played with, the more likely they will break. All ten tails are needed to secure the components together.*

6 With the 18" (45.5 cm) tail of 28-gauge wire by the arrowhead on the right side of component 2, coil down the arm of the pointed swirl on component 2 until reaching the start of the pointed swirl. Pierce the weave of component 1 where the coil ends. Make the hole large enough to pass the 28-gauge wire through three times. Lash the pointed swirl to component 1 three times. Secure the 28-gauge wire by threading through the lashings twice in the back. Trim off the excess 28-gauge wire. Repeat on the other side (**Figure 4**). Tighten the lashes wrapped around your 14-gauge wire of component 1. Plump the lashings in the back with the beading awl and thread the tail wire through several times to secure the 12" (30.5 cm) section of 28-gauge wire used to connect the arcs. Trim off the excess secured wire.

7 Using the 28-gauge wire from component 1, coil around the 18-gauge arm of component 1 four times. Lash the 18-gauge arm to the long arm of Wire 2 right above the ball on Wire 2. Lash three times. With your fingers, shape the 18-gauge wire to follow a similar path as Wire 2, keeping a little distance between the two wires. Coil the length of the 18-gauge wire. As you reach the tail of the 18-gauge wire lash it to Wire 4 where they touch. Lash three times. Thread the 28-gauge wire through the lashings to secure then trim. Repeat on the other side (**Figure 5**).

NOTE *At this point we have used up all but two of the tail wires. While the design is almost finished, you will find that it still pivots along the 14-gauge wire in the center, making it unstable. This was an unforeseen flaw in the original design. When this happened, I found a creative solution that adds to the design while adding the needed stability. The following steps will secure Wires 4 together and lock the components in place.*

8 Repeat step 5 of the Flora Pendant to create a V-shaped wire; make two.

9 On the back of the work, place one V shape below the arc of Wires 4 where they are connected. Adjust the angle and arms so that it is running parallel to Wires 4. Remove the V from the work. Using an 18" (45.5 cm) length of 28-gauge wire and working 9" (23 cm) from one end, coil 4 wraps round each arm of the V. Replace the V shape below the arcs of Wires 4; starting on one side, use lashing weave with a pattern of 2 lashes, 4 coils to attach the V shape to Wire 4. When reaching the bend in Wire 4, lash the V shape to the pointed swirl of Wire 1 three times. Secure the 28-gauge wire by threading through the lashings in the back and trim. Repeat on the other side *(Figure 6)*.

10 Repeat step 9 placing the second V shape above the arches of Wires 4. Make the final lashes around the small loop in Wire 4 of component 2 *(Figure 7)*.

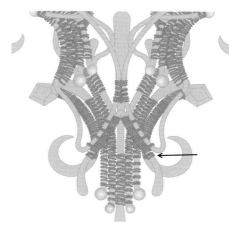

Fig 6 - Back View

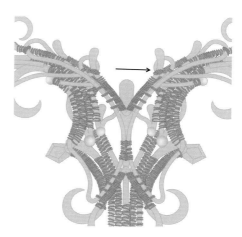

Fig 7 - Back View

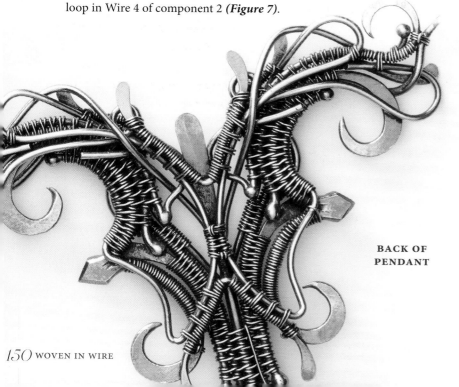

BACK OF PENDANT

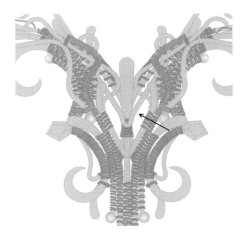

Fig 8

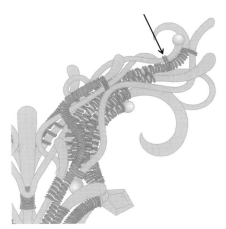

Fig 9

11 Mark the center of a 5" (12.5 cm) length of 18-gauge wire. With flat-nose pliers, bend the wire at the mark to form a sharp point. Trim the arms to 2¼" (5.5 cm) from the bend. Draw a bead on each end of the wire, taking care to make them the same size.

12 From the front of the work, slip the two arms of the wire just formed through the curved wires of component 2 resting on either side of the top of the 14-gauge wire. Push all the way through until the point rests on top of the lashing on the 14-gauge wire.

> **NOTE** *The angle of the wire will spread apart as you push it through.*

Push the arms up to help lock the point in place *(Figure 8)*.

13 With your fingers, gently curve the arms down and over the top of component 2. Swirl the balled end slightly inside the pointed swirl of Wire 3 in component 2. With the remaining 28-gauge wire, lash the balled end of the new wire to Wire 3 of component 2 on either side where they touch. Continue to coil Wire 3 until it's possible to lash Wire 2 to Wire 3.

> **NOTE** *If the hole in the hammered ball of Wire 2 faces the front of the work, rotate it 90 degrees.*

Lash the two wires together three times. Thread your 28-gauge wire through the lashings in the back twice. Trim off the excess 28-gauge wire *(Figure 9)*.

14 Using a 12" (30.5 cm) length of 26-gauge wire, attach the briolette dangle to the bottom of the pendant.

Finishing

15 Oxidize with liver of sulfur and polish with 0000 super fine steel wool. Use your jeweler's brass bristle brush to remove any steel wool caught in the weave.

ada

NECKLACE

PENDANT SIZE
2⅜" × 3"
(6 cm × 7.5 cm)

MATERIALS
17½" (44.5 cm)
of fine silver
14-gauge wire

10" (25.5 cm) of fine
silver 16-gauge wire

29" (73.5 cm) of fine
silver 18-gauge wire

12" (30.5 cm) of
sterling silver
24-gauge wire

6" (15 cm) of fine
silver 26-gauge wire

20' (6.1 m) of fine
silver 28-gauge wire

9' (2.7 m) of fine
silver 30-gauge wire

1 coin 14 mm pearl

1 round 4 mm
metal bead

Four 5 mm pearls

Sterling silver
chain in the
length desired

Clasp

TOOLS
Ruler

Permanent marker

Wire cutters

Flat-nose pliers

Butane micro torch

Cross-lock tweezers

Tile or rimmed
cookie sheet

Quenching bowl

Graph paper

Scrap paper

Pens in two
different colors

Round-nose pliers

Chasing hammer

Bench block

Needle files

Sandpaper in in
graduated grits

1.25 mm hole
punch pliers

Pro-Polish pads

5 mm dowel

Beading awl

Ring mandrel

Liver of sulfur

0000 Steel wool

Brass bristle brush

Elements of the Aries Pendant (page 128) and mirror-image components from the Tempest Clasp (page 62) feature in this breathtaking design. It's intricate; therefore remember to use graph paper to continually check symmetry, and you're assured a beautiful end result.

Component 1

1 Repeat steps 1–9 of the Aries Pendant (page 128) to make component 1 with the following adjustments: In step 6, replace the 7' (2.1 m) length of weaving wire with a 9' (2.7 m) length of 30-gauge wire, working the weave from the center of the weaving wire out *(Figure 1)*.

Component 2

2 Repeat steps 1–30 of the Tempest Clasp (page 62) with the following adjustments: In step 8, create a pointed swirl on the short arm of Wire 1. The swirl needs to be tighter and closer in towards the arrowhead. In step 13, do not hammer or punch a hole in the balled end of Wire 2. In step 25, do not coil Wire 4 along the length that travels behind Wire 1 *(Figure 2)*. This will be referred to as Component 2 left.

3 Create a second Tempest Clasp component with the same adjustments in mirror image to the first. This will be referred to as Component 2 right.

Assembling

4 Place Component 2 right on the right side of component 1. The pointed swirl of the short arm of Wire 1 in Component 2 right needs to be above and swirling in towards the center of the pendant. The pointed swirl of component 1 should nestle below the arrowhead. With a beading awl, pierce the weave below the arrowhead where the pointed swirl on Component 1 touches. Use the 12" (30.5 cm) 28-gauge tail wire on component 2 right to lash the pointed swirl of component 1 to the weave three times (see Lashing Weave, page 44). Secure the 28-gauge wire by threading through the lashings in the back twice then trim off the excess 28-gauge wire *(Figure 3)*.

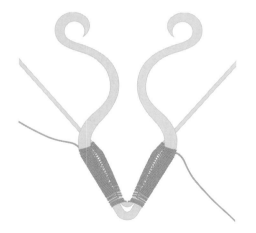

Fig 1

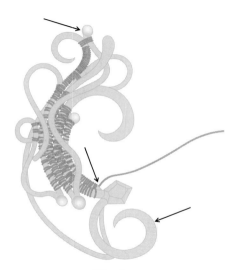

Fig 2

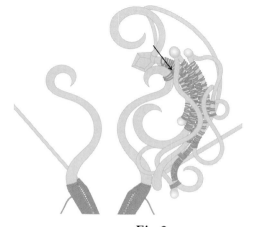

Fig 3

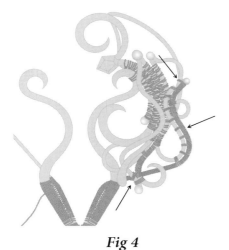

Fig 4

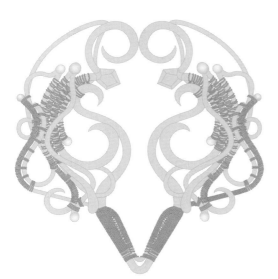

Fig 5

5 Adjust the 18-gauge arm on the right of component 1 so that it touches the loop in Wire 4 on Component 2 right. With the 30-gauge tail wire on component 1, coil along the 18-gauge wire. Stop to lash the balled arm of Wire 2 in Component 2 right to the 18-gauge arm three times. Continue to coil the 18-gauge wire. When reaching the loop of Wire 4 on Component 2 right, lash the 18-gauge wire to the loop three times. Shape the 18-gauge arm to the outer edge of the Wire 4 loop on Component 2 right. Use the lashing weave with a pattern of 2 lashes, 8 coils to weave the 18-gauge wire to the loop of Wire 4. Weave the full length of the 18-gauge arm. The very last lashing set on the 18-gauge wire will be to Wire 3 behind the 18-gauge wire. Lash three times then thread the 30-gauge wire through the lashing twice before trimming the excess 30-gauge wire *(Figure 4)*.

6 Repeat steps 4–5 on the left with Component 2 left. Pay close attention to how the two sides are aligned. Make the necessary adjustments to achieve symmetry before making connections *(Figure 5)*.

BACK OF PENDANT

7 Thread a 4 mm metal bead onto the center of a 6'
(1.8 m) length of 28-gauge wire. Place the bead above the
pointed swirls at the top of the combined components.
Wrap the 28-gauge wire around the pointed swirls on
either side of the bead. Thread the two 28-gauge wires
back through the bead. Coil down the pointed swirl
towards the bend in Wire 4 on component 2, and then lash
the pointed swirl to the bend of Wire 4 *(Figure 6)*.

8 Mark the center of a 7" (18 cm) length of 18-gauge wire.
With flat-nose pliers, bend the wire in half at the mark.
Trim the ends to 3" (7.5 cm). Draw a bead on each cut end
of the 18-gauge wire. With chasing hammer and bench
block, flatten the bent end for approximately ¼" (6 mm).
Mark the two arms ⅝" (1.5 cm) from the bend.

9 With your fingers, gently curve the arms of the 18-gauge
wire out below the bend. Align the marks on the arms of
the wire to the top bend in Wire 4 of component 2 on both
the right and left sides. Lash the 18-gauge wire to Wire 4
three times, and then coil for 8 wraps *(Figure 7)*.

> **NOTE** *It is important to lash both sides then coil
> to lock the new wire in place. This will make it
> easier to be symmetrical as we weave the sides.*

10 Continuing in the lash and coil pattern established in
step 5, weave the 18-gauge wire to the arc in Wire 4 on both
sides, shaping the 18-gauge wire as you go to keep it parallel
to Wire 4. Weave the full length of the arc. When you can
no longer lash the 18-gauge wire to the arc, end with three
lashes. Thread the 28-gauge wire through the lashings in
the back twice. Trim off the excess 28-gauge wire. Create a
small loop with the end of the 18-gauge wire and nestle the
balled end inside the loop of Wire 4 *(Figure 8)*.

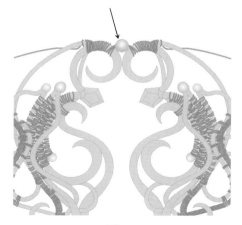

Fig 6

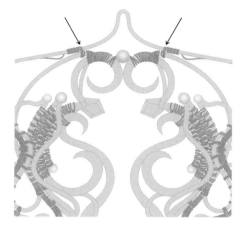

Fig 7

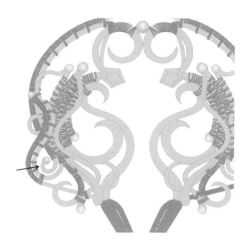

Fig 8

11 Attach a 14 mm coin pearl with 6" (15 cm) of 26-gauge wire inside the V point of component 1 by lashing to the looped wires of component 2 on the right and left sides.

Finishing

12 Oxidize with liver of sulfur then polish with 0000 super fine steel wool. Use a jeweler's brass bristle brush to remove any steel wool caught in the weave.

VARIATION

The Aries Pendant (page 128) hangs from mirror image Tempest Clasps (page 62).

Acknowledgments

I have to give a big thank you to my wonderful husband, Brian. He was the one who encouraged me to write a second book when I was on the fence about whether or not I wanted to do so. Without his overwhelming support and stepping in to be Mom and Dad while I wrote the book, this book would not have happened.

Thank you to all my students who are a continual inspiration to me. I love teaching because of you, and this book is a direct result of all the fun we've had together in class.

And thank you to the wonderful Interweave team for helping me bring together this book and making it better.

Resources

RIO GRANDE
(800) 545-6566
7500 Bluewater Road NW
Albuquerque, NM 87121
riogrande.com

FUSION BEADS
(888) 781-3559
fusionbeads.com

MONSTERSLAYER, INC.
(505) 598-5322
P.O. Box 550
Kirtland, NM 87417-0530
monsterslayer.com

RINGS & THINGS
(800) 366-2156
304 E. 2nd Avenue
Spokane, WA 99202
rings-things.com

BOLLYWOOD BEAD COMPANY
bollywoodbeadcompany.com

BASHA BEADS
etsy.com/shop/bashabeads

ABOUT THE AUTHOR

Sarah Thompson is a wire artist from Spokane, Washington. She has been wire weaving since 2009 and teaching this art form since 2010. She loves teaching and instilling in others the joy and passion of working with wire. Sarah's Craftsy class "Wire Weaving Bracelets: Basics and Beyond" teaches the foundation of wire weaving. And her best-selling book, *Fine Art Wire Weaving: Weaving Techniques for Stunning Jewelry Designs*, introduces the fun and intricacy that can be achieved through wire weaving. When not teaching or making jewelry, Sarah enjoys spending time with her five children and wonderful husband.

METRIC CONVERSION CHART

To Convert	To	Multiply By
Inches	Centimeters	2.54
Centimeters	Inches	0.4
Feet	Centimeters	30.5
Centimeters	Feet	0.03
Yards	Meters	0.9
Meters	Yards	1.1

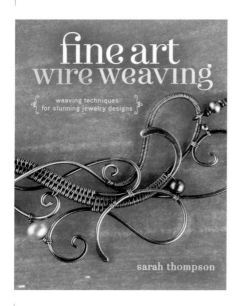
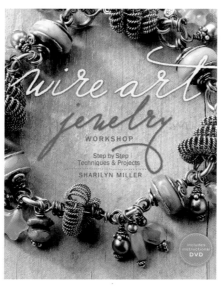
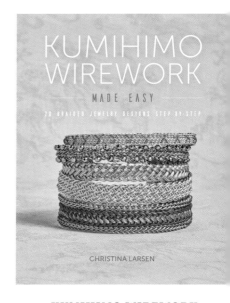

Pat Sloan's
Teach Me to Appliqué

Fusible Appliqué that's Soft & Simple

Martingale®
Create with Confidence

Pat Sloan's Teach Me to Appliqué:
Fusible Appliqué that's Soft and Simple
© 2015 by Pat Sloan

Martingale®
19021 120th Ave. NE, Ste. 102
Bothell, WA 98011-9511 USA
ShopMartingale.com

Printed in China

20 19 18 17 16 15   8 7 6 5 4 3 2 1

**Library of Congress Cataloging-in-Publication Data
is available upon request.**

ISBN: 978-1-60468-523-7

MISSION STATEMENT

Dedicated to providing quality products and service
to inspire creativity.

CREDITS

PUBLISHER AND CHIEF VISIONARY OFFICER
Jennifer Erbe Keltner

EDITORIAL DIRECTOR
Karen Costello Soltys

DESIGN DIRECTOR
Paula Schlosser

ACQUISITIONS EDITOR
Karen M. Burns

PHOTOGRAPHER
Brent Kane

TECHNICAL EDITOR
Laurie Baker

PRODUCTION MANAGER
Regina Girard

COPY EDITOR
Melissa Bryan

ILLUSTRATOR
Rose Wright

SPECIAL THANKS
Martingale thanks Elke and Don Spivey for
generously alllowing the photography of this
book to take place in their home.

Contents

If you want a golden rule that will fit everybody, this is it: Have nothing in your house that you do not know to be useful, or believe to be beautiful.

—WILLIAM MORRIS

Make stuff, be happy!
—UNKNOWN

Being creative
is not a hobby,
it is a way of life.
—UNKNOWN

Today isn't just an
ordinary day.
Today I'll create
something beautiful
—UNKNOWN

Season
everything
with love.
—UNKNOWN

Come Stitch with Me

I'm a quiltmaker. It's what I was meant to be. Since the time I was little, I've had thread and fabric to play with. From making doll clothing to my own clothing, all I've wanted to do is sew. I've done a lot of other crafts and still do, but fabric and thread are what I love and create with the most.

In 1979 I made my first quilt, which was really a bedspread. It wasn't until 1998 that I decided to learn to *really* quilt. When I took my first workshop, I fell head over heels in love with quilting from the first block, even making it by hand using cardboard templates and cutting with scissors. I loved the entire process.

Over the years I've designed and made a lot of quilts—at least 600 projects and counting. When I make quilts I'm happy, my heart sings, and my soul is filled with goodness. If I go for a while without quilting, well . . . let's just say I make it a point to sew often!

Some of us make quilts for the sheer joy of sewing. That's me, and I imagine that you also fall into that category. Selecting, cutting, and putting back together bits of fabric—for us, every part of this creative process is exciting.

Pat Sloan's Teach Me to Appliqué is my 31st quilt book, and I'm delighted to partner with Martingale for this new series of publications about quilt design. When designing the quilts in this book, I wanted them to be ones you could use as shown, or take individual parts of and create your own design. "Farmers' Market" on page 74 is a great example of a quilt with this type of versatility. I want you to feather your nest with these projects and make your home beautiful.

If you've always loved appliqué but avoided it because you didn't think you could do it, make sure you read through my lessons on machine appliqué, beginning on page 7. I truly believe *everyone* can learn to appliqué this way.

From banners to bed quilts, the appliquéd quilts in this book are fun, happy, and easy to make. Thank you so much for selecting my book and joining me to make quilts for the sheer joy of it!

Fusible Appliqué by Machine

All the appliqué in this book is done by machine, starting with using an adhesive commonly called paper-backed fusible web and finishing with machine blanket stitching. I began fusing fabric to fabric before I ever quilted, and then years ago when I was first starting to appliqué, I decided to learn how to do beautiful fusible machine appliqué to get the look I wanted. Going back to what I had done with fusible web when I was sewing clothing, I refined my technique until I had a process—and results—I loved.

This method is easy, anyone can do it, and points will always turn out pointy and shapes are always as you expect them to be!

In these how-to pages, I'll walk you through the most important parts of doing fusible appliqué by machine. You can follow along step by step to create a sample and learn the technique, or simply read sections as you need them. Let's get to it!

This section includes:
- The tools you need
- Thread facts
- How to prepare appliqué shapes
- Getting to know your machine's blanket stitch
- The need to stabilize—or not
- How and where to start and stop stitching
- How to stitch around curves, points, and inside and outside corners

Making Samples

The easiest way to learn this technique is by making samples. In addition to the tools described next, you'll need to gather several 12" squares of light-colored fabric for the background of your samples and large scraps of fabrics that contrast well with the background fabric for the appliqué shapes.

Patterns are provided on this page and page 9 for the shapes used in the photos. Use these shapes to practice your fusing and stitching techniques on the fabric squares. Write notes directly on the squares about the details.

Small heart

Circle

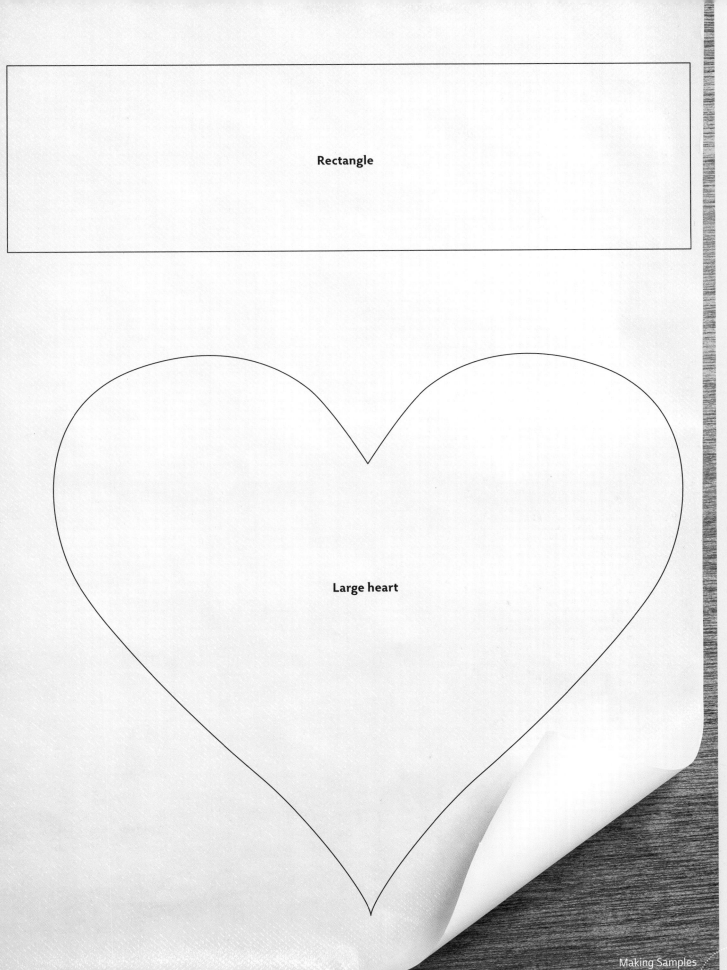

Rectangle

Large heart

Tools

You don't need many tools for fusible appliqué, but there are so many options available. Over the years I've tried many products and learned a lot about what works and what doesn't work so well, so I've been able to refine the list to a set of tools that are super dependable, easy to use, and effective.

Paper-backed fusible web. I've been using HeatnBond Lite as my adhesive of choice for a very long time. While there are several other fusible products on the market, this one has been the most dependable for me, and it works well with the cutaway method I like to do. (More about that on page 13.) I've also never had the paper separate from the adhesive while I was handling it. No matter what fusible product you use, make sure it can be sewn through so your needle won't gum up when you stitch your appliqués in place.

Sewable Fusible Web

How do you know if you can sew through fusible web? Look for "lightweight" or "sewable" on the end of the bolt. Or ask the clerk at the fabric store. Fusible web also comes in a heavy-duty variety, which is great for crafts that won't involve sewing. It's firmer and has more adhesive, so if you try to sew through it, your needle will get gummed up and your sewing will quickly come to a halt!

Tracing tool. Pens, pencils, Sharpies—they've all worked well for me. Try a variety of tools and find what works best for you to trace the patterns from this book onto the paper side of the fusible web. The ink (or graphite) won't come into direct contact with the fabric, so just about anything is fine. Just be sure the marks can tolerate heat, because you'll be ironing on the lines. You also don't want the marks to disappear or transfer to your iron, where they could then transfer to your fabric.

Scissors. I've tried many scissors over the 25-plus years that I've been using this technique, and I've discovered a few things. In fact, I've discovered so many things that the information needs its own space. See "Choosing the Right Scissors" on page 11.

Iron. The most important feature for your iron is that it stays hot. Just about any iron works fine, but it does need to have a cotton setting and the heat that this setting provides. Of course, you don't want the iron to get so hot that it cooks your project, so make sure you do a test with any iron before you use it and follow the temperature setting suggested for the fusible product you're using. This is especially necessary when you're working with an old iron, a travel iron, or an iron you're not familiar with, like those provided at a class or workshop.

Fabric. Quality woven-cotton fabrics are ideal for fusible-web appliqué—they hold up well, can withstand the heat of the iron, and come in a lot of great prints and colors. If you're using a cotton-blend fabric or a fabric that's a totally different fiber, test

Choosing the Right Scissors

You'll be using your scissors a lot while preparing the appliqués, and the right pair will make all the difference between enjoying the process and not.

• **Choose a longer blade.** This is not the time to use your embroidery scissors. A pair of 8" bent-handle shears works nicely for cutting out appliqué shapes. The long blade length lets you make fewer long cuts to get around the shape rather than a lot of short cuts, which would be required with shorter-blade scissors. I also recommend turning the piece in a continuous motion while cutting—rather than cutting a bit, rotating the shape, and then cutting again—to reduce the amount of opening and closing of the scissors and make the process much easier on your hand. This also helps to keep the edges of your shapes smooth, without noticeable starts and stops of the scissors.

• **Pick a pair that's sharp and lightweight.** Try them out. Lightweight scissors make a huge difference ergonomically when cutting out a lot of shapes. You don't want heavy or clunky scissors that weigh down your wrists. And you want sharp scissors. I prefer a pair that's *not* serrated. I feel the serrated edges slow me down, plus I prefer scissors that cut cleanly and smoothly.

• **Look for effortless opening and closing action.** The scissors should open and close with no effort at all. Stiff scissors not only slow you down and create uneven cuts, but they're bad for the health of your wrist.

• **Keep your fingers happy.** I prefer scissors with a finger hole that I can fit three fingers into, like those shown at far right in the photo above. They're very comfortable for me when I'm cutting a lot of shapes. Scissors with only enough room for one finger in each hole are too hard to use for long periods and can cause your fingers to cramp.

it with your fusible web first and adjust the iron's temperature setting as needed. Most high-quality cotton fabrics don't need to be washed, but if you find the adhesive isn't sticking, wash the fabric and try again. Fabrics may have leftover chemicals from processing on them that prevent the adhesive from sticking. Fabric softeners will also leave a residue that can keep the adhesive from sticking, so avoid using them during the washing or drying process.

Thread. This is another subject that demands its own space. For detailed information on thread weights and choosing colors, see "Selecting Thread" on page 17.

Sewing-machine needles. For 50-, 40-, and 28-weight thread, I use a universal 70/10 or 80/11 size needle. The thicker the thread, the larger the eye of the needle needs to be. Use a 90/14 or 100/16 needle for thread thicker than 28 weight.

Creating the Appliqué Shapes

I love tracing and cutting shapes. It's relaxing and reminds me of cutting out paper dolls as a little girl. The best part about paper dolls was the cutting!

Most of the shapes you'll find in this book are just the right size—not too big or too little—and they're very organic and natural. If you vary from the lines a little when tracing or cutting, it's no big deal. However, sometimes shapes need to fit precisely together, so you'll need to trace them accurately.

All of the asymmetrical patterns in this book have been reversed for the fusible-appliqué method, so they look the opposite of how the final shape will appear on the background. And because this is a raw-edge technique, no seam allowance is needed. If you use the patterns with another appliqué method, you may need to reverse the asymmetrical shapes and/or add seam allowances. If you use this fusible-web method with patterns from other books, check to be sure the asymmetrical patterns have been reversed.

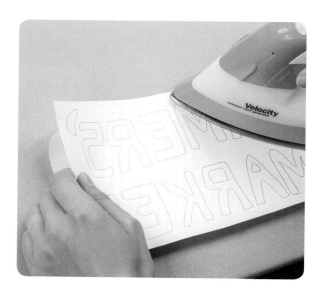

Already Reversed?

If you're not sure whether the patterns in another book are reversed, find a directional shape in your project, like the letters *F, K, or R.* If the pattern shown is backward, then the shape is ready to trace. If it's not reversed, you'll need to reverse the image before tracing onto your fusible web.

Tracing the Pattern

Place the fusible web paper side up over the pattern, and trace the shape **(photo 1)**. If you're tracing more than one pattern, be sure to leave space between the shapes. The amount of space needed will depend on the shape itself and how much excess fusible web is needed to stabilize the piece, which I discuss more in "Cutting Away the Excess Web" below.

When tracing natural shapes like flowers, leaves, and berries, I trace very quickly and smoothly. You can always change your drawn line when you cut the final shape, and if it's a straight line, you can use a ruler to assist you when you're drawing the shape onto paper **(photo 2)** or cutting the piece from the fabric.

Cutting Away the Excess Web

Fusible web tends to make appliqués stiff, even when using a lightweight product. If you have lots of appliqué shapes in your quilt, especially ones that are layered, the fusible web can make the quilt want to stand up by itself! My favorite part of my appliqué technique is that it creates soft, flexible appliqué shapes in my quilts. To achieve this, I cut away most of the fusible-web product and leave just a narrow rim that will "baste" the shape to the background. The machine stitches will then cover most of the fusible web, leaving the rest of the shape super soft and flexible.

Examples A and B in **photo 3** show the same rectangle traced onto fusible web, cut out with excess web around the shape, and fused to the wrong side of the fabric. When the shapes are cut out of the fabric on the marked line, example A will have fusible web entirely covering the wrong side of the fabric. This shape will be stiff until it's washed multiple times. Example B shows the cutaway method, also referred to as the doughnut method or windowing. The interior of the adhesive shape is cut away prior to fusing to the fabric, leaving just a rim of fusible web inside the drawn shape.

Some pieces are too small to cut away the fusible web inside the shape, although personally,

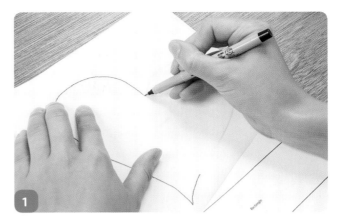

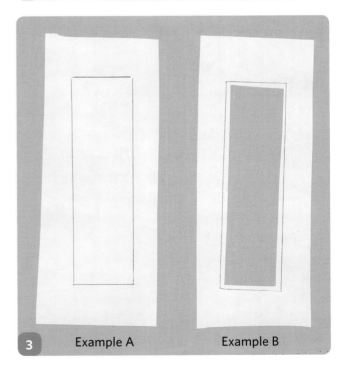

Example A   Example B

Who doesn't like doughnuts? Even better, fusible-web doughnuts are calorie-free!

I cut away from the smallest shapes I possibly can. In the projects in this book, the fusible shapes for the stems, letters, and very small pieces are left intact, or what I like to call "full fusible."

Here's my process for making soft and flexible fused appliqués.

1. Roughly cut out each shape, leaving enough fusible web around the outside edges of the drawn lines so that the shape will be stable when the interior is cut away and you have something to hold on to when placing the shape on the fabric. How much fusible web is enough? It depends on the size of the piece. The larger the shape, the more web you'll need to leave around the outside. If you don't leave enough, the piece will become limp and hard to control, kind of like a wet noodle. With experience, you'll gain wisdom as to how much is enough, but until you get a feel for it, don't fret. There's no right or wrong amount.

2. Cut through the excess web around the shape, through the marked line, and into the interior of the shape **(photo 4)**. Then cut away the excess fusible web on the *inside* of the shape, leaving less than ¼" inside the drawn line **(photo 5)**. Think of that little rim *inside* the drawn line as your basting rim. That's what will hold the shape on the background fabric.

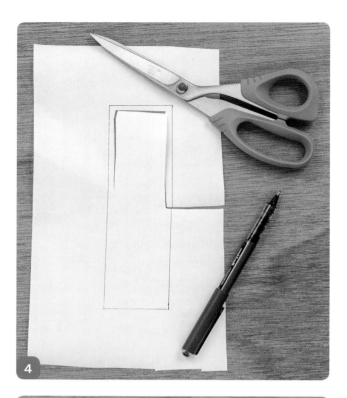

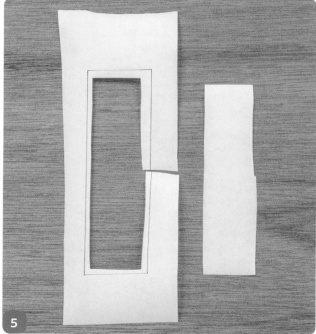

Seeing Is Believing

With the fusible web cut away inside the appliqué, you have a nice window for seeing the part of the print that will be featured in the shape.

The Inside Story

Your fusible web goes further with this method if you trace smaller shapes onto the interior piece of fusible web you cut away. If I can't use the extra pieces for my current project, I store them in a plastic bag to use another time.

Fusing the Shape onto the Fabric

1. **Place the fusible-web shape** onto the wrong side of the fabric you've selected for the appliqué **(photo 6)**. The adhesive can't be removed once it has felt the heat of the iron, so if you accidentally fuse the shape to the right side of the fabric, you'll need to start over. Double-check to make sure your shape is on the wrong side before you go any further. In this case, wrong (side) is right!

2. **Following the manufacturer's** instructions, press the fusible-web shape in place with a hot iron, starting on the edge *opposite* the cut **(photo 7)**. That way, for a large shape you can smooth the shape and keep it flat as you press. Take your time and press; don't push the fusible web out of shape with your iron.

Read and Obey!

When using HeatnBond Lite, you don't need to press for long; just a few seconds will melt the adhesive. You're not cooking a roast, so be quick! Other brands may require a longer heating time, so be sure to follow the instructions on the package. What works for one fusible-web product might not work for another.

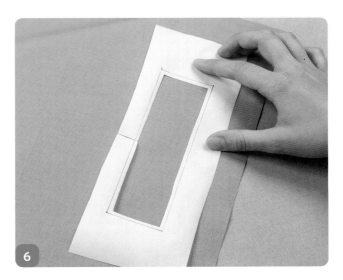

6

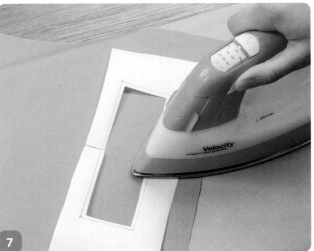

7

Fuse all the shapes that will be cut from the same fabric at the same time. The excess web around the edges of the shapes can overlap, but be sure the marked lines don't.

Cutting the Final Shape

Once the shape is fused to the fabric, you're ready to cut on the marked line to create the final appliqué shape. Remember, this is a raw-edge technique and you don't need to add seam allowance.

1. **If desired, smooth out** your drawn line so it's exactly as you want it.

2. **When you're ready,** cut on the marked line to create your final appliqué shape **(photo 8)**.

3. **Remove the paper backing.** I do this now so that when I'm ready to lay out the shapes, they're ready to be fused **(photo 9)**.

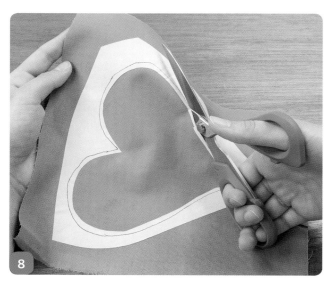

Fusing the Appliqués to the Background

An appliqué placement diagram is given with each project so that you can see where the shapes are placed on the background fabric. The project photo also provides a good reference. For this technique, I prefer to position all of the shapes on the background at the same time and fuse them in place. The text will indicate the order in which to place the shapes.

Position the shapes, fusible side down, on the *right* side of the background piece. (We're done working on the wrong side of the fabric now!) None of these projects requires precise placement, but you'll want to make sure to keep the appliqués out of the seam allowances. Some appliqués will cross over into other areas of the project, so you may not be able to fuse all the pieces in place until other parts are added.

When you're happy with the placement, follow the manufacturer's instructions to fuse all of the shapes in place at once.

Note to Self

Excess humidity can cause the paper backing to peel off of fusible web over time, so remember to store leftover bits of fusible web in a plastic bag. That way, when you go to use it—even months later—it will be ready for your appliqués.

Selecting Thread

Fusing with lightweight web is temporary, so after you fuse your appliqués to the background, you'll stitch them permanently in place. The thread you select plays an important role in the final look of the appliqué and, for that matter, the entire project. So many colors and thread weights are available, so you should be able to find one that makes your project just the way you envisioned.

I use cotton thread, so that's what we'll be discussing here. If you want to try other types of thread, stitch a sample with them first and see what you think. That's the best way to decide if you like the way they look and if they'll work nicely in your machine.

I use the same thread in the bobbin and needle, unless I'm using a 12-weight or heavier thread. For heavier threads, I use a finer thread in the bobbin, testing and adjusting the bobbin tension until I have a beautiful stitch.

Thread Weight

Several different thread weights work well for fusible appliqué.

• **50 weight** is the finest (thinnest) thread I'll use for appliquéing. Because it's fine, it will be the least visible of all the weights mentioned here, and it will blend into your appliqué shape the best when you use a matching thread color.

• **40 weight** is slightly thicker than 50 weight. It will give a little more definition to your stitches.

• **28 weight** is noticeably thicker than 50 weight. This weight is super nice if you want your stitching to serve as an added design feature, and I love using it when I select a thread shade that's darker or lighter than the appliqué and want the added definition to really show up.

• **12 weight** is very thick but really adds a lot of visual definition and texture. Because of the thickness, you'll need to use a needle with a large eye, such as a 90/14 or 100/16, and stitch a bit slower. You may also need to use a stabilizer under the background fabric. Because the thread is thick

and takes up more space, I also make my stitch length a bit longer. And I use a 28-weight thread in the bobbin so that I don't need to adjust the bobbin case.

Thread Color

The color of the thread is something else you'll need to decide. Do you want thread that matches or contrasts with your appliqués, or maybe something in between? You've got almost as many options when it comes to thread as there are thread colors. Ultimately, the best way to audition a thread color is to stitch with it and see if you like the look.

No contrast. I normally match my thread color to the appliqué fabric. To find the best color, lay a single strand of thread over your fabric and see how well it blends. If you're stuck between a couple of shades that might work, choose a color that is a shade darker than the fabric. Darker colors recede and lighter colors come forward, so a darker shade will visually blend better. Your thread color

I've posted a YouTube video about thread weights so that you can see what the different weights look like when stitched out and wrecommend making a sample for yourself using your own sewing machine.

Fuse a few rectangles of fabric to a background square and then stitch around each one using different weights and colors of thread. Mark the thread weight and machine settings directly (length by width) on the background so you can refer to them later.

Look for the link to all my videos on my website at www.PatSloan.com.

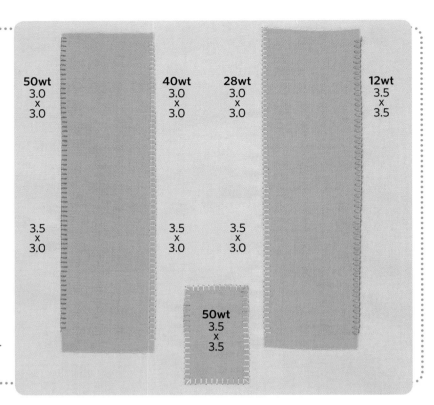

doesn't have to be a perfect match to blend well. Read my thoughts on thread colors that play well with lots of fabric colors in "My Go-To Colors" on page 19.

Slight contrast. If you just want to give your appliqués a faint outline, use a thread color that contrasts slightly with the appliqué fabric. Not

trying to match the color exactly also allows you to use the thread colors you have available, because you won't always find a perfect match in your stash.

High contrast. You've probably seen those pastel appliquéd quilts from the '30s that were blanket stitched with black thread. For a lot of people, those quilts provided the first introduction

Audition several different thread weights and colors to determine which one gives you the look you envision.

to the blanket stitch. Granny didn't have a lot of color options back then, and I bet she wouldn't have stitched black on pastel if she'd had the color choices we do now.

When you use a thread color that's a high contrast to your appliqué fabric, you're adding another layer of design to your quilt. Each shape will not only be outlined, but the stitch that lies on the appliqué (the "bite" of the blanket stitch) will create a visual design.

One color. Using one thread color for the entire project is a great option. Select a color that blends with a lot of fabrics (see "My Go-To Colors") and go for it!

Variegated color. Another way to use just one thread while not limiting yourself to one

My Go-To Colors

Over the years, I've found that there are a few thread colors that blend with a lot of fabrics. Aurifil has even boxed my favorite neutrals in a thread set! (See them on page 20.) When you have these go-to shades in your collection, you can start stitching right away. Try one of these colors when you don't have the perfect match.

For warm fabric colors, I find that shades of tan to brown work really well.

For cool colors, the spectrum of gray, from light to dark, will blend with many different fabrics.

color is by choosing a variegated thread. Make a sample to make sure you like the color changes, and then enjoy your stitching without having to change threads.

I often use variegated thread for my folk-art pieces or when I need some definition between my appliqué shapes and the background. For instance, when I stitch pale-yellow flower petals on a cream background, the pale yellow appliqués may blend into the background from a distance and the petals can become lost. Stitching around the petals with a deep yellow gives them definition and I can still use a light-colored appliqué on a light background.

Middle Ground

When using a variegated thread for appliqué, choose a thread color in the middle of the variegated range to use in the bobbin.

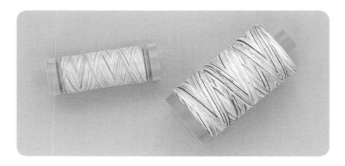

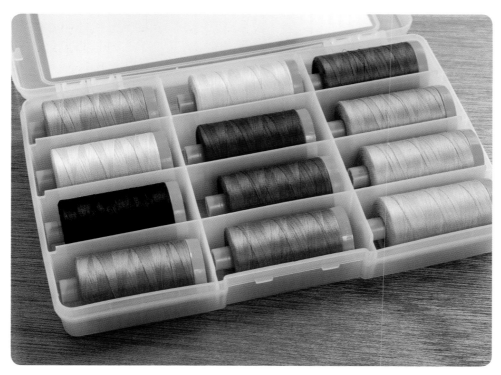

The Perfect Box of Neutrals by Pat Sloan for Aurifil

Preparing to Stitch

Before you can start stitching, you need to do a little prep work—and a little playing.

Putting the Right Foot Forward

I highly recommend using an open-toe appliqué foot for the best visibility when stitching. Your regular presser foot has a bar across it that blocks the view of where you're stitching. And because the needle will be moving side to side to make the blanket stitch, make sure you don't use your machine's patchwork or ¼" foot. You're sure to break a needle with that foot in place.

If your machine didn't come with an open-toe foot, you should be able to purchase one from your sewing-machine dealer.

Selecting Your Blanket Stitch

Depending on your machine, you may have several different blanket-stitch options available. Whichever you choose or whatever is available on your machine (provided it sews more than a straight stitch!) will work fine for my appliqué method.

The most important thing to know about your stitch is what it looks like. Why? Have you ever been stitching along and turned a corner only to find out that your stitch is suddenly going in another direction? If you know what your stitch looks like and how it's formed, you can prevent a lot of seam ripping and aggravation. Some of the options you might find on your machine are shown below.

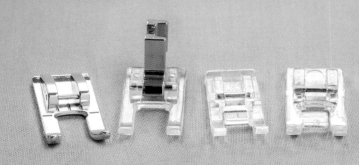

The open-toe feet on the left enable you to see where you're stitching, as opposed to the regular presser feet on the right, which block the stitching area.

Once you know which type of blanket stitch you have, you'll be able to easily make decisions on when to pivot your work and prevent the stitch from shooting out in a direction you weren't expecting. For example, if your stitch is one bite and then two straight stitches, you need to keep track of which part of the stitch comes next when pivoting.

Blanket-Stitch Substitutes

Can you use other stitches to secure your appliqués? Sure! For narrow pieces, I sometimes use a straight stitch. For other shapes, I might use a decorative stitch other than a blanket stitch. If you choose a different decorative stitch, just make sure enough of the stitch grabs the shape to secure it. Many decorative stitches have more of the stitching on one side than the other and won't secure the shape.

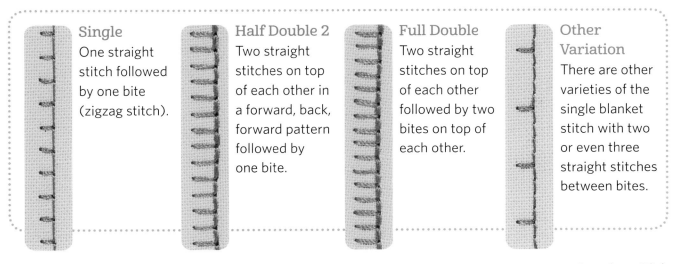

Single
One straight stitch followed by one bite (zigzag stitch).

Half Double 2
Two straight stitches on top of each other in a forward, back, forward pattern followed by one bite.

Full Double
Two straight stitches on top of each other followed by two bites on top of each other.

Other Variation
There are other varieties of the single blanket stitch with two or even three straight stitches between bites.

The button for the locking stitch on my machine

Playing with Stitch Size

For most machines the default blanket stitch won't be exactly what you're looking for, but try it first and see what you think. Stitch one of your samples with it and make a note of the setting. Then try changing the settings and see if you like something else better.

I've found that I like the bite (stitch width) and the straight stitch (stitch length) numbers to be equal, such as a 3.1 and 3.1. But, you might like a larger bite or you might like your stitches closer together. My experience with seeing hundreds of machines in my workshops is that many quilters will find a target size between 2.0 and 3.5. If you don't find something you like in that range, keep adjusting until you find the setting that works for you.

Depending on the brand or model of your machine, you may also need to select a mirror image of the blanket stitch to make the bite of the blanket stitch go to the left. I know some brands of machines stitch toward the right. If you have a mirror-image button on your machine, remember to push that before you begin and your stitches will be formed with the bite swinging to the left.

Securing the Stitches

It's important to secure lines of stitching when stopping and starting. I use the locking-stitch button on my machine to do a few stitches in place. For projects that won't be washed frequently, this is perfect and saves a lot of time. If my project is going to be heavily laundered, I'll pull the threads to the back and tie them by hand with a knot to really secure them. No locking stitch? No problem. Set your stitch length to 0 and stitch in place a few times, and then reset your machine for a blanket stitch.

When ending, I stitch right up to where I started and end at the same spot. I usually stitch with a 50-weight thread, so if I happen to shoot past a stitch and cross over another one, the extra thread isn't really visible.

Using a Stabilizer . . . or Not

I find that for most machines, you don't need to use stabilizer when blanket stitching. If you notice that the stitch is pulling, first try adjusting the tension. If that doesn't work, you could have the machine serviced to be sure the problem isn't with the machine. If your machine stitching continues to pull up when not using a stabilizer, then try starching your background fabric before stitching. That often gives your piece just enough firmness to keep your piece from pulling. And that way, you won't have to spend time in the end removing all the stabilizer. If your stitches are still pulling and puckering after trying all of these options, then try using a stabilizer under the fabric.

Practicing Your Stitching

Practice makes perfect, so make one of each of the appliqué shapes from the patterns on pages 8 and 9 and fuse them to one of your background squares. Then practice stitching curves, corners, and inner and outer points.

If your machine has a needle up/down function, set it for the needle-down position. Working in this position allows you to turn and not lose your place.

Curves

Curves come in all sizes. The softer curves found in a large circle or leaf are easier to manage because you don't have to pivot as often. With tighter curves, like the sample circle, you need to stop and adjust the fabric frequently. If you have a machine with a knee lift, use it. It allows you to raise the presser foot without having to remove your hands from the work, which is the ideal way to stay in control when you're blanket stitching. Some machines have a "hover" feature that lifts the presser foot slightly when you stop stitching in the needle-down position. This gives you the same benefit as the knee lift. If you don't have either of these features, you'll need to manually lift the presser foot when turning your work.

Let's practice on the circle shape.

1. **Begin in the background** right next to the appliqué shape. Bring the bobbin thread to the top and take a few locking stitches, or plan on securing your thread later.

2. **Start blanket stitching** with the needle in the background fabric immediately next to the edge of the shape **(photo 1)**. If it's in the shape, you'll create a V when you turn.

3. **Straight stitch right** next to the shape, and then as soon as the stitch pattern takes a bite into the appliqué **(photo 2)** and returns to the background, stop with the needle down in the background.

Straight Start

When possible, start stitching along an edge where you can take a few stitches before needing to turn. Or, if your project involves a lot of curves, try to begin at a gentle curve rather than a tight curve.

Sewing forever, housework whenever.

—UNKNOWN

4. Lift the presser foot and pivot the fabric so you can stitch following the curve.

5. Put the presser foot back down and take the next stitch, which should be a straight stitch. If you're using any blanket stitch other than a single straight stitch followed by a single bite, be aware of where you are in the stitch pattern so you'll know when to stop and pivot. Lift the presser foot and pivot **(photo 3)**. Put the presser foot back down.

6. Continue taking a stitch and pivoting until you have stitched around the entire shape **(photo 4)**. Secure the stitches and cut the threads.

Outside Points

Points require a bit more maneuvering. Here I'll share a casual way to approach an outside point as well as a more detailed way.

The casual way is to use a 50-weight thread in a color that matches the appliqué fabric, and let the threads overlap as shown in the illustration. I do this a lot because when the thread color matches the shape, you don't even see it.

For a more detailed approach to stitching points, you'll need to angle the stitches as you approach the point. This is very pretty and not hard to do. Once you're close to where the bite might touch the bite on the opposite side of the point, you'll start to angle the stitches.

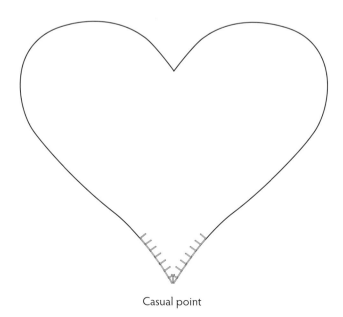

Casual point

Detailed point

Let's use the point on the heart shape to practice making the detailed point. If you want to go casual, just skip angling the stitches on both sides of the heart point.

1. **Start stitching at about the middle** of the gentle curve on the right-hand side of the heart. Stop stitching when you get close to the point at which your bite length is almost half the distance to the opposite side, ending after you've completed the straight stitch part of the stitch pattern. The needle should be down in the background **(photo 5)**.

2. **With the needle down,** lift the presser foot. Angle the appliqué so the bite stitch will be angled or tilted upward slightly **(photo 6)**. Make the stitch, and end with the needle down in the background **(photo 7)**.

3. **Lift the presser foot and rotate** the appliqué back into position to stitch the straight stitch next to the shape. (If you don't rotate, the straight stitch will end up *on* the appliqué.) Take the stitch **(photo 8)**.

4. **Continue rotating and angling** the stitches, with each of the bite stitches angling a little more than the previous one, kind of like a drawbridge opening. When you get to the point, the heart will be completely to the left of the needle and the bite stitch will be horizontal **(photo 9)**.

5. **Continue stitching up the other side** of the heart, again angling the stitches until you clear the narrow area.

Inside Points

For inside angles on shapes like hearts, flowers, and stars, the appliqué looks best if the bite hits right in the center of the V. It rarely hits there on its own, however, so we need to help it.

1. Stitch up to the point where you have one straight stitch left to make before the inside point **(photo 10)**.

2. Raise your needle out of the fabric. If your machine will execute the stitch when you use the "needle-up" feature, this is perfect. If your machine stays in place with the needle up, then you need to lightly tap the foot pedal to raise the needle **(photo 11)**.

3. Lift the presser foot.

4. Adjust your appliqué so that when you put the needle back down in the fabric it will be at the point of the V. Lower the needle into the fabric, and then lower the presser foot **(photo 12)**.

5. Rotate the appliqué so the bite stitches straight down from the V into the appliqué **(photo 13)**.

6. Rotate the appliqué and continue stitching **(photo 14)**.

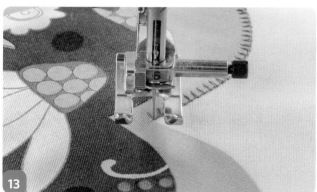

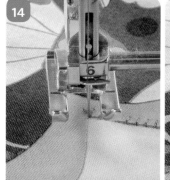

Stitching Sequence

You'll be stitching the exposed edges of the appliqués, and with fusible appliqué there's no mandatory stitching order. I tend to stitch by color—all the blue shapes using blue thread, and then all the green shapes with green thread, and so on. For me, that's the most efficient way to stitch my quilts.

There are times when shapes overlap and I need to look at the most effective way to go around each one with as little starting and stopping as possible. If you take a few seconds to look at the order of the shapes—what overlaps, what doesn't—you can reduce the starts and stops. Sometimes I need to change to a straight stitch and "travel" on the edge of a shape for a short distance, 1" or so, and then switch back to the blanket stitch when I get to the next location. I do this so that I don't have to tie off thread. If I want to jump to another area, I lock my stitches and then, without cutting the thread, move to the new area, lock the stitches, and continue stitching. When I'm finished, I go back and clip the "jump" threads.

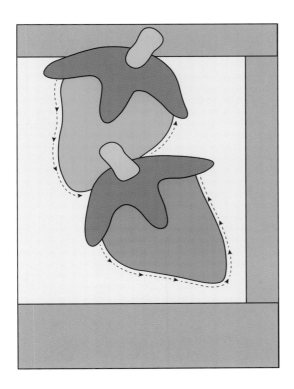
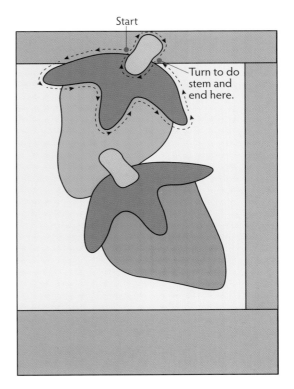

Good food ends with good talk.

—AUTHOR UNKNOWN

Let's GO Sew!

Now that you have some new tools in your toolbox, let's go use them! If you have a question, please write to me at Pat@PatSloan.com. Please also visit my website, www.PatSloan.com, where you can sign up for my newsletter and join me at one of my online groups.

I hope to see you there!

One who makes
no mistakes
makes nothing.
—GIACOMO CASANOVA

Sweet Bea's Bouquet

There are always flowers for those who want to see them.

—HENRI MATISSE

When I'm learning a new technique, I like to start with a small project that I can complete easily. A single block with pretty borders is my go-to size!

My great-aunt Bea loved flowers. She lived in a tiny row house near Lancaster, Pennsylvania, with a long, skinny backyard. She had flowers planted the entire length of her yard, and they were spectacular. "Sweet Bea's Bouquet" reminds me of her.

Finished wall hanging: 24½" x 24½"

Materials

Yardage is based on 42"-wide fabric unless otherwise noted.

⅝ yard of cream solid for background

½ yard of aqua print for outer border

¼ yard of navy print for inner border and single-fold binding

1 fat quarter (18" x 21") of red print #1 for center medallion appliqué

9" x 13" rectangle of red print #2 for flower appliqués

8" x 11" rectangle of green print for leaf and stem appliqués

4" x 4" square of gray print for flower base appliqués

1 yard of fabric for backing

30" x 30" piece of batting

1 yard of 17"-wide paper-backed fusible web

Cutting

From the cream solid, cut:
1 square, 16½" x 16½"

From the navy print, cut:
5 strips, 1½" x 42"; crosscut *2 of the strips* into:
    2 strips, 1½" x 16½"
    2 strips, 1½" x 18½"

From the aqua print, cut:
2 strips, 3½" x 18½"
2 strips, 3½" x 24½"

Assembling the Wall-Hanging Top

1 Refer to the assembly diagram on page 32 to sew the navy 1½" x 16½" inner-border strips to the sides of the cream square. Press the seam allowances toward the border. Sew the navy 1½" x 18½" inner-border strips to the top and bottom edges of the cream square. Press the seam allowances toward the border.

2 Sew the aqua 3½" x 18½" outer-border strips to the sides of the wall-hanging top. Press the seam allowances toward the outer border. Sew the aqua 3½" x 24½" outer-border strips to the top and

bottom edges of the wall-hanging top. Press the seam allowances toward the outer border.

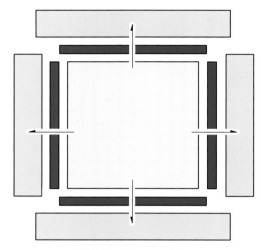

Wall-hanging assembly

Adding the Appliqués

1 Refer to "Fusible Appliqué by Machine" on page 7 and use the patterns on page 33 to prepare the flower, flower base, stem, and leaf appliqués from the fabrics indicated on the patterns. Remove the paper backing from each shape.

2 For the center medallion shape, fold a 16" square of fusible web in half vertically and horizontally and gently finger-press the folds. Open up the square. Trace the quarter pattern for the center medallion on page 34 onto one quarter of the fusible-web square, aligning the fold lines with the straight edges as indicated on the pattern. Repeat to trace the pattern onto each quarter of the fusible-web square. Fuse the square to the wrong side of red print #1, and then cut out the shape. Remove the paper backing.

Pattern assembly guide

3 Fold the wall-hanging top in half horizontally and vertically and press the folds to mark the center. Repeat with the fusible-web shape for the center medallion. Position the medallion in the middle of the wall-hanging top, matching the centers.

4 Refer to the appliqué placement diagram below to position the remaining prepared appliqué shapes on the wall-hanging top in the following order. Position the stems and then place a flower at the top of each stem. Place one leaf and one reversed leaf on opposite sides of each stem. I like to tuck the leaves under the stem, but there's no right or wrong way. Just do what you like best. Position the flower base.

Appliqué placement

5 Fuse the appliqués in place. Blanket-stitch around the outer edges of each shape using a matching or slightly contrasting thread color.

Finishing

1 Layer the wall-hanging top, batting, and backing; baste the layers together.

2 Quilt your project. Refer to "Up-Close and Beautiful" on page 33 for details on how my wall hanging was quilted.

3 Refer to "Binding by Machine" on page 93 to bind the quilt edges using the remaining navy strips.

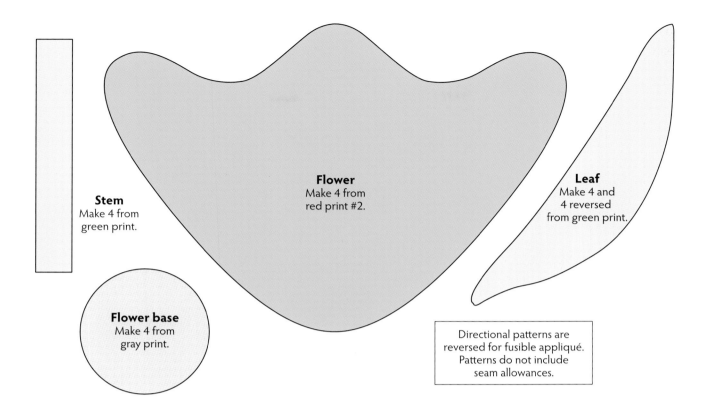

Stem
Make 4 from
green print.

Flower base
Make 4 from
gray print.

Flower
Make 4 from
red print #2.

Leaf
Make 4 and
4 reversed
from green print.

Directional patterns are
reversed for fusible appliqué.
Patterns do not include
seam allowances.

Up Close and Beautiful

I outline quilted all the appliqué shapes close to the
edges, and then quilted a swirl design in the background.
Each stem is stitched through the center. For the inside of the
medallion, I quilted ½" from the edge and stitched a swirl in the center.
The border is quilted with swirls, loops, and feather shapes.

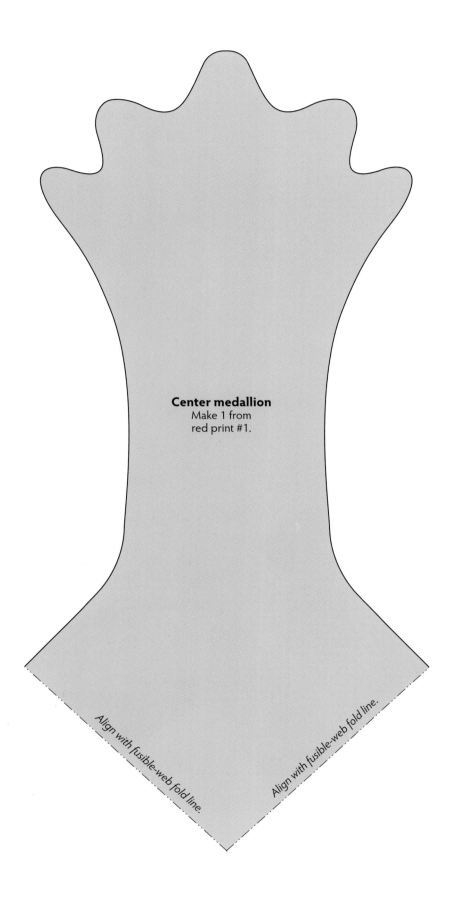

Center medallion
Make 1 from
red print #1.

Align with fusible-web fold line.

Align with fusible-web fold line.

Flowers are my inspiration, any time of the year and in any weather. If I see a flower, it immediately lifts my spirits and makes my heart do a dance! A few years back I was given a clump of daisies from a friend's yard. These daisies are so hardy and they multiply so well that I've since shared clumps of my daisy plants with friends and neighbors, spreading the love one white flower at a time. Gardens are like that for me—an endless source of joy.

Daisy Patch

All my scattering moments are taken up with my needle.

—ELLEN BIRDSEYE WHEATON

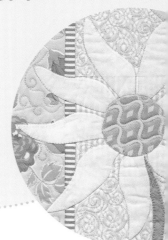

Finished banner: 18½" x 18½"

Materials

Yardage is based on 42"-wide fabric unless otherwise noted.

¼ yard *each* of 2 assorted cream prints for background

⅜ yard of narrow red-and-white stripe for inner border and single-fold binding

⅜ yard of red floral for outer border

1 fat quarter (18" x 21") of white print for daisy petal appliqués

12" x 12" square of medium-green print for bias stems

8" x 14" rectangle of aqua print #1 for vase appliqué

10" x 10" square of light-green print for leaf appliqués

6" x 12" rectangle of aqua print #2 for berry appliqués

5" x 12" rectangle of yellow print for daisy center appliqués

1⅝ yards of fabric for backing

27" x 52" piece of batting

½" bias-tape maker (optional)

Liquid basting glue

1½ yards of 17"-wide paper-backed fusible web

Cutting

From *each* of the cream prints, cut:
7 squares, 5½" x 5½" (14 total)

From the red-and-white stripe, cut:
2 strips, 1½" x 35½"
2 strips, 1½" x 12½"
4 strips, 1½" x 42"

From the red floral, cut:
2 strips, 3½" x 37½"
2 strips, 3½" x 18½"

From the medium-green print, cut:
Enough 1"-wide bias strips to make approximately 70" of bias tape when joined end to end

Make It Your Own

I LOVE daisies! They're such happy summer flowers and I believe they may have been one of the first I picked as a little girl. But you may have a different favorite flower, or you may be making this quilt for someone else. It's super easy to just change the flower to your favorite, maybe a sunflower for the fall or big fun tulips for spring!

Assembling the Banner Top

1 Arrange the assorted cream 5½" squares into seven horizontal rows of two squares each, alternating the fabrics in each row and from row to row. Sew the squares in each row together. Press the seam allowances in opposite directions from row to row. Sew the rows together to complete the banner center. Press the seam allowances in one direction.

2 Refer to the assembly diagram at right to sew the striped 1½" x 35½" inner-border strips to the sides of the banner center. Press the seam allowances toward the inner border. Sew the striped 1½" x 12½" inner-border strips to the top and bottom edges of the banner center. Press the seam allowances toward the inner border.

3 Join the red floral 3½" x 37½" outer-border strips to the sides of the banner top. Press the seam allowances toward the outer border. Sew the red floral 3½" x 18½" outer-border strips to the top and bottom edges of the banner top. Press the seam allowances toward the outer border.

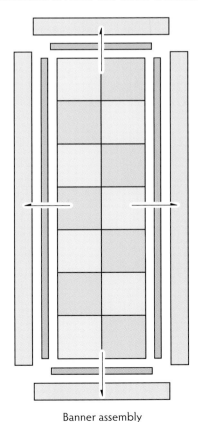

Banner assembly

Adding the Appliqués

1 Refer to "Fusible Appliqué by Machine" on page 7 and use the patterns on pages 39 and 40 to prepare the appliqués from the fabrics indicated on the patterns. Remove the paper backing from each shape.

2 If you're using a bias-tape maker, follow the manufacturer's instructions to make approximately 70" of ½"-wide bias stems from the medium-green 1"-wide bias strips. If you're not using a bias-tape maker, join the medium-green 1"-wide bias strips end to end; press the seam allowances open. Fold both long raw edges in to meet at the center, wrong sides together, to create a ½"-wide stem; press.

3 Refer to the appliqué placement diagram on page 39 to position the prepared appliqué shapes on the banner right side in the following order. Center the vase shape right above the bottom inner border. Position the daisy petals in groups of nine, overlapping some of the petals of each flower onto the borders. Place a daisy center in the middle of each flower, covering the ends of the petals. Add the berries.

4 When you're pleased with the placement of the appliqué shapes, use basting glue to "draw" lines where the stems will go, avoiding previously placed shapes. Lay the bias strip you made in step 2 over the glue lines, raw edges face down, cutting the strip as necessary to create the five stems. Tuck the ends of each stem under shapes to hide them, and lift up previously placed shapes that the stems run under.

5 Refer to the appliqué placement diagram to position the leaves.

Up Close and Beautiful

I used a very-light shade of gray thread that blended into the background fabric for all of my quilting. I outline quilted all the appliqué shapes, and then I added quilting inside the daisy centers and vase. Spiral quilting fills the background. The border is quilted with a vine motif.

6 Fuse the appliqués in place. Blanket-stitch around the outer edges of each shape using a matching or slightly contrasting thread color.

Appliqué placement

Finishing

1 Layer the banner top, batting, and backing; baste the layers together.

2 Quilt your project. Refer to "Up-Close and Beautiful" on page 38 for details on how my wall hanging was quilted.

3 Refer to "Binding by Machine" on page 93 to bind the quilt edges using the remaining striped strips.

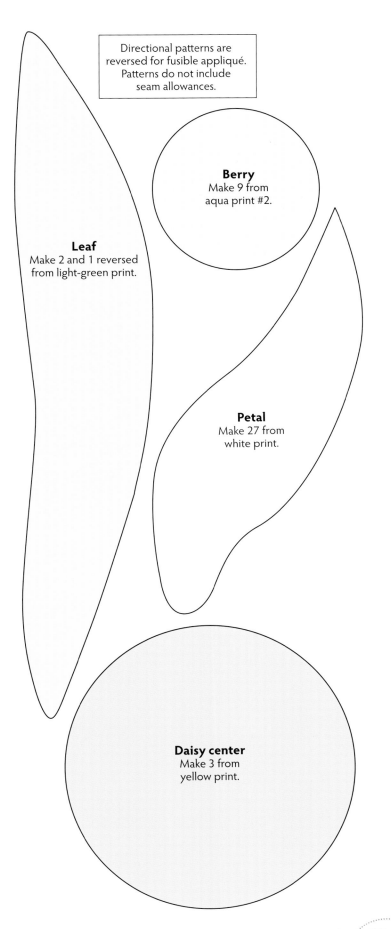

Directional patterns are reversed for fusible appliqué. Patterns do not include seam allowances.

Leaf
Make 2 and 1 reversed from light-green print.

Berry
Make 9 from aqua print #2.

Petal
Make 27 from white print.

Daisy center
Make 3 from yellow print.

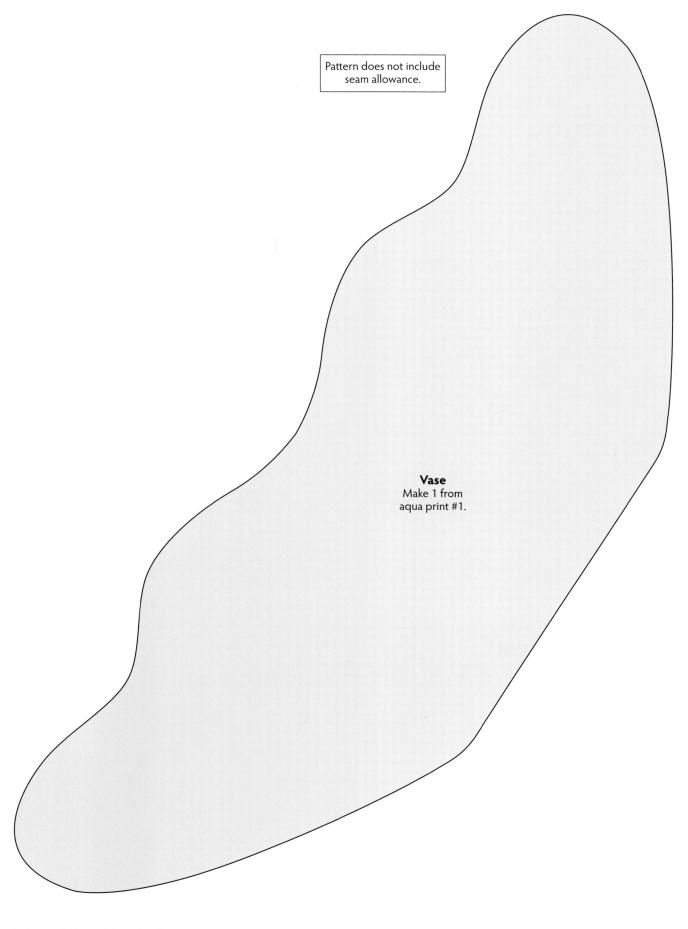

Pattern does not include
seam allowance.

Vase
Make 1 from
aqua print #1.

My home is my canvas, my nest, my baseline. This is where I work and play and experiment. I love my home to be cozy but fresh. I have surrounded myself with the things I love, but it's not overstuffed. I am constantly moving and arranging and decorating my home as I love to play with design and color.

With this little banner, I can personalize the colors and give it as a gift, sharing a piece of my heart with my friends.

Feels Like Home

What I love most about my home is who I share it with.

—TAD CARPENTER

Finished banner: 12½" x 33½"

Materials

Yardage is based on 42"-wide fabric unless otherwise noted.

½ yard of blue floral for border and single-fold binding

⅓ yard of cream print for background

7" x 15" rectangle of green print for stem, flower base, and leaf appliqués

7" x 13" rectangle of red print #1 for petal appliqués

6" x 11" rectangle of red print #2 for house appliqué

4" x 15" rectangle of blue print #1 for letter appliqués

7" x 7" square of blue print #2 for roof appliqué

3" x 8" rectangle of yellow print for door appliqué

3" x 3" square of blue print #3 for chimney appliqué

½ yard of fabric for backing

16" x 40" piece of batting

1 yard of 17"-wide paper-backed fusible web

Cutting

From the cream print, cut:
1 strip, 7½" x 28½"

From the blue floral, cut:
2 strips, 3" x 28½"
2 strips, 3" x 12½"
3 strips, 1½" x 42"

Assembling the Banner Top

Refer to the assembly diagram to sew the floral 3" x 28½" border strips to the sides of the cream strip. Press the seam allowances toward the border strips. Sew the floral 3" x 12½" border strips to the top and bottom edges of the cream strip. Press the seam allowances toward the border strips.

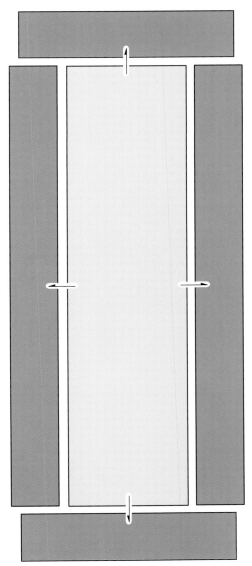

Banner assembly

Adding the Appliqués

1 Refer to "Fusible Appliqué by Machine" on page 7 and use the patterns on pages 45–47 to prepare the appliqués from the fabrics indicated on the patterns.

2 Refer to the appliqué placement diagram below to position the prepared appliqué shapes on the banner right side in the following order. Place the house, door, roof, and chimney. Position the letters vertically to spell *HOME*. Add the stem, tucking the bottom end under the roof. Arrange three groups of petals on the stem and position a flower base at the bottom of each group. Add the leaves to the stem.

Appliqué placement

3 Fuse the appliqués in place. Blanket-stitch around the outer edges of each shape using a matching or slightly contrasting thread color.

Personalize It!

This is a fun little project to make for yourself or as a housewarming or shower gift for a friend. A touch of embroidery is a great way to personalize the banner. Consider stitching the house number, your (or the recipient's) last name, the year, or a sweet saying like:

"Take a Deep Breath, You're Home Now"
"Home Sweet Home"
"Home Is Where Your Story Begins"
"There's No Place Like Home"

Finishing

1 Layer the banner top, batting, and backing; baste the layers together.

2 Quilt your project. Refer to "Up-Close and Beautiful" below for details on how my banner was quilted.

3 Refer to "Binding by Machine" on page 93 to bind the quilt edges using the remaining floral strips.

Up Close and Beautiful

I outline quilted all the appliqué shapes, and then I quilted the house with vertical lines. The roof is quilted with wavy horizontal lines. Open swirls fill the border.

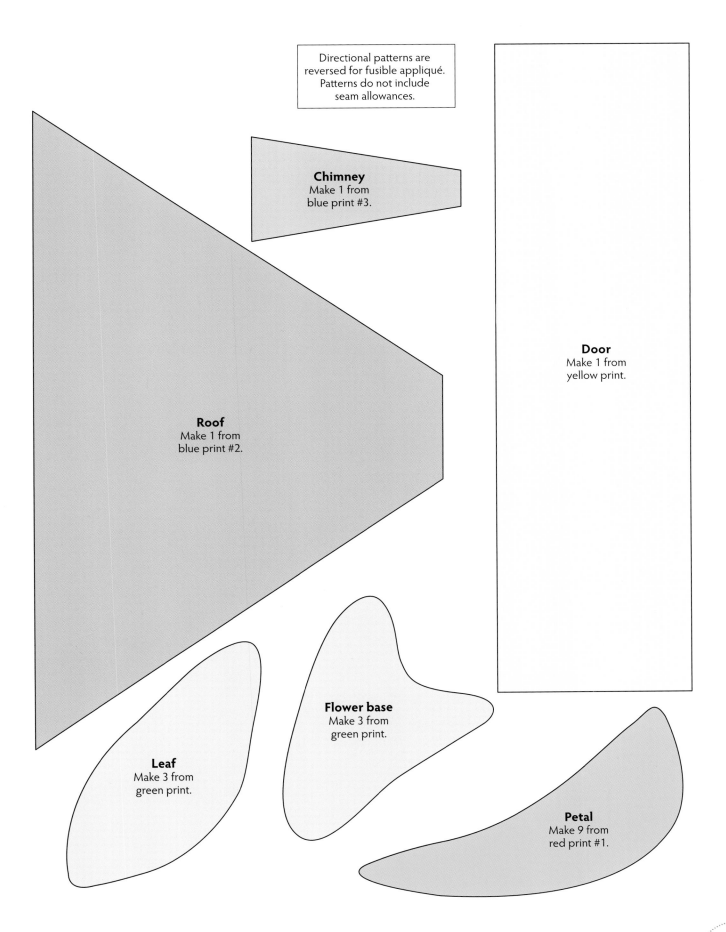

Directional patterns are reversed for fusible appliqué. Patterns do not include seam allowances.

Chimney
Make 1 from blue print #3.

Door
Make 1 from yellow print.

Roof
Make 1 from blue print #2.

Flower base
Make 3 from green print.

Leaf
Make 3 from green print.

Petal
Make 9 from red print #1.

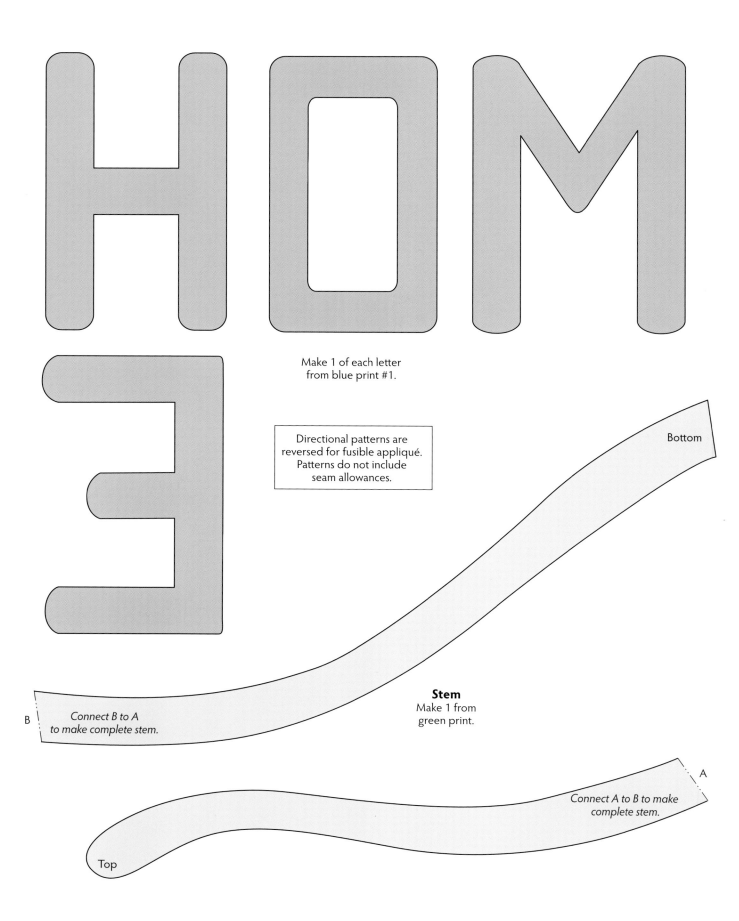

Make 1 of each letter
from blue print #1.

Directional patterns are
reversed for fusible appliqué.
Patterns do not include
seam allowances.

Bottom

Connect B to A
to make complete stem.

B

Stem
Make 1 from
green print.

A

Connect A to B to make
complete stem.

Top

House
Make 1 from
red print #2.

My Veggie Garden

You are never too old to set another goal or to dream a new dream.

—C. S. LEWIS

The quote by C. S. Lewis perfectly captures the way I feel about my gardens. Each winter I become obsessed with the possibilities that the garden holds. Will my butterfly bush come back? Where should I plant the tomatoes this year so they do better? To share a secret with you, I'm a springtime gardener. I dig and plant like crazy for a month, and then I hope for the best. And every year I cultivate a new goal, a new dream, for the perfect garden. How about you?

Finished banner: 14½" x 38½"

Materials

Yardage is based on 42"-wide fabric unless otherwise noted.

⅛ yard *each* of 4 assorted black prints for sashing and border
⅓ yard of light-gray print for block backgrounds
6" x 6" square *each* of 3 assorted red prints for tomato appliqués
5" x 7" rectangle *each* of 3 assorted orange prints for carrot appliqués
4" x 8" rectangle *each* of 3 assorted purple prints for
    eggplant appliqués
5" x 10" rectangle of green print #1 for tomato stem/cap and
    leaf appliqués
4" x 10" rectangle of green print #2 for carrot leaf appliqués
4" x 5" rectangle of green print #3 for carrot leaf appliqué
4" x 8" rectangle of green print #4 for eggplant stem/cap appliqués
¼ yard of black print for single-fold binding
⅝ yard of fabric for backing
18" x 42" piece of batting
1 yard of 17"-wide paper-backed fusible web

Cutting

From the light-gray print, cut:
3 squares, 10½" x 10½"
From the 4 assorted black prints, cut a *total* of:
58 squares, 2½" x 2½"
From the black print for binding, cut:
3 strips, 1½" x 42"

Make It Yours!

My kitchen has a skinny area between the pantry door and the door to the dining room. It's a perfect place to display this banner. However, if you don't have such a spot, you can easily turn "My Veggie Garden" into a table runner by rotating the shapes so they're oriented toward the sides. Or just appliqué a single tomato on a tea towel. Play with the shapes and make them your own!

Appliquéing the Blocks

1. Refer to "Fusible Web by Machine" on page 7 and use the tomato, eggplant, and carrot patterns on page 52 (with the "Farmers' Market" project instructions) to prepare the appliqués from the fabrics indicated on the patterns. Remove the paper backing from each shape.

2. Refer to the appliqué placement diagram below to position the prepared appliqué shapes on the light-gray squares. For the eggplant block, position the eggplant shapes first and then the stem/cap shapes. For the carrots, position the carrots first and then the leaves, placing the leaf shape cut from green print #3 between the green print #2 leaves. Position the three tomato shapes on the remaining square, followed by the stem/cap shapes and then the leaves.

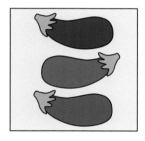

Appliqué placement

3. Fuse the appliqués in place. Blanket-stitch around the outer edges of each shape using a matching or slightly contrasting thread color.

Assembling the Banner Top

1. Randomly sew five black squares together side by side to make a pieced sashing strip. Press the seam allowances in one direction. Repeat to make a total of two pieced sashing strips and two pieced top/bottom borders.

Make 4.

2. Randomly sew 19 black squares together side by side to make a pieced side border. Press the seam allowances in one direction. Repeat to make a total of two pieced side borders.

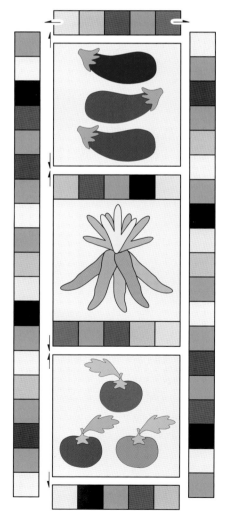

Banner assembly

3 Refer to the assembly diagram on page 50 to sew the sashing strips to the top and bottom of the carrot block. Press the seam allowances toward the sashing strips. Sew the top border to the top of the eggplant block and the bottom border to the bottom of the tomato block. Press the seam allowances toward the border strips. Join the blocks. Press the seam allowances toward the sashing/border strips. Sew the side border strips to the sides of the joined blocks. Press the seam allowances toward the border strips.

Finishing

1 Layer the banner top, batting, and backing; baste the layers together.

2 Quilt your project. Refer to "Up-Close and Beautiful" below for details on how my banner was quilted.

3 Refer to "Binding by Machine" on page 93 to bind the quilt edges using the black strips.

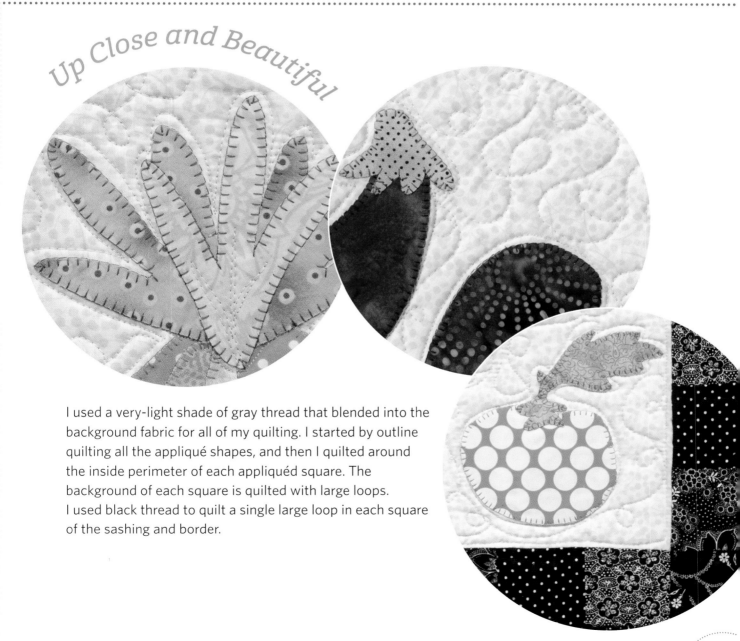

Up Close and Beautiful

I used a very-light shade of gray thread that blended into the background fabric for all of my quilting. I started by outline quilting all the appliqué shapes, and then I quilted around the inside perimeter of each appliquéd square. The background of each square is quilted with large loops. I used black thread to quilt a single large loop in each square of the sashing and border.

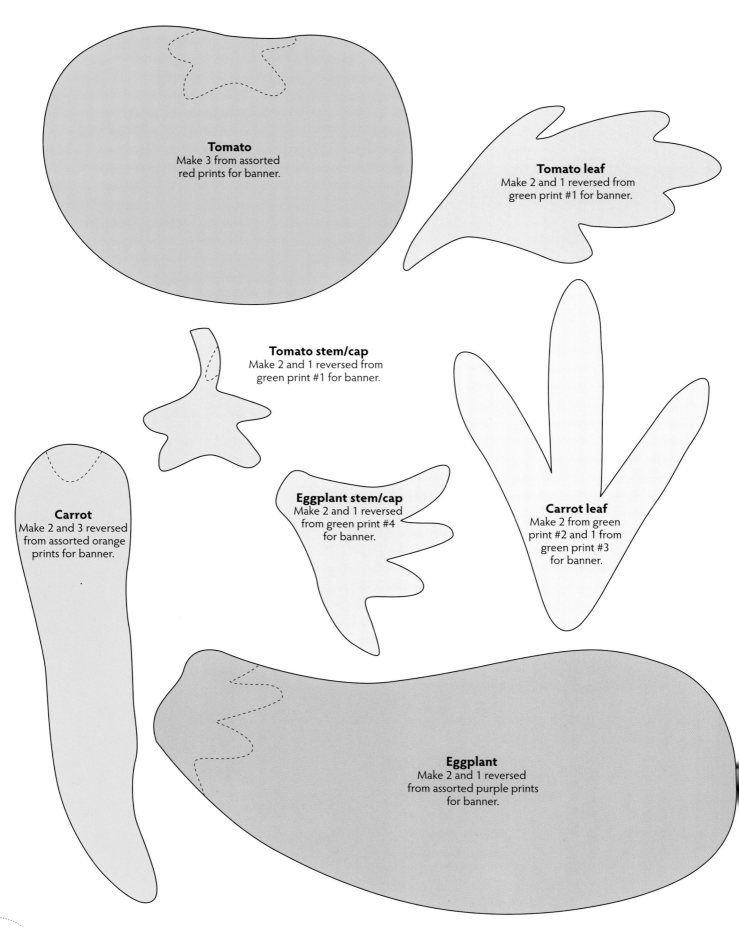

Tomato
Make 3 from assorted
red prints for banner.

Tomato leaf
Make 2 and 1 reversed from
green print #1 for banner.

Tomato stem/cap
Make 2 and 1 reversed from
green print #1 for banner.

Carrot
Make 2 and 3 reversed
from assorted orange
prints for banner.

Eggplant stem/cap
Make 2 and 1 reversed
from green print #4
for banner.

Carrot leaf
Make 2 from green
print #2 and 1 from
green print #3
for banner.

Eggplant
Make 2 and 1 reversed
from assorted purple prints
for banner.

A 16-Patch block is such a great way to use up a stash of fabric within one color family. Pick two of your favorite colors to work with—in my case, that's red and aqua. To frame the quilt, use a solid or tonal print for the border. Top it all off with a super-cute focus fabric for the center of the flowers. My go-to print is always a polka dot. Now, watch your flowers just POP from within the patchwork and spill out into the border! I can't wait to see your version. Happy sewing!

Flower POP

Sewing mends the soul.
—UNKNOWN

Finished quilt: 60½" x 76½"
Finished block: 8" x 8"

Quilted by Shelly Pagliai

Materials

Yardage is based on 42"-wide fabric unless otherwise noted.

1¾ yards of aqua tone on tone for border
¼ yard *each* of 8 assorted aqua prints for 16-Patch blocks
¼ yard *each* of 8 assorted red prints for 16-Patch blocks
1⅓ yards of cream print for appliqué block backgrounds
1¼ yards of red tone on tone for flower appliqués
½ yard of red-and-white polka dot for flower-center appliqués
½ yard of red-and-aqua print for single-fold binding
5 yards of fabric for backing
70" x 86" piece of batting
6 yards of 17"-wide paper-backed fusible web

Cutting

From the cream print, cut:
5 strips, 8½" x 42"; crosscut into 17 squares, 8½" x 8½"
From *each* of the 8 assorted aqua prints, cut:
2 strips, 2½" x 42"; crosscut into 18 squares, 2½" x 2½" (144 total)
From *each* of the 8 assorted red prints, cut:
2 strips, 2½" x 42"; crosscut into 18 squares, 2½" x 2½" (144 total)
From the *lengthwise grain* of the aqua tone on tone, cut:
2 strips, 10½" x 60½"
2 strips, 10½" x 56½"
From the red-and-aqua print, cut:
8 strips, 1½" x 42"

It's All about the Color

Just because red and aqua is my favorite color pairing doesn't mean it's yours. What about red and white, or black and yellow, or pink and green? Or the classic blue and white? Choosing just two colors lets you play with value and scale in the 16-Patch blocks.

Making the 16-Patch Blocks

1 Select one 2½" square of each of the eight assorted aqua prints and one 2½" square of each of the eight assorted red prints (16 squares total). Arrange the squares in four rows of two aqua and two red squares each, alternating the colors in each row and from row to row. Sew the squares in each row together. Press the seam allowances toward the red squares. Sew the rows together. Press the seam allowances in one direction.

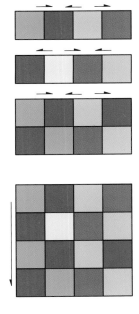

2 Repeat step 1 to make a total of 18 blocks, maintaining the position of the colors but mixing up the placement of the prints in each block. This will create a scrappy effect when the blocks are sewn together.

Making the Appliquéd Blocks

1 Refer to "Fusible Appliqué by Machine" on page 7 and use the patterns on page 57 to prepare the appliqués from the fabrics indicated on the patterns. Remove the paper backing from each shape.

2 Refer to the appliqué placement diagram to center a prepared flower shape on the right side of a cream square. Position a flower-center shape in the middle of the flower appliqué. Fuse the appliqués in place. Repeat to make a total of 17 blocks. Set aside the remaining flower and flower-center shapes for the border.

Appliqué placement

3 Blanket-stitch around the outer edges of each shape on each block using a matching or slightly contrasting thread color.

Assembling the Quilt Top

1 Refer to the assembly diagram on page 56 to lay out the 16-Patch blocks and appliquéd blocks in seven rows of five blocks each, alternating the blocks in each row and from row to row. Make sure the 16-Patch blocks are all oriented so that an aqua square is in the top-left corner. Sew the blocks in each row together. Press the seam allowances toward the 16-Patch blocks. Sew the rows together. Press the seam allowances in one direction.

2 Join the aqua 10½" x 56½" border strips to the sides of the quilt top. Press the seam allowances toward the border strips. Sew the aqua 10½" x 60½" border strips to the top and bottom edges of the quilt top. Press the seam allowances toward the border strips.

3 Position the remaining seven prepared flower shapes on the quilt top where desired, referring to the assembly diagram and the photo on page 54 as needed. Position a flower center in the middle of each flower shape; fuse and blanket stitch in the same manner as you did the blocks.

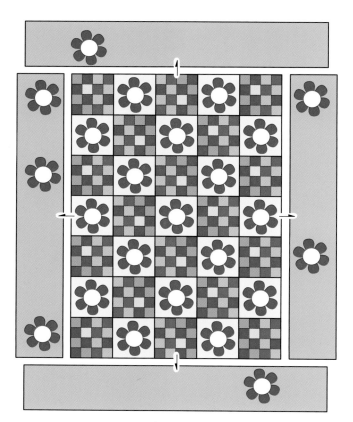

Quilt assembly

Finishing

1 Layer the quilt top, batting, and backing; baste the layers together.

2 Quilt your project. Refer to "Up-Close and Beautiful" below for details on how my quilt was quilted.

3 Refer to "Binding by Machine" on page 93 to bind the quilt edges using the red-and-aqua strips.

Up Close and Beautiful

Shelly Pagliai used thread to match each fabric. She outline quilted around all the appliqué shapes, and then she added small bubble motifs in the background of the appliquéd blocks. The 16-Patch blocks are quilted with a four-petal flower design in each square. The border is custom quilted with chevrons and bubble motifs.

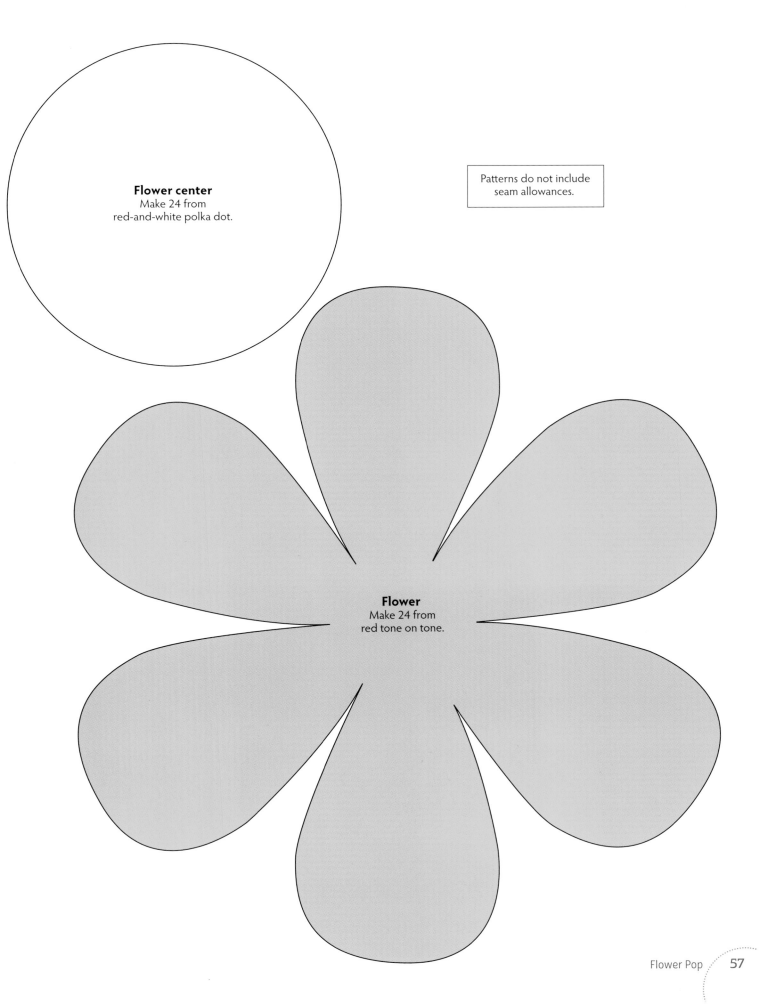

Flower center
Make 24 from
red-and-white polka dot.

Patterns do not include
seam allowances.

Flower
Make 24 from
red tone on tone.

Cherry FIZZ

Sometimes you will never know the value of a moment until it becomes a memory.

—DR. SEUSS

Cherries are my all-time favorite fruit. A fabulous bowl of fresh cherries just makes a summer day full of memories! When I was selecting fabrics for this quilt, the outer-border fabric came first. Then I picked the cherry and stem fabrics. I used a set of red prints and a set of green prints, with both sets including fabrics that were different yet very similar, so they give your eye some variety. Pair the cherry blocks with the simple Chain block and your beautiful pile of fabric will turn into a fantastic design in no time at all.

Finished quilt: 72½" x 72½"
Finished block: 10" x 10"

Quilted by Cindy and Dennis Dickinson

Tossed Salad

Do you like one of the fruit or vegetable shapes in "My Veggie Garden" on page 48? Switch out the cherries and make this quilt your own! Eggplants, carrots, or tomatoes—oh my! Or, you could leave off the appliqué entirely for a quick-to-make pieced quilt.

Materials

Yardage is based on 42"-wide fabric unless otherwise noted.

2¼ yards of large-scale red print for outer border
1¼ yards of green print for stem and leaf appliqués, inner border, and single-fold binding
1¼ yards of yellow print #1 for blocks
1⅛ yards of yellow print #2 for blocks
⅓ yard *each* of 3 assorted raspberry-red prints for Chain blocks
¼ yard *each* of 2 assorted green prints for stem and leaf appliqués
12" x 12" square *each* of 4 assorted cherry-red prints for cherry appliqués
5 yards of fabric for backing
82" x 82" piece of batting
3 yards of 17"-wide paper-backed fusible web

Cutting

From yellow print #1, cut:
2 strips, 10½" x 42"; crosscut into 6 squares, 10½" x 10½"
28 rectangles, 2½" x 6½"
28 squares, 2½" x 2½"

From yellow print #2, cut:
2 strips, 10½" x 42"; crosscut into 6 squares, 10½" x 10½"
24 rectangles, 2½" x 6½"
24 squares, 2½" x 2½"

From *each* of 2 raspberry-red prints, cut:
3 strips, 2½" x 42"; crosscut into 36 squares, 2½" x 2½" (72 total)

Continued on page 60

Continued from page 58

From the remaining raspberry-red print, cut:

3 strips, 2½" x 42"; crosscut into 45 squares,
2½" x 2½"

**From the green print for appliqués, inner border,
and binding, cut:**

14 strips, 1½" x 42"

**From the *lengthwise grain* of the large-scale red
print, cut:**

2 strips, 10½" x 52½"

2 strips, 10½" x 72½"

Making the Chain Blocks

1 Randomly select nine assorted raspberry-red
2½" squares, four assorted yellow 2½" squares,
and four assorted yellow 2½" x 6½" rectangles.

2 Arrange five raspberry-red squares and four
yellow squares into three horizontal rows,
alternating the colors in each row and from row to
row. Sew the squares in each row together. Press
the seam allowances toward the raspberry-red
squares. Sew the rows together to make a nine-
patch unit. Press the seam allowances toward the
top and bottom rows.

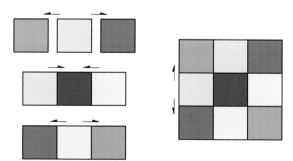

Color Control

My quilt is controlled scrappy. For the Chain
blocks, I sort my raspberry-red and yellow
fabrics by piece size and color, and then
select the pieces for each block individually so
they'll all be unique. I follow the same process
for my appliquéd blocks, using a variety of
green prints for the stems and leaves and
an assortment of cherry-red prints for the
cherries in each block.

3 Join yellow rectangles to the sides of the nine-
patch unit. Press the seam allowances toward
the rectangles. Add a raspberry-red square to each
end of the remaining yellow rectangles. Press the
seam allowances toward the rectangles. Join these
pieced strips to the top and bottom edges of the
nine-patch unit to complete the block. Press the
seam allowances toward the pieced strips.

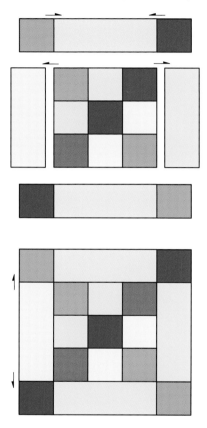

4 Repeat steps 1–3 to make a total of 13 Chain
blocks.

Making the Appliquéd Blocks

1 Refer to "Fusible Appliqué by Machine" on
page 7 and use the patterns on page 64 to
prepare the appliqués from the fabrics indicated
on the patterns. Remove the paper backing from
each shape.

2 Refer to the appliqué placement diagram below to position the prepared appliqué shapes on a yellow 10½" square in the following order. Center a cluster of three leaves on the upper third of the square. Position three stems and three cherries, tucking the stem ends under the leaves and cherries. Fuse the appliqués in place. Repeat to make a total of 12 appliquéd blocks.

Appliqué placement

3 Blanket-stitch around the outer edges of each shape on each block using a matching or slightly contrasting thread color.

Assembling the Quilt Top

1 Arrange the Chain blocks and appliquéd blocks in five horizontal rows of five blocks each, alternating the blocks in each row and from row to row, as well as the yellow background fabric of the appliquéd blocks. Sew the blocks in each row together. Press the seam allowances toward the appliquéd blocks. Sew the rows together. Press the seam allowances in one direction.

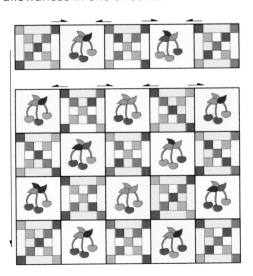

2 Join six of the green 1½" x 42" strips end to end to make one long strip. From the pieced strip, cut two inner-border strips, 1½" x 50½". Refer to the assembly diagram below to sew the strips to the sides of the quilt top. Press the seam allowances toward the border. From the remainder of the pieced strip, cut two inner-border strips, 1½" x 52½". Join these strips to the top and bottom edges of the quilt top. Press the seam allowances toward the border.

3 Sew the red 10½" x 52½" outer-border strips to the sides of the quilt top. Press the seam allowances toward the outer border. Join the red 10½" x 72½" outer-border strips to the top and bottom edges of the quilt top. Press the seam allowances toward the outer border.

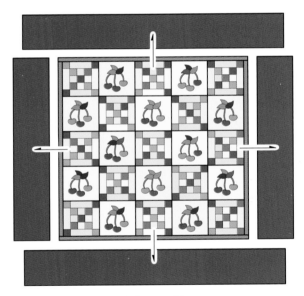

Quilt assembly

Little Packages

You know that saying, "Good things come in little packages"? Well, if this 72" square quilt is too big for your needs, consider making a smaller version. If you use five Chain blocks and four Cherry blocks, you can have a 30" square quilt in no time! Add a border if you want it a little bigger, or just quilt and bind for an adorable little wall hanging.

Finishing

1 Layer the quilt top, batting, and backing; baste the layers together.

2 Quilt your project. Refer to "Up-Close and Beautiful" at right for details on how my quilt was quilted.

3 Refer to "Binding by Machine" on page 93 to bind the quilt edges using the remaining green strips.

Quilt Backings

I have always loved to piece quilt backs from random fabrics. The backing is a place to use up extras from the quilt front or add in a funky-fabric find that complements the top. I pieced the backing on my very first quilt because I'd run out of fabric and didn't want to buy ¼ yard more to finish the back, so I just added leftover fabric from the front!

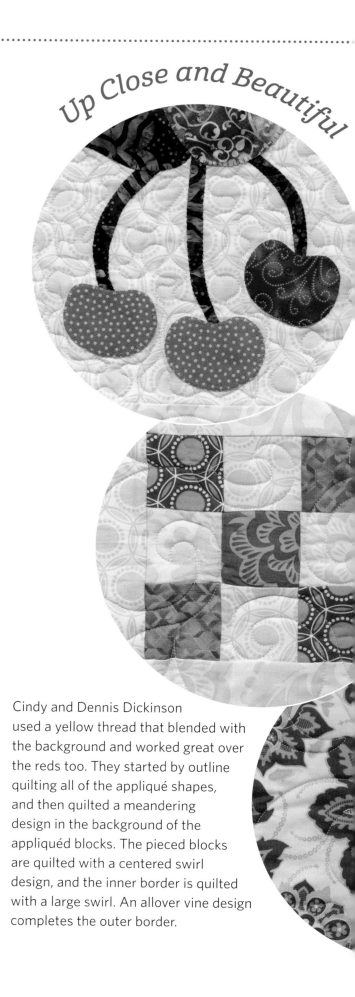

Up Close and Beautiful

Cindy and Dennis Dickinson used a yellow thread that blended with the background and worked great over the reds too. They started by outline quilting all of the appliqué shapes, and then quilted a meandering design in the background of the appliquéd blocks. The pieced blocks are quilted with a centered swirl design, and the inner border is quilted with a large swirl. An allover vine design completes the outer border.

Use it up, wear it out,
make it do, or do without.

—UNKNOWN

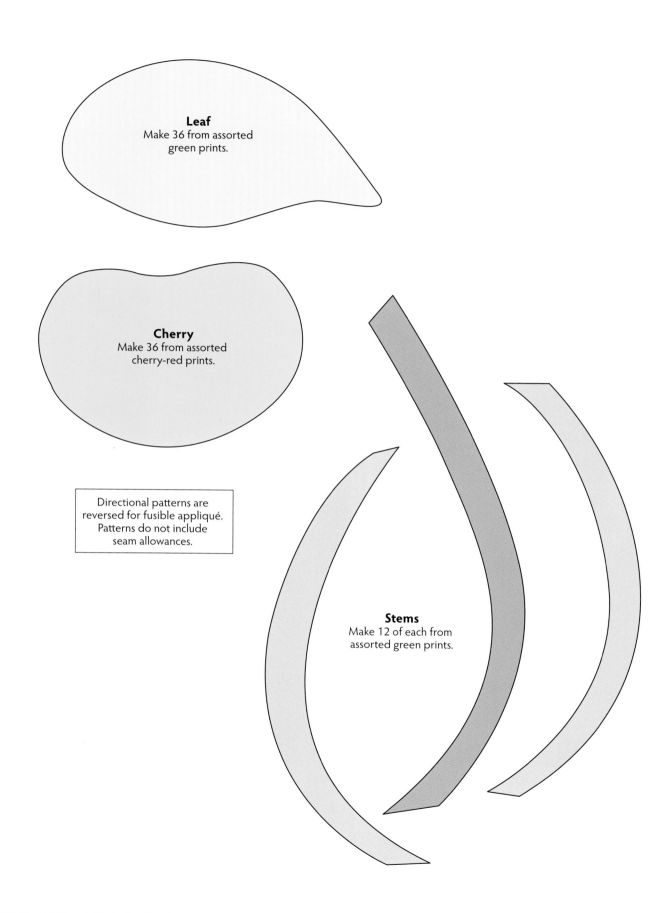

Leaf
Make 36 from assorted
green prints.

Cherry
Make 36 from assorted
cherry-red prints.

Directional patterns are
reversed for fusible appliqué.
Patterns do not include
seam allowances.

Stems
Make 12 of each from
assorted green prints.

Easy, breezy fields of flowers make my heart sing. Filling a quilt with happy posies is the next best thing to being outside. The strippy quilt format used here has been around a long time. From pieced blocks in horizontal strips to appliquéd strips, I love a strip setting. For this quilt, the ¼"-wide vines and slender leaves wave in the summer breeze . . . any time of year! Make the matching pillowcases and accent pillows to complete the ensemble.

Meadow *Breeze*

Why fit in when you were born to stand out?

—DR. SEUSS

Meadow Breeze Quilt

Materials

Yardage is based on 42"-wide fabric unless otherwise noted.

2 yards of teal print #1 for outer border

1¾ yards of cream print for appliquéd strip background

1¾ yards of teal print #2 for plain strips and vine appliqués

¾ yard of green print #1 for leaf appliqués

¼ yard *each* of peach prints #1, #2, and #3 for large and medium circle appliqués

¾ yard of peach stripe for pieced inner border and single-fold binding

½ yard of teal print #3 for appliquéd strip borders

⅜ yard of peach solid for pieced inner border

9" x 20" rectangle of green print #2 for leaf appliqués

8" x 17" rectangle of white tone on tone for flower appliqués

8" x 8" square of dark-peach print for small circle appliqués

5 yards of fabric for backing

80" x 90" piece of batting

½" bias-tape maker (optional)

Liquid basting glue

2 yards of 17"-wide paper-backed fusible web

Finished quilt: 72½" x 80½"

Quilted by Cindy and Dennis Dickinson

Cutting

From the *lengthwise grain* of the cream print, cut:
3 strips, 6½" x 56½"

From teal print #3, cut:
9 strips, 1½" x 42"

From the *lengthwise grain* of teal print #2, cut:
4 strips, 6½" x 56½"

From the remainder of teal print #2, cut:
Enough 1"-wide bias strips to make approximately 220" of bias tape when joined end to end

From the peach solid, cut:
4 strips, 2½" x 42"; crosscut into 54 squares, 2½" x 2½"

From the peach stripe, cut:
4 strips, 2½" x 42"; crosscut into 54 squares, 2½" x 2½"
8 strips, 1½" x 42"

From the *lengthwise grain* of teal print #1, cut:
2 strips, 10½" x 72½"
2 strips, 10½" x 60½"

Making the Appliquéd Strips

1 Sew the 1½" x 42" teal print #3 strips together end to end to make one long strip. From the pieced strip, cut six strips, 1½" x 56½".

2 Join 1½" x 56½" teal print #3 strips to both long edges of each 6½" x 56½" cream strip. Press the seam allowances toward the teal strips. Sew 6½" x 56½" teal print #2 strips to both long edges of one of the pieced strips and to one long edge of each of the remaining two strips. Press the seam allowances toward the teal print #2 strips.

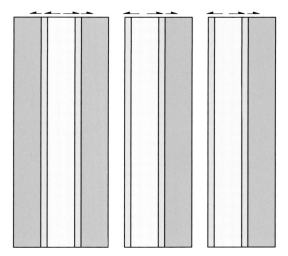

3 Refer to "Fusible Appliqué by Machine" on page 7 and use the patterns on page 73 to prepare the small circle, medium circle, large circle, flower, and large leaf appliqués from the fabrics indicated on the patterns. Remove the paper backing from each shape.

4 If you're using a bias-tape maker, follow the manufacturer's instructions to make approximately 220" of ½"-wide bias vine from the 1"-wide teal print #2 bias strips. If you aren't using a bias-tape maker, join the 1"-wide teal print #2 bias strips end to end; press the seam allowances open. Fold both long raw edges in to meet at the center, wrong sides together, to make a ½"-wide vine; press.

5 Refer to the appliqué placement diagram at right to position the prepared large-circle shapes on the right side of the three pieced strips from step 2, overlapping some of the circles onto the teal strips.

6 Use the basting glue to "draw" lines where the long vine and three side vines on each strip will go, avoiding the large circles. Lay the bias vine you made in step 4 over the glue lines, raw edges face down, cutting the vine as necessary and lifting up the previously placed circles as needed where the vine runs under them. Tuck the top end of each long vine under the large circle at the top of each strip, and tuck one end of each short vine under the long vine.

7 Position a flower shape on each large circle, and then center a small circle on each flower.

8 Position the leaves and medium circles.

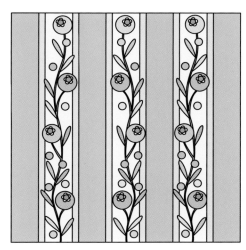

Appliqué placement

9 Fuse the appliqués in place. Blanket-stitch around the outer edges of each shape using a matching or slightly contrasting thread color.

Assembling the Quilt Top

1 Refer to the assembly diagram on page 68 to sew the three appliquéd strips together, making sure the mirror-image appliqués are on the center strip. Press the seam allowances toward the teal strips.

2 To make the pieced inner border, alternately sew together 14 peach-solid 2½" squares and 14 peach-striped 2½" squares. Press the seam allowances toward the solid squares. Repeat to make a total of two pieced strips. Refer to the assembly diagram to sew these strips to the sides of the quilt top, making sure a striped square is at the top on the left-hand strip and a solid square is at the top on the right-hand strip. Press the seam allowances toward the quilt center. Join 13 peach-solid 2½" squares and 13 peach-striped 2½" squares; press the seam allowances toward the solid squares. Repeat to make a total of two pieced strips. Sew these strips to the top and bottom edges of the quilt top, paying careful attention to the placement of the solid and striped squares so they alternate around the quilt top. Press the seam allowances toward the quilt center.

3 Sew the teal 10½" x 60½" teal print #1 strips to the sides of the quilt top. Press the seam allowances toward the outer border. Sew the 10½" x 72½" teal print #1 strips to the top and bottom edges of the quilt top. Press the seam allowances toward the outer border.

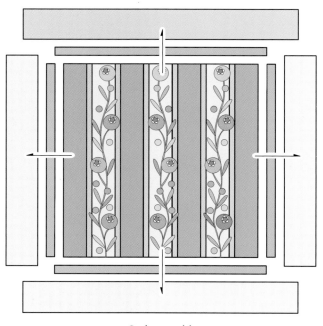

Quilt assembly

Finishing

1 Layer the quilt top, batting, and backing; baste the layers together.

2 Quilt your project. Refer to "Up-Close and Beautiful" at right for details on how my quilt was quilted.

3 Refer to "Binding by Machine" on page 93 to bind the quilt edges using the peach-striped strips.

Up Close and Beautiful

Cindy and Dennis Dickinson echo quilted the appliquéd strips. The small white flowers are also echo quilted. The aqua strips are custom quilted with a feather and butterfly design. The outer border is quilted with a large free-flowing feather design.

Meadow Breeze Pillowcases

Matching pillowcases are the perfect finishing touch for the "Meadow Breeze" quilt.

Finished pillowcase: 20" x 31"

Materials

Yardage is based on 42"-wide fabric unless otherwise indicated and is sufficient for 2 pillowcases.

1⅔ yards of teal print #1 for body
⅝ yard of teal print #2 for cuff
⅛ yard of peach stripe for accent strip

Cutting

From the peach stripe, cut:
2 strips, 1¼" x 40½"
From teal print #1, cut:
2 rectangles, 26½" x 40½"
From teal print #2, cut:
2 strips, 9½" x 40½"

Making the Pillowcases

1 Sew a peach-striped accent strip between a teal print #1 body rectangle and a teal print #2 cuff strip. Press the seam allowances toward the teal print #2 strip.

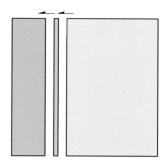

2 Fold the pieced unit from step 1 in half lengthwise, right sides together. Stitch along the bottom and side edges, leaving the cuff end open.

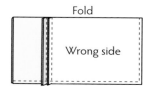

3 Press under the cuff raw edges ¼". Fold the pressed-under edge so it just covers the cuff/accent strip seam allowance; press. Turn the pillowcase to the right side. Pin the cuff in place along the turned-under edge. Topstitch the cuff in place along the cuff side of the cuff/accent strip seam line.

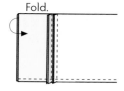
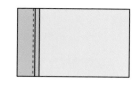

4 Repeat steps 1–3 to make a total of two pillowcases.

Meadow Breeze Pillow

Pillows make every room comforting and inviting. They also make fantastic gifts!

Finished pillow: 12½" x 12½"

Materials

Yardage is based on 42"-wide fabric unless otherwise indicated.

½ yard of teal print for border and pillow-cover back

⅜ yard of cream solid for background

8" x 8" square of green print #1 for ring appliqué

6" x 8" rectangle of green print #2 for leaf appliqués

5" x 7" rectangle of peach print for medium circle appliqués

½ yard of muslin for pillow-cover top backing

⅛ yard of peach stripe for single-fold binding

14" x 14" square of batting

½ yard of 17"-wide paper-backed fusible web

12" x 12" square pillow form

Cutting

From the cream solid, cut:

1 square, 10½" x 10½"

From the teal print, cut:

2 strips, 1½" x 10½"

2 strips, 1½" x 12½"

2 rectangles, 9" x 12½"

From the muslin, cut:

1 square, 14" x 14"

From the peach stripe, cut:

2 strips, 1½" x 42"

Appliquéing the Pillow Top

1 Refer to "Fusible Appliqué by Machine" on page 7 and use the patterns on page 73 to prepare the small leaf, medium circle, and ring appliqués from the fabrics indicated on the patterns. To make the complete ring pattern, fold a 7" square of fusible web in half and gently finger-press the fold. Open up the square. Trace the half-ring pattern onto half of the fusible-web square, aligning the fold with the straight edges as indicated on the pattern. Rotate the square and trace the remaining half of the ring onto the fusible web. Remove the paper backing from each fabric shape.

2 Refer to the appliqué placement diagram below to position the prepared appliqué shapes on the cream square in the following order. Center the ring appliqué. Position the medium circles over the ring with approximately the same amount of space between each one. Place two leaves on each circle.

Appliqué placement

3 Fuse the appliqués in place. Blanket-stitch around the outer edges of each shape using a matching or slightly contrasting thread color.

Assembling the Pillow

1 Refer to the assembly diagram to sew the teal 1½" x 10½" strips to the sides of the pillow top. Press the seam allowances toward the strips. Sew the teal 1½" x 12½" strips to the top and bottom edges of the pillow-cover top. Press the seam allowances toward the strips.

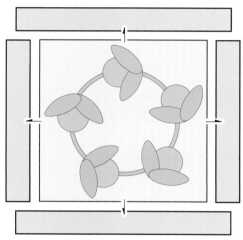

Pillow-top assembly

2 Layer the muslin square, batting square, and pillow-cover top; baste the layers together. Quilt your project. Here's how mine is quilted: I outline quilted the appliqués and used a swirl pattern for the background. With my walking foot, I added two rows of straight-line quilting to the border. Trim the muslin and batting even with the pillow-cover top edges.

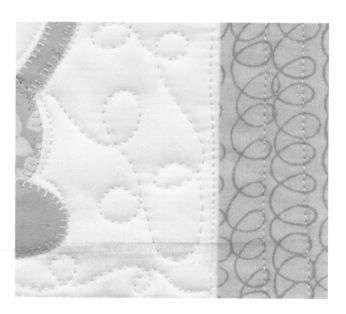

3 To make the pieces for the pillow-cover back, press under one long edge of each teal 9" x 12½" rectangle ½" twice to make a hem. Stitch the hems in place.

4 Lay the pillow-cover top on your work surface wrong side up. Place the back rectangles over the pillow-cover top, right sides up with the hemmed edges overlapping at the center and the outer edges aligned with the pillow-cover top edges; pin the top and back pieces together. Stitch around the outer edges.

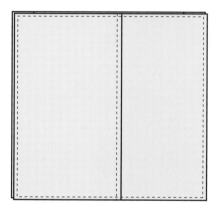

5 Refer to "Binding by Machine" on page 93 to bind the edges of the pillow cover with the peach-striped strips.

6 Insert the pillow form into the pillow cover through the opening in the back.

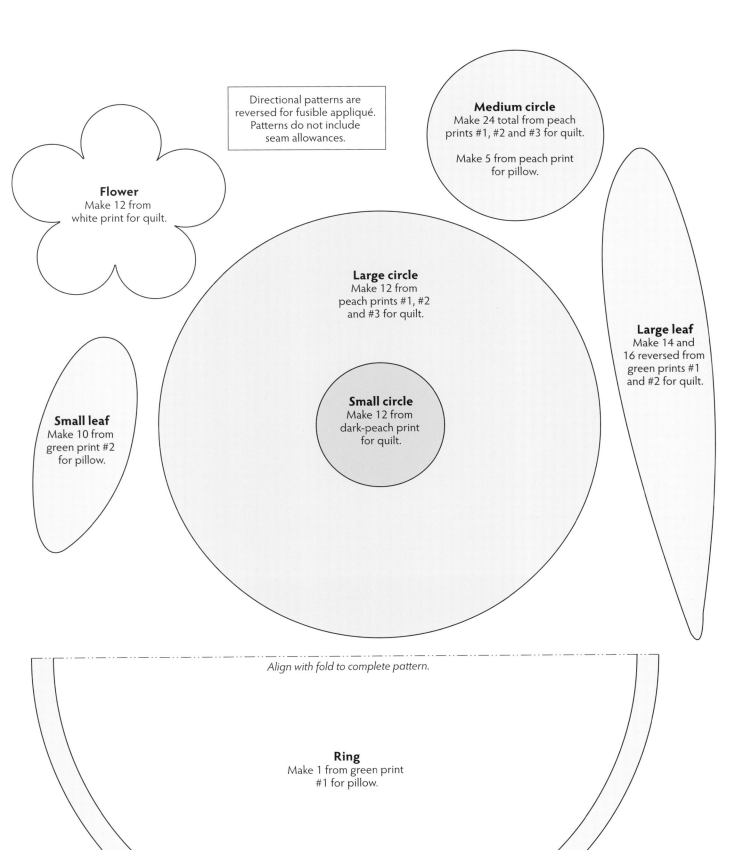

Directional patterns are reversed for fusible appliqué. Patterns do not include seam allowances.

Flower
Make 12 from white print for quilt.

Medium circle
Make 24 total from peach prints #1, #2 and #3 for quilt.

Make 5 from peach print for pillow.

Large circle
Make 12 from peach prints #1, #2 and #3 for quilt.

Large leaf
Make 14 and 16 reversed from green prints #1 and #2 for quilt.

Small circle
Make 12 from dark-peach print for quilt.

Small leaf
Make 10 from green print #2 for pillow.

Align with fold to complete pattern.

Ring
Make 1 from green print #1 for pillow.

Farmers' Market

There is no sincerer love than the love of food.

—GEORGE BERNARD SHAW

My love of the farmers' market started early. My granny worked for Kessler Meat Company in Pennsylvania (home of Penn State's Nittany Lion franks!). As a kid we would go to the farmers' market with my pappy to pick her up from work. It was magical!

While traveling to teach quilting, I love to visit local farmers' markets—indoors or out. I photograph the displays, breathe in the smells, and, of course, buy goodies! I created my "Farmers' Market" quilt to capture these precious memories.

Finished wall hanging: 47½" x 49½"

Quilted by Joann Hoffman

Materials

Yardage is based on 42"-wide fabric unless otherwise noted.

⅓ yard *each* of cream prints #1, #3, #4, and #5 for block backgrounds

⅜ yard of cream print #2 for block backgrounds

¼ yard *each* of red prints #1–#5 for border triangle appliqués

¾ yard of red print #6 for inner border and binding

6" x 6" square *each* of red prints #7–#9 for tomato appliqués

7" x 7" square of red print #10 for apple appliqué

¼ yard *each* of blue prints #1–#6 for sashing and border triangles

⅜ yard of blue print #7 for sashing and border triangles

4" x 8" rectangle *each* of purple prints #1–#3 for eggplant appliqués

5" x 6" rectangle *each* of purple prints #4 and #8–#10 for vase and canning jar appliqués

2" x 5" rectangle of purple print #5 for vase top/bottom rim appliqué

3" x 10" rectangle *each* of purple prints #6 and #7 for pie pan appliqués

4½" x 9" rectangle *each* of green prints #1 and #2 for squash appliqués

6½" x 16" rectangle of green print #3 for squash and seedling leaf and stem appliqués

11" x 15" rectangle of green print #4 for eggplant stem/cap, strawberry cap, and cherry stem appliqués

9" x 7" rectangle of green print #5 for strawberry stem and corn husk appliqués

10" x 10" square of green print #6 for corn husk, apple leaf, and peach leaf appliqués

8" x 14" rectangle of green print #7 for carrot leaf, tomato stem/cap, tomato leaf, and cherry leaf appliqués

6" x 10" rectangle of green print #8 for carrot leaf and cherry leaf appliqués

6" x 6" square *each* of orange prints #1 and #2 for carrot appliqués

11" x 6" rectangle of orange print #3 for peach top appliqués

4" x 4" square *each* of orange prints #4–#8 for round flower appliqués

6" x 6" square *each* of pink prints #1 and #2 for strawberry appliqués

Continued on page 76

A party without cake is just a meeting.

—JULIA CHILD

Continued from page 74

6" x 12" rectangle of navy print for letter appliqués

4" x 4" square of yellow print #1 for squash blossom bottom and squash bottom appliqués

4" x 7" rectangle of yellow print #2 for squash blossom top and seedling flower appliqués

5" x 14" rectangle of yellow print #3 for corn appliqués

3" x 6" rectangle of gray print for apple sign appliqué

7" x 7" square of peach print #1 for peach bottom appliqués

3" x 12" rectangle of peach print #2 for canning jar lid appliqués

4" x 16" rectangle of peach print #3 for canning jar fabric appliqués

4" x 5" rectangle *each* of peach prints #4–#6 for cherry appliqués

10" x 10" square of brown print #1 for squash stem, apple stem, pie vent, vase middle rim, and peach stem appliqués

4" x 5" rectangle of brown print #2 for seedling pot rim and signpost appliqués

4" x 8" rectangle of brown print #3 for seedling pot appliqués

3" x 12" rectangle *each* of tan prints #1 and #2 for pie crust appliqués

16" length of green medium rickrack for round-flower stems

3 yards of fabric for backing

54" x 56" piece of batting

3 yards of 17"-wide paper-backed fusible web

Liquid basting glue

Black embroidery floss

Size 26 embroidery needle

Cutting

From cream print #1, cut:
1 rectangle, 8½" x 10½"
1 rectangle, 6½" x 17½"

From cream print #2, cut:
1 rectangle, 10½" x 12½"
1 rectangle, 7½" x 9½"

From cream print #3, cut:
1 rectangle, 8½" x 15½"
1 rectangle, 7½" x 9½"
1 rectangle, 7½" x 11½"

From cream print #4, cut:
1 rectangle, 8½" x 11½"
1 rectangle, 7½" x 8½"
1 rectangle, 7½" x 12½"

From cream print #5, cut:
1 rectangle, 8½" x 12½"
1 rectangle, 7½" x 8½"

From blue print #1, cut:
1 square, 5½" x 5½"
1 rectangle, 5½" x 15½"
1 strip, 1½" x 8½"
1 strip, 1½" x 12½"

From blue print #2, cut:
1 square, 5½" x 5½"
2 rectangles, 5½" x 15½"
1 strip, 1½" x 7½"
1 strip, 2½" x 8½"

From blue print #3, cut:
1 rectangle, 5½" x 7½"
1 rectangle, 5½" x 9½"
1 strip, 1½" x 9½"
1 strip, 1½" x 12½"
1 strip, 2½" x 10½"
1 strip, 2½" x 8½"

From blue print #4, cut:
1 square, 5½" x 5½"
1 rectangle, 5½" x 15½"
1 strip, 2½" x 12½"
1 strip, 1½" x 7½"

From blue print #5, cut:
2 rectangles, 5½" x 15½"
1 strip, 1½" x 17½"
1 strip, 2½" x 27½"

From blue print #6, cut:

1 square, 5½" x 5½"

1 rectangle, 5½" x 9½"

1 rectangle, 5½" x 7½"

2 strips, 1½" x 10½"

1 strip, 2½" x 8½"

From blue print #7, cut:

2 rectangles, 5½" x 15½"

1 strip, 2½" x 15½"

1 strip, 2½" x 11½"

From red print #6, cut:

2 strips, 1½" x 35½"

2 strips, 1½" x 39½"

6 strips, 1½" x 42"

Appliquéing the Blocks

1 Refer to "Fusible Appliqué by Machine" on page 7 and use the patterns on pages 83-92 to prepare the appliqués from the fabrics indicated on the patterns. Remove the paper backing from each shape.

2 Refer to the eggplant-and-squash block photo to position the eggplant, eggplant stem/cap, squash, squash stem, squash bottom, and squash blossom appliqués on the 6½" x 17½" cream print #1 rectangle. Fuse the appliqués in place. Blanket-stitch around the outer edges of each shape using a matching or slightly contrasting thread color.

3 Refer to the carrot block photo to position the carrot and carrot leaf appliqués on the 7½" x 9½" cream print #2 rectangle. Two carrots and the center leaf extend into the sashing and border. Fuse as much of these pieces to the background as you can, leaving the extended area free. Blanket-stitch around the outer edges of as

Pin Pals

Several shapes extend into the sashing area of the quilt and will need to be positioned after other pieces are sewn in place. Appliqué as many of the pieces that are within the background as you can, and then pin the shapes that overlap the sashing to the block they belong to so you can easily keep track of them.

many of the shapes as possible using a matching or slightly contrasting thread color.

4 Refer to the strawberry block photo to position the top and bottom strawberry appliqués and the bottom strawberry's cap and stem appliqués on the 7½" x 8½" cream print #4 rectangle. Set aside the cap and stem for the top strawberry until after section 2 of the quilt is assembled and joined to section 1. Fuse the appliqués in place. Blanket-stitch around the outer edges of each shape.

5 Refer to the corn block photo to position the corn and corn husk appliqués on the 7½" x 8½" cream print #5 rectangle. Fuse the appliqués in place, and then blanket-stitch around each shape.

6 Refer to the tomato block photo to position the tomato and tomato stem/cap appliqués and the left and middle leaf appliqués on the 10½" x 12½" cream print #2 rectangle. Set aside the right tomato's leaf. Position the letters to spell *FARMERS' MARKET.* Fuse the appliqués in place and blanket-stitch around each shape.

7 Refer to the jar of posies block photo to position the vase appliqué on the 8½" x 11½" cream print #4 rectangle. Position the round flowers next. Use basting glue to draw lines from the flowers to the vase where the rickrack stems will be placed. Cut the rickrack into the lengths needed and lay each length on a glue line. Position the top/bottom rim shape on the vase and then place the

middle rim over it. Fuse the appliqués in place and blanket-stitch around each shape.

8 Refer to the pie block photo to position the pie pan, pie crust, and pie vent appliqués on the 7½" x 11½" cream print #3 rectangle. Fuse the appliqués in place and blanket-stitch around each shape.

9 Refer to the canning jar block photo to position the canning jar, canning jar fabric, and canning jar lid appliqués on the 8½" x 15½" cream print #3 rectangle. Fuse the appliqués in place, and then blanket-stitch around each shape.

10 Refer to the seedling block photo to position the pot, pot rim, stem, leaf, and seedling flower appliqués on the 8½" x 10½" cream print #1 rectangle. Fuse the appliqués in place, and then blanket-stitch around each shape.

11 Refer to the apple block photo to position the apple appliqué on the 7½" x 9½" cream print #3 rectangle. Position the sign and then tuck the signpost under the sign and apple. Add the stem and leaf appliqués. Fuse the appliqués in place, and then blanket-stitch around each shape. Using two strands of black embroidery floss and the embroidery needle, freehand stitch *For Sale 10¢* to the sign.

12 Refer to the cherry block photo to position the cherry leaf and stem appliqués on the 8½" x 12½" cream print #5 rectangle. Place a cherry appliqué at the end of each stem except the stem at the far left. Fuse the appliqués in place and then blanket-stitch around each shape.

13 Refer to the peach block photo to position the peach top appliqués on the 7½" x 12½" cream print #4 rectangle. Add a peach bottom to each top. Position the leaf and stem appliqués. Fuse the appliqués in place, and then blanket-stitch around each shape.

Assembling the Wall-Hanging Top

1 To make section 1 of the quilt top, sew the 1½" x 17½" blue print #5 strip to the bottom of the eggplant-and-squash block. Press the seam allowances toward the blue strip. Add the 1½" x 7½" blue print #2 strip to the left edge of the carrot block. Press the seam allowances toward the blue strip. Join the carrot unit to the right edge of the eggplant-and-squash block. Press the seam allowances toward the blue print #2 strip.

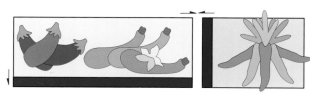

Section 1

2 To make section 2, sew the 1½" x 8½" blue print #1 strip between the strawberry and corn blocks. Press the seam allowances toward the blue strip. Sew the 2½" x 10½" blue print #3 strip to the left edge of the tomato block and a 1½" x 10½" blue print #6 strip to the right edge. Press the seam allowances toward the strips. Sew the 2½" x 15½" blue print #7 strip between the block units. Press the seam allowances toward the blue strip.

Section 2

3 To make section 3, sew the 2½" x 11½" blue print #7 strip to the right edge of the jar of posies block. Press the seam allowances toward the blue strip. Add the remaining 1½" x 10½" blue print #6 strip to the top of the block. Press the seam allowances toward the blue print #6 strip. Join the 2½" x 12½" blue print #4 strip to the left edge of the block; press the seam allowances toward the strip. Sew the 1½" x 7½" blue print #4 strip to the right edge of the pie block. Press the seam allowances toward the blue strip. Sew the 1½" x 12½" blue print #3 strip between the block units. Press the seam allowances toward the blue print #3 strip.

Section 3

4 To make section 4, sew the 2½" x 8½" blue print #3 strip between the canning jar and seedling blocks. Press the seam allowances toward the blue strip. Add the 2½" x 27½" blue print #5 strip to the top of the joined blocks. Press the seam allowances toward the blue print #5 strip.

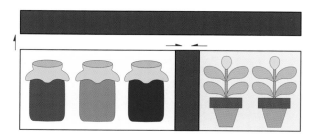

Section 4

5 To make section 5, sew the 1½" x 9½" blue print #3 strip to the left edge of the apple block. Press the seam allowances toward the blue strip. Sew the 2½" x 8½" blue print #2 strip to the bottom of the block. Press the seam allowances toward the strip. Sew the 1½" x 12½" blue print #1 strip to the left edge of the peach block. Press the seam allowances toward the blue strip. Add the 2½" x 8½" blue print #6 strip to the top of the block. Press the seam allowances toward the blue strip. Sew the cherry block between the block units. Press the seam allowances toward the blue strips.

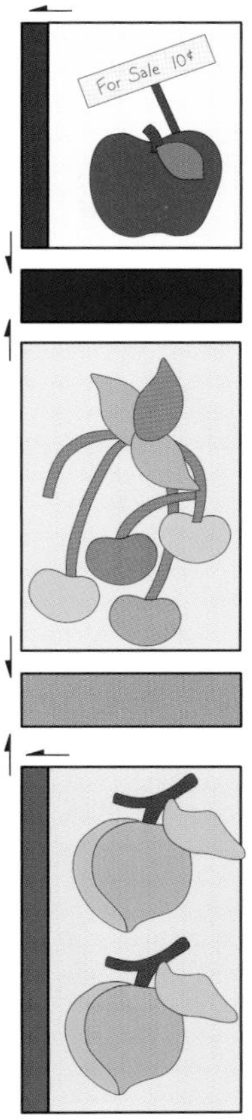

6 Join sections 2 and 3. Press the seam allowances toward section 3. Add section 1 to the top of the joined sections. Press the seam allowances toward section 1. Join section 4 to the bottom. Press the seam allowances toward section 4. Add section 5 to the right edge of the joined sections. Press the seam allowances toward sections 1–4.

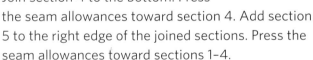

Section 5

7 Position, fuse, and blanket-stitch the appliqués that extended onto the sashing strips.

Making and Adding the Borders

1 Refer to the assembly diagram on page 82 to sew the 1½" x 35½" red print #6 strips to the top and bottom edges of the quilt top. Press the seam allowances toward the red strips. Sew the 1½" x 39½" red print #6 strips to the top and bottom edges of the quilt top. Press the seam allowances toward the red strips.

2 Using the blue-print rectangles, make the border units as shown. Press all seam allowances in one direction.

Blue print #4 5½" x 15½"	Blue print #6 5½" x 9½"	Blue print #7 5½" x 15½"

Left side border

Blue print #5 5½" x 15½"	Blue print #3 5½" x 9½"	Blue print #2 5½" x 15½"

Right side border

Blue print #2 5½" x 15½"	Blue print #3 5½" x 7½"	Blue print #1 5½" x 15½"

Top border

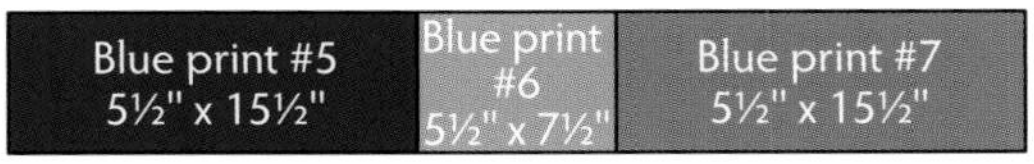

Blue print #5 5½" x 15½"	Blue print #6 5½" x 7½"	Blue print #7 5½" x 15½"

Bottom border

3 Refer to "Fusible Appliqué by Machine" and use the triangle pattern on page 83 to prepare the appliqués from the fabrics indicated on the pattern. Remove the paper backing from each triangle. Position six triangles on each border unit as shown, with the points slightly overlapped. Fuse the triangles in place and then blanket stitch around each shape.

4 Sew the outer side borders to the quilt top. Press the seam allowances toward the inner border. Add a blue-print 5½" square to each end of the top and bottom borders. Press the seam allowances toward the squares. Join the border strips to the top and bottom edges of the quilt top. Press the seam allowances toward the inner border.

Quilt assembly

Finishing

1 Layer the quilt top, batting, and backing; baste the layers together.

2 Quilt your project. Refer to "Up-Close and Beautiful" below for details on how my quilt was quilted.

3 Refer to "Binding by Machine" on page 93 to bind the quilt edges using the red print #6 strips.

Up Close and Beautiful

Joann Hoffman used thread colors that matched the fabrics so they would blend nicely. Each appliqué shape is outline stitched, and various background textures are quilted in the block backgrounds. The sashing strips are quilted with loops and lines. The four outer-border corner squares are quilted with small feather wreaths, the blue rectangles are quilted with tight leaves, and the red triangles have a fleur-de-lis design.

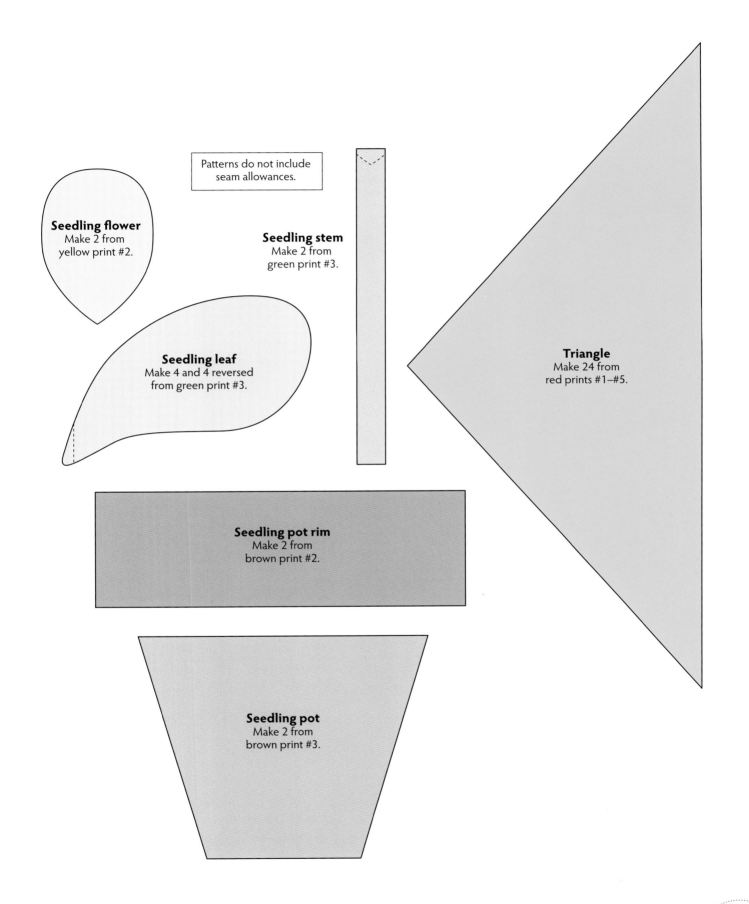

Seedling flower
Make 2 from
yellow print #2.

Patterns do not include
seam allowances.

Seedling stem
Make 2 from
green print #3.

Seedling leaf
Make 4 and 4 reversed
from green print #3.

Triangle
Make 24 from
red prints #1–#5.

Seedling pot rim
Make 2 from
brown print #2.

Seedling pot
Make 2 from
brown print #3.

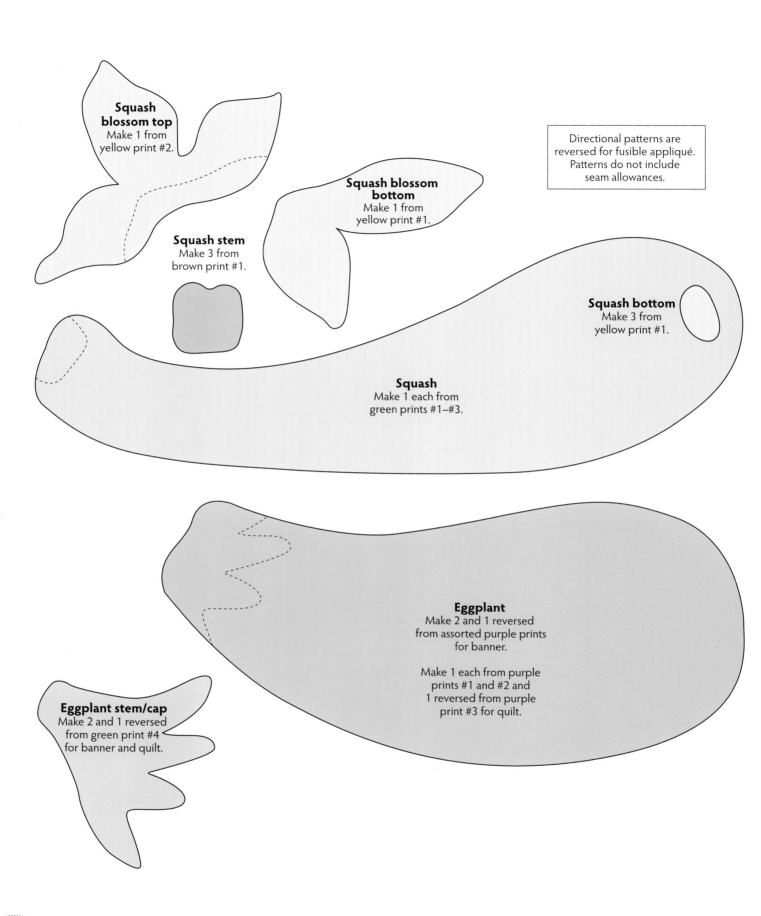

Squash blossom top
Make 1 from
yellow print #2.

Squash blossom bottom
Make 1 from
yellow print #1.

Squash stem
Make 3 from
brown print #1.

Squash bottom
Make 3 from
yellow print #1.

Squash
Make 1 each from
green prints #1–#3.

Directional patterns are
reversed for fusible appliqué.
Patterns do not include
seam allowances.

Eggplant
Make 2 and 1 reversed
from assorted purple prints
for banner.

Make 1 each from purple
prints #1 and #2 and
1 reversed from purple
print #3 for quilt.

Eggplant stem/cap
Make 2 and 1 reversed
from green print #4
for banner and quilt.

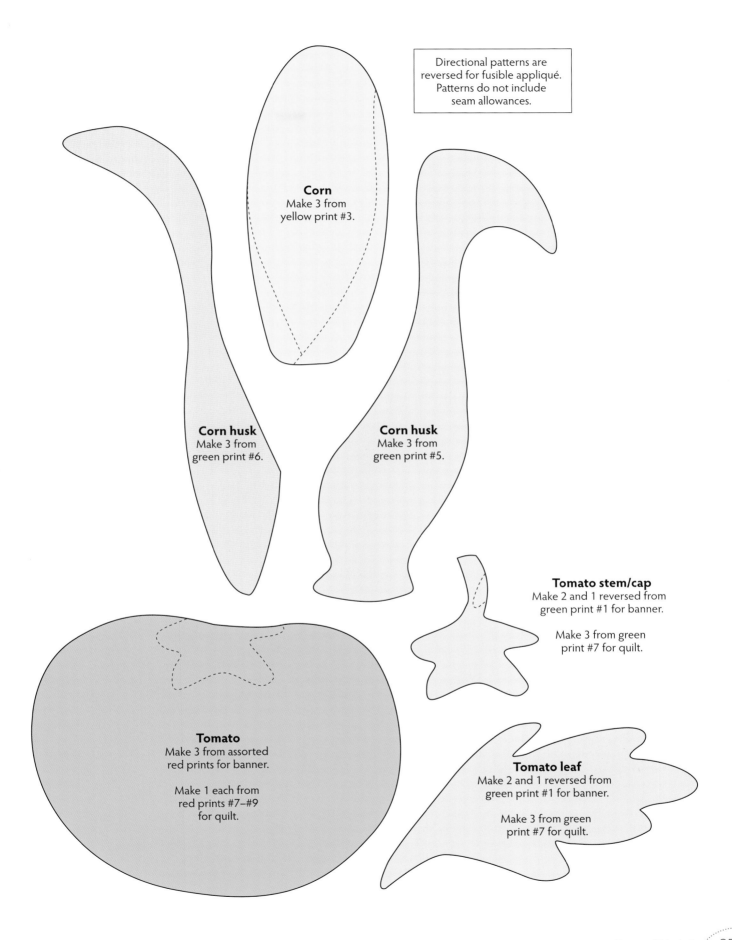

Directional patterns are reversed for fusible appliqué. Patterns do not include seam allowances.

Corn
Make 3 from yellow print #3.

Corn husk
Make 3 from green print #6.

Corn husk
Make 3 from green print #5.

Tomato stem/cap
Make 2 and 1 reversed from green print #1 for banner.

Make 3 from green print #7 for quilt.

Tomato
Make 3 from assorted red prints for banner.

Make 1 each from red prints #7–#9 for quilt.

Tomato leaf
Make 2 and 1 reversed from green print #1 for banner.

Make 3 from green print #7 for quilt.

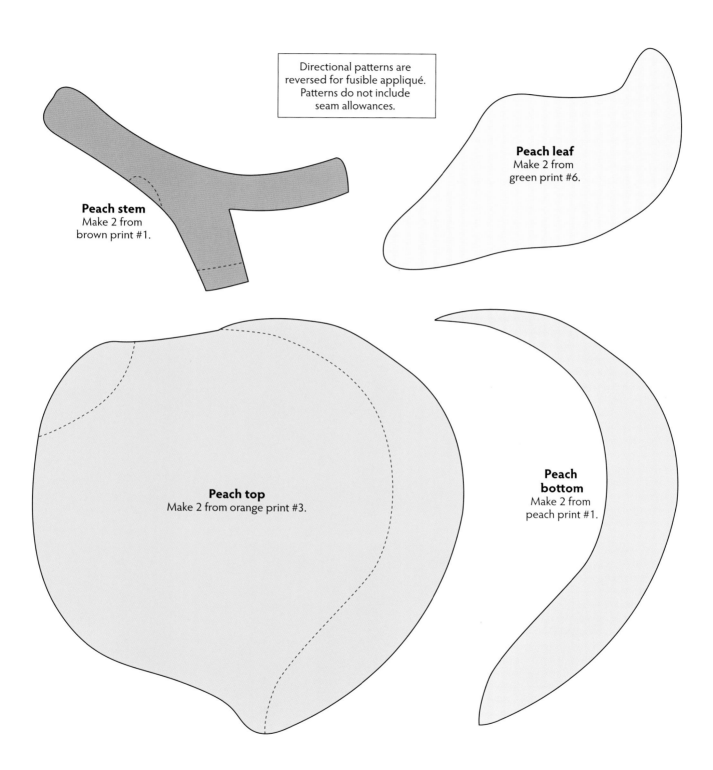

Directional patterns are
reversed for fusible appliqué.
Patterns do not include
seam allowances.

Peach stem
Make 2 from
brown print #1.

Peach leaf
Make 2 from
green print #6.

Peach top
Make 2 from orange print #3.

Peach bottom
Make 2 from
peach print #1.

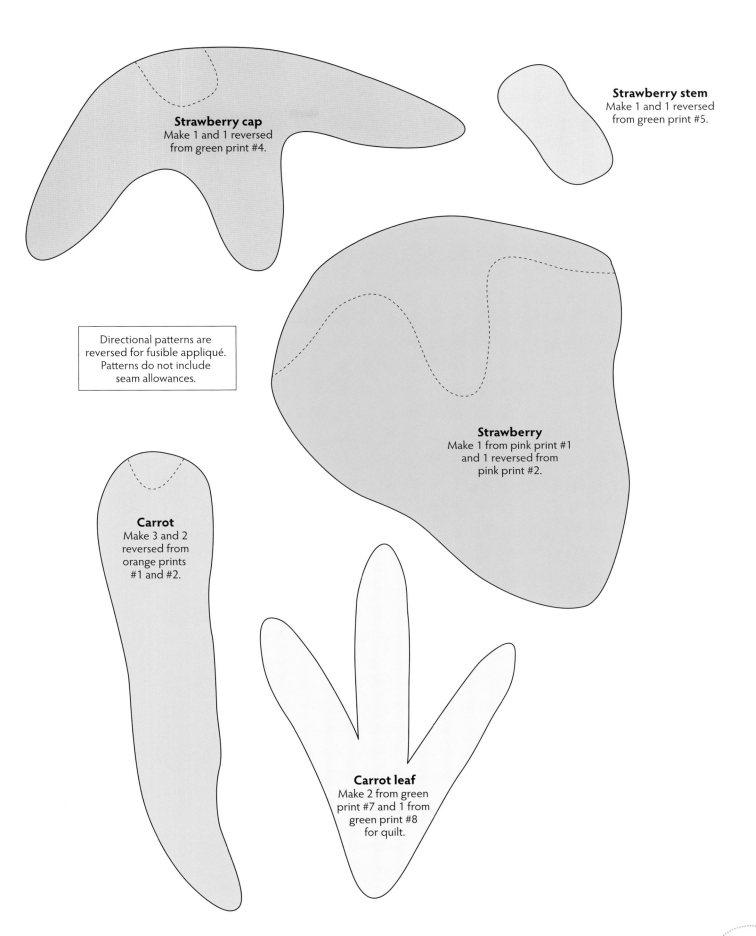

Strawberry cap
Make 1 and 1 reversed from green print #4.

Strawberry stem
Make 1 and 1 reversed from green print #5.

Directional patterns are reversed for fusible appliqué. Patterns do not include seam allowances.

Strawberry
Make 1 from pink print #1 and 1 reversed from pink print #2.

Carrot
Make 3 and 2 reversed from orange prints #1 and #2.

Carrot leaf
Make 2 from green print #7 and 1 from green print #8 for quilt.

Directional patterns are reversed for fusible appliqué. Patterns do not include seam allowances.

Letters
Cut 1 of each from navy print.

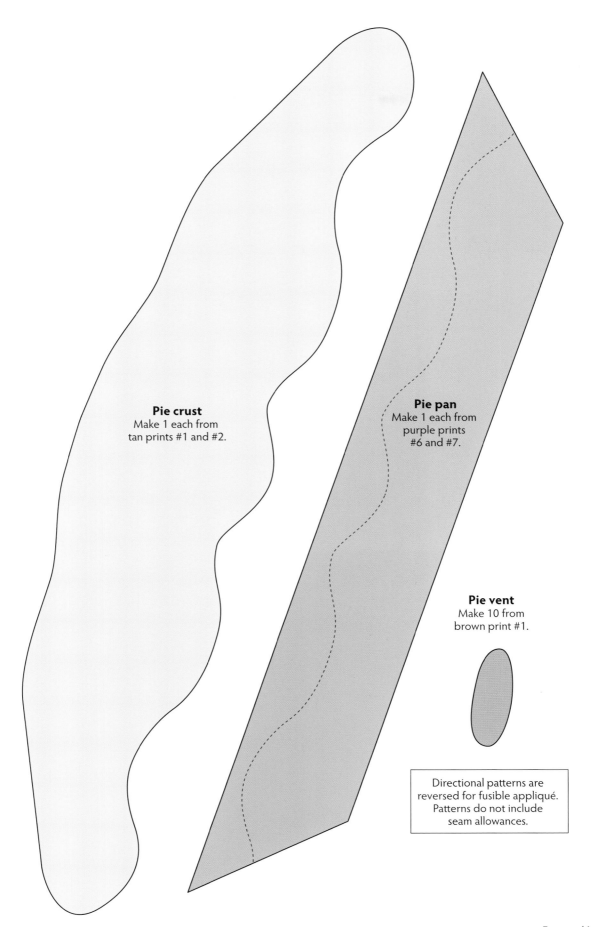

Pie crust
Make 1 each from
tan prints #1 and #2.

Pie pan
Make 1 each from
purple prints
#6 and #7.

Pie vent
Make 10 from
brown print #1.

Directional patterns are
reversed for fusible appliqué.
Patterns do not include
seam allowances.

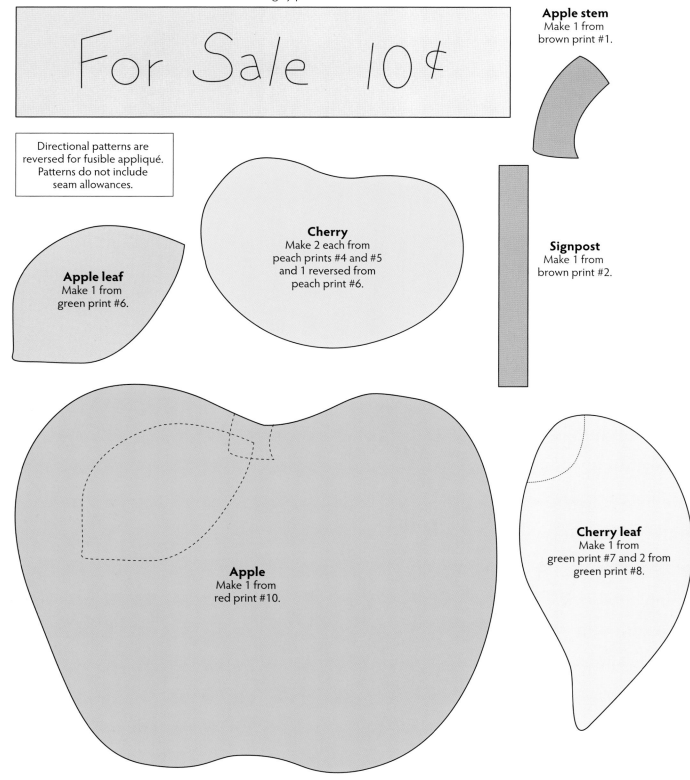

Apple sign
Make 1 from gray print.

For Sale 10¢

Apple stem
Make 1 from
brown print #1.

Directional patterns are
reversed for fusible appliqué.
Patterns do not include
seam allowances.

Cherry
Make 2 each from
peach prints #4 and #5
and 1 reversed from
peach print #6.

Signpost
Make 1 from
brown print #2.

Apple leaf
Make 1 from
green print #6.

Apple
Make 1 from
red print #10.

Cherry leaf
Make 1 from
green print #7 and 2 from
green print #8.

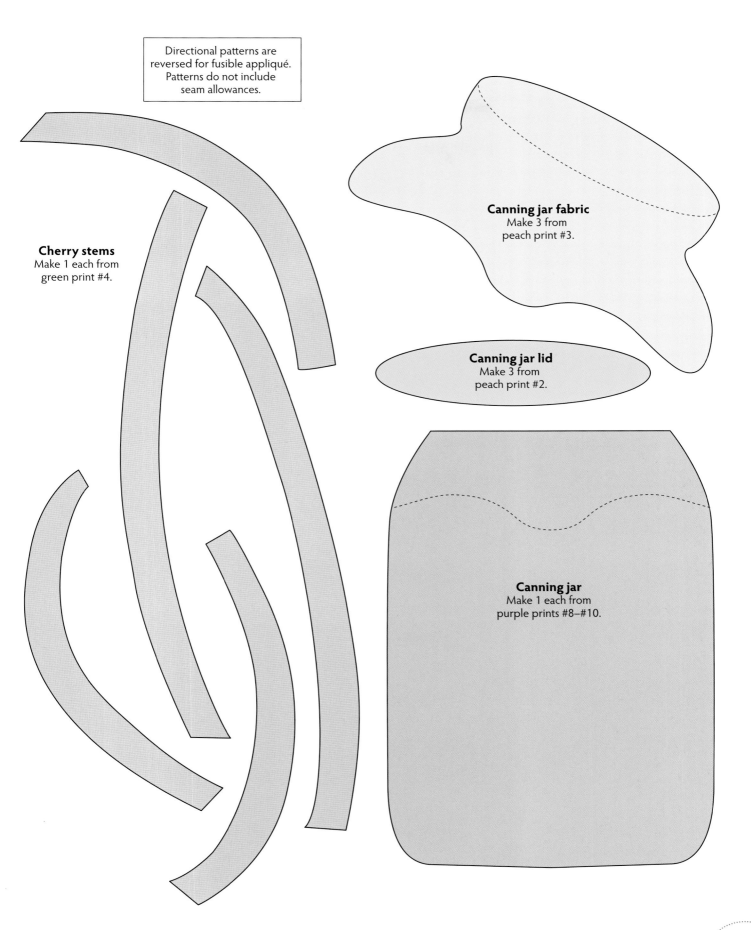

Directional patterns are reversed for fusible appliqué. Patterns do not include seam allowances.

Cherry stems
Make 1 each from green print #4.

Canning jar fabric
Make 3 from peach print #3.

Canning jar lid
Make 3 from peach print #2.

Canning jar
Make 1 each from purple prints #8–#10.

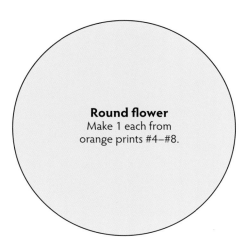

Round flower
Make 1 each from
orange prints #4–#8.

Vase top/bottom rim
Make 1 from
purple print #5.

Vase middle rim
Make 1 from
brown print #1.

Directional patterns are
reversed for fusible appliqué.
Patterns do not include
seam allowances.

Vase rim
Make 1 from
purple print #4.

Binding by Machine

When it comes to finishing your quilts, you can quilt them by hand or machine. If you need help with the finishing steps, you can find free downloadable information at www.ShopMartingale.com/HowtoQuilt. But when it comes to binding quilts, I'll describe my preferred method, which includes attaching the bindings entirely by machine. It's fast, it's sturdy, and I save my hand-sewing time for other tasks!

Preparing the Binding

I prefer to use a single-fold binding to finish my quilt edges. However, this technique will also work with double-fold binding if you prefer.

1 Cut the amount of 1½"-wide strips from the binding fabric indicated in the project instructions. The amount specified is enough to go around the perimeter of the quilt plus approximately 10" extra for joining strips and mitering corners.

2 Join the binding strips with a diagonal seam to make one long strip.

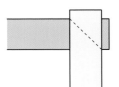 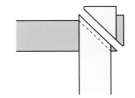

3 Press under ¼" along one long edge of the binding strip.

Sewing the Binding to the Quilt Back

That's right, you're going to sew the binding to the *back* of the quilt! We'll start there and then turn the binding to the front of the quilt and finish machine stitching it in place. Use a walking foot to make sure the quilt layers don't shift while you're stitching.

1 Starting at the center of one side, position the binding strip on one side of the back of the quilt, aligning the raw edges; pin the first edge in place.

2 Using a straight stitch and a ¼" seam allowance, begin sewing about 4" from the beginning end of the binding, and stop sewing ¼" from the corner; backstitch. Clip the thread and remove the quilt from under the presser foot.

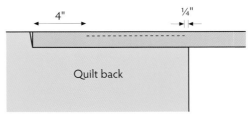

93

3 Fold the binding tail up at a 90° angle, and then bring the binding back down onto itself to square the corner and align with the next side. Starting at the top edge, sew until you're ¼" from the next corner. Repeat the folding and stitching process at each corner.

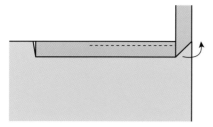

4 When you are about 6" from your starting point, stop sewing and backstitch. Clip the thread and remove the quilt from under the presser foot.

5 Unfold the turned-under edges on the ends of the binding strip. Fold one end up to create a 45° angle and the other end down to create a 45° angle so that the angled folds meet. Press the folds. With right sides together, align the folds; pin. Stitch on the fold line, backstitching at both ends. Trim the excess binding strip, leaving a ¼" seam allowance. Press the seam allowances open. Finish stitching the binding in place.

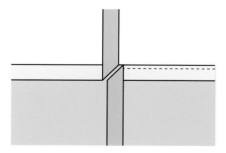

Finishing the Binding on the Quilt Front

To finish the binding by machine, turn your quilt over to the right side, and fold the binding over to the front. We'll be blanket-stitching it in place. Keep your walking foot on for this part as well.

1 Set up your machine for blanket stitching. I find that a 3.5 stitch length and 3.5 stitch width work best. On my machine, this is slightly bigger than what I appliqué with. The majority of your quilt will be positioned to the left of the needle, so for many machines, you may need to reverse the orientation of the blanket stitch so that you can sew with the straight stitches forming on the left and the bite stitches moving to the right.

Tip

Mirror your stitch so the quilt is to the left of the needle.

2 With the front facing up, place one side of the quilt under the machine needle. Pull the binding from the back to the front, aligning the turned-under edge with the stitching line you made while attaching the binding to the back. The goal is to stitch on or next to the stitching line. That way, the blanket stitch will be right next to the binding seam, and you won't see the vertical lines of the stitch on

the back. If you can see the entire blanket stitch on the back, that means you've pulled the binding to the front too far and you're not stitching *on* the seam line.

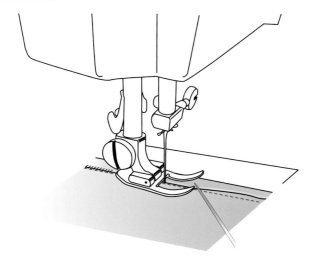

3 Begin stitching. Work slowly, folding the binding over the stitching line as you go. It's helpful to use a stiletto or seam ripper to help hold the fold in place.

Test Drive First

Make a stitch sample to be sure the stitch length, width, and direction of your stitch are correct.

Your stitching should look like this:

Then do another test using a short length of binding and a little quilt sandwich. This way you can see how your stitching works out on both the front and back of the quilt and make adjustments to the cut width of your binding strips, if necessary, to fit your stitching style.

4 When you reach the corner, fold the binding in as you've been doing, all the way to the outer corner. Then, without turning the quilt, fold the binding along the next edge over to meet the stitching line. This will form a mitered corner. Stitch right up to the corner and try to catch the fold.

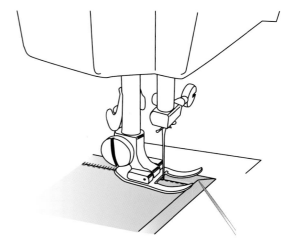

5 Turn the quilt and continue stitching along the next side of the quilt. Repeat until you've stitched along all four sides of the quilt.

6 Hand stitch the miters closed at each corner, on both the front and back of the quilt.

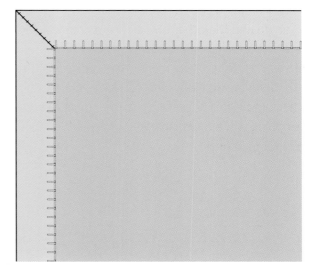

Meet Pat

I'm a quilt designer, author, radio/podcast show producer and host, and fabric designer. My passion for making quilts, sharing quilts, and talking with quilters about quilts is limitless. I travel across the world teaching and host several Internet groups of quilters where we share on a daily basis what we make. And I write about quilting at my blog. To find me, go to www.PatSloan.com, sign up for my newsletter, and let's chat soon!

ACKNOWLEDGMENTS

Many thanks to:

Roberta Miglin and Lina LaMora, who help me meet stitching deadlines.

Cindy and Dennis Dickinson of PinkPaw Designs, Shelly Pagliai of Prairie Moon, and Joann Hoffman, whose machine quilting adds another amazing level to my quilts.

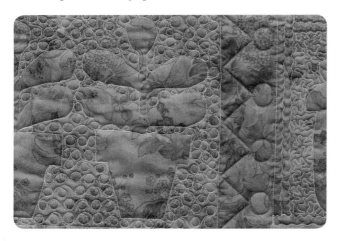

I also work with amazing partners in the industry:

Moda Fabrics not only prints my fabric line, but their fabrics in general are the ones I tend to hoard the most. Plus, they shared wonderful props to make the book delightful.

Aurifil creates beautiful-quality thread that I love in a delicious array of colors.

Tacony Corporation for the Baby Lock sewing machine I use at home and for the photos in this book.

Therm O Web has the most consistent and dependable fusible web, HeatnBond Lite.

Pellon batting adds the best middle layer to my quilts.

Sullivans USA and Havel's Sewing provide me with awesome notions such as scissors and rulers.

Reliable manufactures irons that live up to their name.

Olfa makes the best rotary cutter ever.